*Catholicism
and Political Development
in Latin America*

Catholicism and Political Development in Latin America

by Frederick C. Turner

The University of North Carolina Press
Chapel Hill

To C. T. C. T., with love.

Religion is a great creative and empowering force, but in that fact lies its danger as well as its capacity for good. Religion has been throughout history a force for evil as well as a force for good. Religion always leads to action. Whether or not it leads to actions that are valuable and enriching for human life depends on the ideas and convictions back of religion.

—GEORGE PARKINSON HOWARD, *A Spiritual Adventure in South America*

Preface

This book interprets the attitudes toward social change held by contemporary Catholic leaders in Latin America, and it relates these attitudes and the policies that they suggest to concepts of political development. Analysts of Latin American affairs have long assumed the Catholic Church to have major authority in the region; with the current heated debate over the ways in which clerical prestige can be properly put to use, it is particularly relevant to ask not only what kinds of influence the Church still possesses, but also for what goals the influence is used and what its long-range effects may be. Just as survey research indicates that religious differences continue to have major political significance in the United States[1] and Europe,[2] so the processes of individual achieve-

1. Gerhard Lenski, *The Religious Factor: A Sociological Study of Religion's Impact on Politics, Economics, and Family Life* (New York: Doubleday & Company, 1963). Lenski's study, based on responses from 656 residents in Detroit, Mich., shows great diversity as well as depth in the social influences of religion in the contemporary United States.

2. Arend Lijphart, "Class Voting and Religious Voting in the European Democracies: A Preliminary Report," a paper presented at the Eighth World Congress of the International Political Science Association, Munich, Germany, Sept., 1970. Lijphart's comparisons of survey findings in nine European democracies suggest that religious affiliation, along with class, is one of the two strongest predictors of party preference, and that the relationship between church attendance and party choice is especially strong among the Catholic populations of such countries as Italy, Germany, the Netherlands, and Belgium.

ment and national development in Latin America are also bound up with religious variables. The visions of change that Latin Americans espouse depend partly upon the preachments of their religious mentors. The Church is only one source of authority—both formal and informal—in Latin America, but it occupies a central position and the growing diversity of viewpoints within it makes its influences important subjects for study.

I have consulted both published and unpublished sources and pastoral letters, and I have interviewed many Latin American Church leaders. Although numerous North American scholars have discussed theories of political development, few of them have tried systematically to relate parts of these theories to the wealth of documentary materials available on the Church. In Latin America Catholic periodicals and the writing of churchmen remain largely untouched, and it is disquieting to see how scanty and incomplete are the holdings of Catholic periodicals and sources in many of the research libraries of major North American universities. In trying to overcome these deficiencies, I collected a wide range of Catholic periodicals, solicited pastoral messages from over six hundred Latin American bishops, and interviewed bishops and other leaders over a period of four years. The University of Connecticut Research Foundation financed this project and, without the sympathetic understanding of the foundation and its director, Dr. Hugh Clark, the project would have been impossible.

More than seventy Latin American bishops responded to my request for copies of pastoral messages dealing with social or political issues. Although several bishops wrote to say that they composed pastorals only on strictly religious matters, that they broadcast radio messages in their dioceses rather than sending written messages, or that political pressures in their countries forced them to make statements only through collective pastorals, more than sixty bishops kindly sent a great variety of pastoral messages, dating back in some cases to the 1930's. These pastorals proved to be an important addition to materials received from North American libraries, to studies consulted in Latin American libraries, and particularly to works that I obtained in the libraries of the Centro Bellarmino in Santiago, Chile, and the Center for Intercultural Documentation in Cuernavaca, Mexico. Interviews with more than eighty Church leaders, carried out in Spanish and Portuguese in seventeen Latin American countries between 1967 and 1970, further helped to clarify viewpoints and expand the framework of analysis.

Consultation of this wide range of source material does not obviate the question of bias, particularly on subjects like religion and politics where predilections tend to be strong. In cautioning the author against accepting the biases of Latin American churchmen, Ivan Illich, the highly critical and controversial former monsignor of the Church, warned that interviews may be a useless research instrument if the interviewer is mesmerized by the personalities of his respondents. In analyzing the views of Latin American churchmen, as in informal discussions with them, it is possible to become what Illich called "the intellectual prisoner of a tiny ecclesiastical establishment and its own self-image."[3] In the present study, I consciously have tried not to become the intellectual prisoner of any faction in the contemporary Church controversies. Complete objectivity is impossible, and it would be misleading not to admit that, in working on Latin American Catholicism, I have come to admire the personal dedication and integrity as well as the ideas of some of its leaders. But, especially since this sympathy is not confined to the spokesmen for any single Catholic position, I hope that even those with whom my interpretations differ will recognize a sincere attempt to minimize subjectivity in the following analysis.

In addition to the crucial assistance of Latin American churchmen and the financial support of the University of Connecticut Research Foundation, the specific debts of this study are great. Thanks are especially due Kalman H. Silvert of the Ford Foundation, who originally suggested the study, and David Bronheim, the former Director of the Center for Inter-American Relations, for which a preliminary version of the study was initially written. In a lively

3. Interview with Ivan Illich, in Cuernavaca, Mexico, Nov. 6, 1969. The danger of mesmerization is particularly acute with respondents like Illich himself, who has a most engaging personality. For balanced interpretations of Illich's position, see Peter Schrag, "Ivan Illich: The Christian As Rebel," *Saturday Review*, July 19, 1969; and Francine du Plessix Gray, "Profiles (Ivan Illich)," *New Yorker*, April 25, 1970.

discussion of the study held at the center in New York, particularly helpful contributions came from the late Frank Tannenbaum, from former Ambassador Spruille Braden, and from Stanley Ross of the University of Texas. At the University of Connecticut, discussions with John Plank, Dennison Nash, Louis Gerson, G. Lowell Field, and Everett Ladd, Jr., pointed up important approaches and comparisons. Fredrick B. Pike of the University of Notre Dame, Ivan Vallier of the University of California at Santa Cruz, and Thomas G. Sanders of the American Universities Field Staff each read the manuscript and offered constructive comments, and the manuscript also benefited in major part from the assistance of William Flanagan and the care that Betty Seaver and Gwen Duffey gave to it in various stages of production. My wife Caroline and our three children have shown an exemplary and long-suffering tolerance for the investment of time that the study has required. Although help has come from all of these persons, any errors that the following pages may still contain remain my own.

FREDERICK C. TURNER

Storrs, Connecticut
February, 1971

Contents

Contents

List of Tables

List of Figures

Catholicism
and Political Development
in Latin America

I ⁓

Politics and Progressive Catholicism

To North Americans who still think of Latin American Catholicism in terms of its traditional roles, it comes as a shock to see the connections between Christian ethics and social reform now so commonly made by Catholic leaders in Latin America. Moving far from the situations and issues described in the anticlerical tracts of the past, a new wave of Catholic activity in Latin America has gradually but decisively shifted to support widespread and massive social change. The days of ethereal spirituality and apolitical clerical seclusion are gone, as are those of the Church as a separate and powerful economic entity battling against the states of Latin America for the exclusive privilege of the national clergy or the Holy See. Although great diversity can still be found between the practical orientations of Church leaders, the most striking aspect of Latin American Catholicism in the mid-twentieth century has been its new alignment behind popular demands for a better life in the secular sphere.

CATHOLICISM AND DEVELOPMENT

In order to gauge more precisely the range of interaction between Catholicism and political change in contemporary Latin America, it becomes necessary to distinguish their respective components. Catholicism encompasses, at one and the same time, a complex body of official doctrine, a diverse pattern of attitudes among activist Catholics, a worldwide movement taking orientations from Rome, and —on a national level—the strongest ecclesiastical institution in each of the Latin American countries. Not only does the Church relate to processes of secular development in each of these doctrinal, attitudinal, and institutional spheres, but, because of conflicting Catholic positions within each sphere, the nature of the interrelationships remains open to considerable variety.

This pattern of interrelationship is multifaceted also because of the several dimensions of the development process to which Catholicism is relating. "Development" involves changes in the economic, political, and social dimensions of national communities, and it involves changes in popular perceptions of those communities. More specifically, citizens come to feel that, feasibly and legitimately, per capita national income will rise and allow them a higher material standard of living, that the ascriptive barriers to individual social mobility will be reduced, enabling men to rise more easily on their own merit and effort, and that a larger and larger proportion of the citizenry can and should exert political influence at the national and local levels.

Development theorists have argued that, although this pattern happened to occur first in the Western world, it is actually a broadly interdependent process of "modernization" rather than merely Westernization that is gradually spreading in the Third World as well. A connection is assumed to occur between the increasing pluralism of political power and the rise of economic development through the spread of modern technology and growth in per capita income. Economic and technological innovation create the occupational and social bases for a dispersal of political influence among a mass of citizens who were devoid of power in older and more highly stratified societies; the growing pluralization of political influence in turn stimulates the rationalistic and egalitarian norms that encourage economic growth.[1] In the context of Latin America, K. H. Silvert typically sees states moving toward a type of "modernism" that encompasses secularism, industrialism, nationalism, and an opening social structure. Silvert particularly stresses the conjunction between liberty and development, trying to demonstrate that "growing freedoms and growing economies are not only compatible but mutually reinforcing."[2] Technological advancement permits rather than prevents an increasingly "human role in social causality."[3] Economic growth does not predetermine what choices will be made; instead, it expands the range of possible human choices, which need to be established consciously and in keeping with ethical norms and with a sympathetic appreciation for human diversity.

A trend toward liberty and political pluralism as well as rising national income is assumed in most of the development literature, despite the firm resolve of some authors that "we will not repeat the naïveté of Enlightenment theorists regarding the evolutionary progression in political systems from traditional patterns to constitutional and democratic forms."[4] In a comprehensive defense of more

1. This process has often been conceived as being fundamentally economic in origin, but, as Myron Weiner points out, the history of change does not support such an assumption since, in many cases, it shows shifts in political organization preceding large-scale economic innovation. See Weiner, "Political and Social Integration: Forms and Strategies," in Eric A. Nordlinger, ed., *Politics and Society: Studies in Comparative Sociology* (Englewood Cliffs, N. J.: Prentice-Hall, 1970), p. 208.

2. Kalman H. Silvert, *The Conflict Society: Reaction and Revolution in Latin America,* rev. ed. (New York: American Universities Field Staff, 1966), pp. 256, 284.

3. Kalman H. Silvert, *Man's Power: A Biased Guide to Political Thought and Action* (New York: Viking Press, 1970), p. 142.

4. Gabriel A. Almond and G. Bingham Powell, Jr., *Comparative Politics: A Developmental Approach* (Boston: Little, Brown and Company, 1966), p. 215. Many political scientists have come to feel uneasy with the tendency of the literature on political development to manifest a strong if often implicit preference for Western institutions and patterns of development which would ultimately lead to a stable, "democratic" system. A good critique of this tendency appears in Philip H. Melanson and Lauriston R. King, "Theory in Comparative Politics: A Critical Appraisal" (unpublished paper, 1970), pp. 18–21. Concepts of development do not even adequately describe many aspects of Western politics. As Everett Ladd points out, for example, if we define "development" as steady movement toward increased capacity and legitimacy in a political system, there has been very little development in the role of United States political parties during the last 150 years. See Ladd, *American Politi-*

broadly participant political systems, Lucian Pye rejects the claims of corrupt and inefficient leaders who try to mask their poor performance by claiming that their regimes are feeble because they are democratic. Instead, Pye finds that democratic leaders, in contrast to unpopular authoritarians, can evoke greater voluntary participation and thereby better mobilize human resources for development.[5] In Latin America, the more stable and democratic countries do in fact appear to be those with higher per capita incomes. Martin Needler's careful comparison of political development (as measured by the number of years in the 1935–1964 period during which each Latin American country enjoyed constitutional government) and economic development (as measured by GNP per capita) indicates a positive correlation between them, although a weaker correlation than had been assumed by Seymour Martin Lipset or by Gabriel Almond and James S. Coleman on the basis of contrasting measures of political development.[6] From statistical comparisons, therefore, as well as from personal attachment to the civil liberties and the representative traditions of Western Europe and North America, and perhaps also from strong opposition to the imposition of Stalinist or Maoist models which seem antithetical to both Western security interests and personal freedoms in the developing countries, North American intellectuals have built up a theory of political development that stresses the broad applicability of democratic values and orientations.

Traditionally, the ethic of Latin American Catholicism has opposed free-enterprise capitalism in favor of more corporatist practices, and, despite the fact that Latin America's most democratic

cal Parties: Social Change and Political Response (New York: W. W. Norton & Company, 1970), pp. 9–10.

5. Lucian W. Pye, *Aspects of Political Development* (Boston: Little, Brown and Company, 1966), p. 74. Pye's view notwithstanding, the comparatively concentrated or pluralistic distribution of political power is only one variable in this situation. The popularity of the regime, identification with its goals, and the reward system for participation, all affect the level of participation, just as do the regime's constitutionality and the more-or-less pluralistic distribution of power and opportunity within it.

6. Martin C. Needler, *Political Development in Latin America: Instability, Violence, and Evolutionary Change* (New York: Random House, 1968), chap. 5. Needler recognizes both the prodemocratic bias of the concept of political development and the partially subjective component in all measurements of it, and, by doing so, he presents a balanced critique of other measures and a convincingly documented case for the positive correlation between economic and political development.

leaders have been Catholics, the force of the Church has generally opposed the imposition of the North European and North American models of democracy which underlie the approaches of the political development literature. With the growth of Christian Democracy in Latin America during the middle of the twentieth century, however, and especially with the presidential victories of the Christian Democrats in Chile in 1964 and in Venezuela in 1968, Catholic activists have come dramatically to support norms which also gain support in the theories of development. The interrelationships between contemporary Catholicism and political development appear to be particularly meaningful in five areas: mutual adaptation, legitimation, humanization, associational activity, and diversification.

First, Catholicism and the process of secular development are each adapting to new technological possibilities, to new social expectations, to new institutional relationships, and to each other. As Donald Smith points out, Islam, Hinduism, Buddhism, and Catholicism must now adjust to secular, pluralistic patterns of human values. Smith cogently argues that religions are evolving to a stage of "humanism-pragmatism," characterized by concern for man's well-being on earth and the belief that his well-being depends on his taking a pragmatic approach to his alternatives.[7] Humanism and pragmatism are in fact two of the central concerns of the evolving Catholic position.

Observers disagree considerably on the extent to which the Church has adapted a humanistic, pragmatic orientation. Advocates of "the new Catholicism" often exaggerate its pervasiveness, forgetting the weight of doctrinal and institutional tradition in the Church. On the other hand, such scholars as Richard Adams are too pessimistic in their interpretation of the Church's past accomplishments and present role. Traditional anticlerics insist that the Church has been a poor social innovator and that during the 1950's and 1960's it tried to change the image of the clergy as much to save the Church in Latin America as to "save" Latin America itself. Adams concludes that "the church is rather like the Latin American campesino; it has a great ability to survive, but its condition has improved only

7. Donald Eugene Smith, *Religion and Political Development* (Boston: Little, Brown and Company, 1970), pp. 241–42.

7

slightly, if at all, over the years."[8] The truth of this allegation needs to be tested; the areas in which the Church has changed should be analyzed, the size of new attitudinal groups within it should be determined, and the extent to which such groups have played innovative roles at the national or local levels should be ascertained.

A second way to get at the relationship of Catholicism and development is to ask to what extent the Church now works to legitimize the secular process of modernization. On one hand, if we assume that many Latin Americans remain loyal to Catholic teachings, then religious legitimation for secular change appears to be imperative. A Catholic ethic of cooperation can certainly reduce the internal conflicts that have seriously impeded political development and modernization.[9] Furthermore, if Lerner is right in saying that "modernity is primarily a state of mind—expectation of progress, propensity to growth, readiness to adapt oneself to change,"[10] then the Church's preachments on progress, growth, and change would greatly affect the course of modernization. The fact that Latin American Catholicism has more and more strongly supported this sort of "modernity" is a primary element in the Church's new role.

On the other hand, with the trend toward the secularization of values, religious legitimation for social change is not as necessary as it once was. Economic growth and the achievement-oriented society bring their own rewards. In C. Wright Mills's terms, for the modern world "power is often not so authoritative as it appeared to be in the medieval period; justifications of rulers no longer seem so necessary to their exercise of power."[11] Even though secular rulers do not now depend so heavily upon religious justifications for their regimes, particular groups still receive help—especially in the highly factional and personalistic context of Latin American politics—from

8. Richard Newbold Adams, *The Second Sowing: Power and Secondary Development in Latin America* (San Francisco, Calif.: Chandler Publishing Company, 1967), pp. 221–22.

9. On such conflicts and their impairment of modernization, see S. N. Eisenstadt, "Breakdowns of Modernization," in Jason L. Finkle and Richard W. Gable, eds., *Political Development and Social Change* (New York: John Wiley & Sons, 1966), esp. pp. 573, 576–77.

10. Daniel Lerner, *The Passing of Traditional Society: Modernizing the Middle East* (New York: The Free Press, 1964), p. viii.

11. *The Sociological Imagination* (New York: Grove Press, 1961), p. 41.

the verbal support of religious mentors. To increase their religious support and to maximize its impact, political leaders need to tailor their appeals partly to the interests and needs of the Catholic community and their own ideological supporters within that community.

Third, religious ethics can help to humanize the potentially harsh and brutalizing process of development. Just as Catholic norms traditionally reminded rulers of their ultimate accountability to God and thereby lessened their tendencies to behave selfishly, so the newer Catholic ideals tend to remind citizens of their mutual accountability and their joint responsibility to create a more just and Christian society. Such an ethic generally counsels against violence and against the Stalinist notion of sacrificing one or more generations for the achievement of economic goals. To the extent that Catholic humanism can thus harness individual ambitions and stimulate individual effort and self-abnegation, it can contribute substantially to the achievement of developmental goals.

Religious beliefs can also work to soften and diversify loyalties that might otherwise be too dogmatically political. David Apter rightly says that, although some individual needs can be met only through the acceptance of "transcendental beliefs," these beliefs do not have to be religious in nature. Our need to accept death, to establish an individual personality, and to identify personal objectives can be defined not merely through religiously transcendental concepts of an afterlife and divine sanctions, but also through what Apter calls the "political religion" which encourages men to define themselves in terms of the past and the future situations of their nation-states.[12] Were men to define themselves exclusively in terms of the goals of national politics, however, instead of simultaneously in terms of religious, familial, associational, and political communities, their concepts could be more easily circumscribed in the singleminded mold of totalitarian politics. When men gain some of their concept of moral rightness from religious leaders, as well as from national and family leaders, the increased sources for role models and self-definition should, unless all the role models reinforce one another, counteract dogmatism and authoritarianism. It is

12. David E. Apter, *The Politics of Modernization* (Chicago: University of Chicago Press, 1965), pp. 267–70.

in this sense that the acceptance of the increasingly egalitarian norms of Latin American Catholicism, as one part of a man's moral orientation, can counteract the dogmatism that anticlerics still associate with religion.

Fourth, the Church is an associational sector which, like the military, the student community, or the business community in any Latin American country, needs to be considered in formulating strategies for national development. The Church does not operate as an interest group in the narrow North American sense; it is far less homogeneous than most interest associations lobbying in Washington, D. C.[13] Latin American politicians nevertheless need to seek out allies within such sectors as the Church, the military, the business community, organized labor, the universities, and rural landowners. With very strong support from some of these sectors, leaders can write off substantial parts of others, as the military governments of Arthur da Costa e Silva and Emilio Garrastazú Médici have done with opposing student and Church groups in Brazil. But, as the experience of Juan Perón demonstrates, even a populist regime with strong military backing runs a severe risk of overthrow when it alienates large portions of too many sectors. At the time of Perón, Argentina was highly developed in terms of per capita income, literacy, and urbanization, but was severely underdeveloped in terms of formal institutions embodying expanding political participation. A pattern of coups and countercoups reinforced this institutional underdevelopment,[14] and the Church here played a classic sector role in that it at first strongly supported Perón and later joined in the coalition that pushed him from power.

13. George Blanksten, writing in the classic Almond and Coleman volume on *The Politics of the Developing Areas,* typified an older approach to the Church. He found it to be "a political interest group," citing only a 1934 statement of the Ecuadorean Conservative party to exemplify the Church's political influence. The growing diversity within Latin American Catholicism since Blanksten's evaluation was published in 1960 has now made it necessary to see the Church in each country, not as a single interest group, but rather as an associational sector in which contrasting and often conflicting political attitudes and activities are represented. See George I. Blanksten, "The Politics of Latin America," in Gabriel A. Almond and James S. Coleman, eds., *The Politics of the Developing Areas* (Princeton, N. J.: Princeton University Press, 1960), pp. 502–3.

14. Samuel P. Huntington, *Political Order in Changing Societies* (New Haven, Conn.: Yale University Press, 1968), pp. 83–84.

Fifth, growing diversification within the Church has also crucially affected its relationship to development. Traditional religious beliefs do not now buttress the sort of narrow, comparatively unified "traditional oligarchy" in which Edward Shils sees religion playing an important part.[15] Instead of a unified religious philosophy supporting a single, interlocking pattern of oligarchical control, opposing Catholic ideals support the various political groupings which strive for power in each nation-state. Just as Martin Needler's effective analysis of development and the Latin American military begins with the important premise "that officers of the armed forces are not dominated by a single political viewpoint, but hold a variety of political orientations,"[16] so it is necessary, in analysis of Catholicism and development, to recognize that Latin American churchmen are also diverse in their political stances. Before trying to assess the nature and size of the contrasting groups into which Catholic activists now fall, however, it seems worthwhile to summarize the newly progressive attitudes which they are embracing, tolerating, or rejecting.

THE PROGRESSIVE ORIENTATION

An active demand for secular progress, which has been especially evident in Chile, has spread among key leaders of the Church throughout Latin America. Juan de Castro, a professor of moral theology at the Catholic University of Chile, emphasizes that Christ wanted us "to live our morality."[17] The cardinal archbishop of Santiago recently told Latin American priests that, like contemporary economists and political leaders, they must show a special "creative initiative."[18] Even in articles designed to stir greater enthusiasm among Catholic intellectuals, Latin Americans comment that the "man of action" can give more than the intellectual to his coun-

15. *Political Development in the New States* (The Hague: Mouton & Company, 1962), pp. 81–85.
16. Martin C. Needler, "Political Development and Military Intervention in Latin America," *American Political Science Review* 60, no. 3 (Sept., 1966): 619.
17. "Cristo al centro de nuestra vida moral," *Teología y Vida* 6, no. 2 (abril-junio, 1965): 121.
18. Raúl Silva Henríquez, "Figura conciliar del sacerdote," *Teología y Vida* 8, no. 1 (enero-marzo, 1967): 11.

try and his Church.[19] In taking this new position, Latin Americans have reconciled belief in God's omnipotence with new recognition of the need for human efforts to achieve human goals. Latin American clergymen who have accepted this particular orientation toward social change are generally called *progresistas,* or "progressives." Mario Zañartu, a Chilean Jesuit who received his Ph.D. in economics from Columbia University, enunciates the position when he says that "putting everything in the hands of God does not imply a renunciation of personal responsibility, nor a lessening of creative effort, but only a prudent uncertainty of the success of a given enterprise."[20]

Joseph Fichter's study of the attitudes toward change of Catholic activists in Santiago, Chile, confirms this growth of Catholic progressivism. In 1961, Fichter and a group of other social scientists sent seven-page questionnaires to 782 priests in the diocese of Santiago and to 1,500 Catholic laymen who were said to be particularly active either by the priests or by other laymen whose names the priests supplied. The percentage of priests who completed the questionnaire was 41.9, while 45.1 per cent of the laymen completed it. Among all who replied, 59 per cent found that the velocity of social change in Chile was too slow; only 14.4 per cent said that change was too rapid; and the rest judged the rate of change to be satisfactory. A majority of 60.6 per cent believed that Chilean economic prosperity depended on a more equal distribution of agricultural land, while only a minority of 27 per cent (made up largely of upper-class respondents) rejected such advocacy of land reform. Although most of the activists who responded thus clearly advocated major social reform, their anticommunism appeared in the fact that even in 1961 more than 68 per cent thought that the Castro revolution would bring more harm than benefit to the Cuban people.[21]

19. Cayetano Bourbonnais, S.S.S., "Los intelectuales católicos laicos: Problemas de aquí y de hoy," *Sic* 30, no. 294 (abril, 1967) : 173.

20. Mario Zañartu, S.J., "Religious Values in Latin America: An Appraisal," in John J. Considine, M.M., ed., *The Religious Dimension in the New Latin America* (Notre Dame, Ind.: Fides Publishers, 1966), p. 42. For a more extensive exposition of Zañartu's viewpoint, see Mario Zañartu, *Desarrollo económico y moral católica* (Cuernavaca, Mor.: CIDOC, 1969).

21. Joseph H. Fichter, *Cambio social en Chile: Un estudio de actitudes* (Santiago de Chile: Editorial Universidad Católica, 1962), pp. 9, 24, 29, 30, 34, 36. To appreciate the high degree to which upper-class background inhibited advocacy of

One cannot extrapolate the findings of the Fichter study to apply to Catholic attitudes in rural Chile, and the degree of progressiveness in Santiago certainly seems high in comparison to most of Latin America. The low response rate of the study seriously undermines its validity even for the Santiago area, and its conclusions contrast sharply with the claims of the highly conservative Sociedad Chilena de Defensa de la Tradición, Familia y Propiedad. A leading member of this society, which denounces progressive priests as Marxists and has sent petitions to Pope Paul VI attacking changes in the Church, has claimed that 60 per cent of the Chilean priesthood really agrees with the society's aims.[22] Comparisons and generalizations from the Fichter survey cannot be made, therefore, until more empirical work has been done. Besides illustrating an effective and adaptable research strategy, however, Fichter's work draws attention to the apparent pervasiveness of Catholic progressivism in at least part of Latin America.

In the different Latin American republics it is intriguing, but as yet rather frustrating, to try to estimate what proportion of the clergy may now be "progressive" in Fichter's terms. The unreliability of subjective impressions on this subject is clear in the case of Argentina. Father Ernest Sweeney, a North American Jesuit who studied the Argentine Church for his Ph.D. dissertation, has gone so far as to claim that only 1 per cent of the Argentine clergy is progressive. He believes that "the Church is falling apart here in Argentina—living on the dream that it's still a Catholic country."[23] On the other hand, young Argentine priests contend that nearly half

change, see the comparisons of attitude according to the respondents' definition of their class status on pp. 171–92. For detailed comparisons of their degrees of support for various types of change, see pp. 209–25. Fichter also indicates in detail how the activists' attitudes differed according to their age, sex, marital status, education, profession, nationality, and religious or lay status. In order to contrast Fichter's conclusions with those based on a survey of the attitudes of Chilean priests conducted in 1969 at the Centro Bellarmino, see "Encuesta sobre el sacerdocio en Chile: Informe preliminar," *Mensaje* 19, no. 193 (octubre, 1970). This 1969 survey had a response rate of 60 per cent; in general, it pointed to considerably increased progressivism since the time of the Fichter study.

22. Interview with Maximiliano Griffin Ríos, at the headquarters of the Sociedad Chilena de Defensa de la Tradición, Familia y Propiedad, in Santiago, Chile, Aug. 5, 1968.

23. Interview with Ernest Sweeney, S.J., in Buenos Aires, Argentina, July 11, 1968. Father Sweeney's estimate seems far too low, and it has resulted in part from the composition of the groups with which he came most directly in contact.

of the clergy is progressive, noting that the younger clergy is especially so because it gained its orientation to politics and society during the populist regime of Juan Perón.[24] What is needed to resolve these differences of opinion is empirical research on Latin American clerical attitudes, but until this is accomplished one can only record and evaluate the subjective estimates of informed observers.

As a hypothesis to be tested in later research, it nevertheless seems reasonable to estimate that between one-fifth and one-third of the Latin American clergy now holds attitudes toward social change that place it in the progressive category. This approximation could prove high for some countries and low for others, but careful evaluations suggest that its range would apply for countries as pervasively different in other ways as Venezuela and Bolivia. These two countries contain clerical establishments that appear to be far less consistently progressive than those of such states as Chile or Uruguay. In the Bolivian clergy, where more than three-quarters of the priests are foreign and even fourteen out of its twenty-one bishops are foreign, a priest who has conducted survey research on the clergy finds that 20 per cent of its members are progressive.[25] One manifestation of this social orientation is a statement—signed in 1970 by about 12 per cent of the priests in Bolivia—in which, after discussing their heterogeneity and the "generation gap" that divides them, they concluded rather sadly that they "feel themselves to be useless in society."[26] In Venezuela, only 20 per cent of the clergy has been judged to be *abiertos,* those who openly accept the need for widespread social change. The informed Venezuelan clergyman who made this assessment believed that nearly all of these *abiertos* were foreign priests working in the country, which, in his opinion, made the native Venezuelan clergy the most conservative of any in Latin America.[27]

24. Interview with Father Héctor Ferreiros, in Buenos Aires, Argentina, July 16, 1968. Father Ferreiros has written extensively on religious affairs in Argentina.

25. Interview with Óscar Uzin Fernández, O.P., in La Paz, Bolivia, Aug. 8, 1968. On the attitudes of the Bolivian clergy as revealed in survey research, see Jaime Ponce García and Óscar Uzin Fernández, *El clero en Bolivia, 1968* (Cuernavaca, Mor.: CIDOC, 1970), esp. chap. 3.

26. "Carta de 120 sacerdotes de Bolivia a su conferencia episcopal," *Nadoc,* no. 148 (10 junio, 1970): 4.

27. Based on several interviews during 1968 with a Venezuelan priest who is in

In order to judge the force of progressivism, it is necessary to see not only in what countries the *progresistas* seem to be concentrated but also whether the clergy is numerous enough in a given country to have much impact on the population. As Table 1 and Figure 1 both indicate, Chile once again appears to be in a particularly favorable position, since it has the lowest ratio of inhabitants to priests of any of the twenty major Latin American countries. Chile's 1969 ratio of 3,443 inhabitants to every priest does not look so outstanding when compared to Ireland's ratio of 551 inhabitants per priest, but it is far better than the inhabitants-per-priest ratio of 38,003 in Fidel Castro's Cuba. The Caribbean nations have especially few priests in relation to the size of their populations, as the three highest inhabitants-per-priest ratios in Table 1 appear in Cuba, Haiti, and the Dominican Republic. Such traditionally strong Catholic countries as Colombia and Ecuador approach Chile's low ratio, while the ratio in Brazil stands significantly higher than the twenty-nation average. In Central America, the scarcity of priests in Honduras, El Salvador, and Guatemala contrasts with their comparative abundance in Costa Rica, while such important and politically dissimilar countries as Mexico, Venezuela, Argentina, and Uruguay all have inhabitants-per-priest ratios in the middle range of 4,000 to 6,000.[28]

As Table 1 also indicates, in 1969 Latin America contained over 33,000 brothers and 124,000 nuns, as compared to nearly 45,000 priests. The new Catholic ideals have affected not only the views of many priests, but other groups as well, such as the monks and religious women, groups that have traditionally had little concern with questions of social change and political development. Monks like Martín de Elizalde have begun to question the limitations imposed by the strictly contemplative lives prescribed by monastic orders. Elizalde declares that the need for renovation in the religious life of

---

a particularly appropriate position to judge the social attitudes of the clergy in that country. His name is withheld in order to protect the confidentiality of the interviews. Latin Americans interchangeably use the terms *abiertos* and *progresistas* in references to this segment of the clergy.

28. These data are computed from information given for every diocese in the *Annuario Pontificio per l'Anno 1970* (Città del Vaticano: Tipografia Poliglotta Vaticana, 1970). For an extensive discussion of the techniques of computation and the reliability of the data, see footnote 106 on pp. 182–83.

Table 1: *The Latin American Clergy, 1969*

	Inhabitants per Priest	Total Priests	Diocesan Priests[a]	Religious Priests[b]	Brothers	Sisters
Chile	3,443	2,459	974	1,485	2,195	5,931
Ecuador	3,845	1,585	760	825	1,714	3,629
Colombia	4,263	4,858	2,980	1,878	2,871	17,762
Costa Rica	4,347	367	222	145	186	890
Uruguay	4,354	627	228	399	640	2,026
Paraguay	4,594	446	197	249	324	536
Argentina	4,722	5,530	2,589	2,941	4,479	13,953
Venezuela	4,852	1,904	905	999	1,473	3,930
Panama	5,128	257	81	176	232	430
Bolivia	5,419	855	313	542	737	1,663
Peru	5,500	2,311	825	1,486	2,110	4,649
Mexico	5,947	8,649	6,302	2,347	3,853	23,637
Nicaragua	5,992	300	111	189	262	543
Brazil	7,764	12,427	5,152	7,275	10,306	40,568
Guatemala	7,951	517	187	330	420	770
El Salvador	8,222	395	204	191	350	805
Honduras	8,942	260	111	149	167	317
Dominican Republic	8,945	446	122	324	435	1,189
Haiti	11,005	410	202	208	395	780
Cuba	38,003	215	92	123	165	161
Total	6,063	44,818	22,557	22,261	33,314	124,169

[a] Source: *Annuario Pontificio per l'Anno 1970* (Città del Vaticano: Tipografia Poliglotta Vaticana, 1970).
[b] "Religious" priests are those who belong to religious orders.

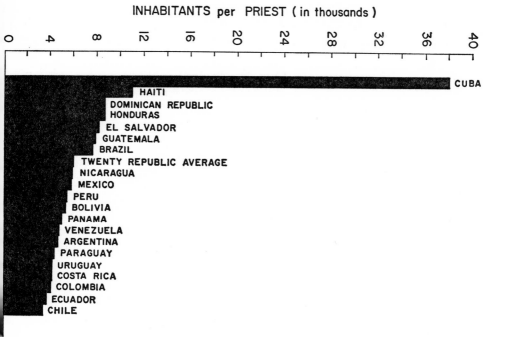

Figure 1: Inhabitants-per-Priest Ratios in the Latin American Republics, 1969

Latin America has reached the monasteries as well as the parishes, and he questions the required use of Latin in monastic devotions. He recognizes that in the modern world men are increasingly less able to believe in divine intervention, and he advocates that monks become much more actively engaged in the life of the local society around them.[29] Although monastic communities are small in Latin America, the number of women—both nuns and members of the laity—who are similarly attuned to changes in Catholicism is large. Since Latin American women remain particularly attentive to Church directives, the present evolution of Catholic thought should help to channel their efforts into political activity and social reform.

29. Martín de Elizalde, "Renovación de la vida monástica en América Latina," *Criterio* 39, no. 1518 (23 febrero, 1967): 114–20.

Women's participation could dramatically expand the number of activists working for reform, broadening feminist activity beyond the conventional areas of socialite largess and the acquisition of voting rights.

In its radiation to Catholic groups, contemporary Christian thought has a "this-worldliness," a concentration on immediate human problems rather than on problems of immortality or divinity, which distinguishes it from religious theology. For most Latin Americans, a traditional emphasis upon the virtue of humility justified an ethic of passive acceptance and political nonparticipation. Recent statements on humility, however, have extolled it without specifying its political implications in any way. Humility is still of "supreme importance" and "a most beautiful virtue," but now Catholic leaders often praise it as applying to the relationship between man and God without extending it also to encompass relationships between a man and his fellow men.[30]

Concern with the spiritual disaffection of Latin Americans underlies both the rise and continuance of the ethic of worldly activism. Latin America is a crucial testing ground for Catholic social thought because it is the region of the world which holds the greatest possibility of a Catholic resurgence. Militant atheism and the long-term suppression of religion in vast areas of Communist China and Russia prevent Catholic influence there, and the chances for widespread conversion to Catholicism in major non-Communist areas such as India also seem remote. In Latin America, however, with massive elements of each national population at least calling themselves Catholic and manifesting a traditional respect for Catholic teachings, the potential influence of contemporary Catholic thought is much more profound.

Papal concern for this potential influence became evident in 1960, when the Pontifical Commission for Latin America created the Papal Volunteers for Apostolic Collaboration in Latin America, an organization of laymen who would go to Latin America as social workers and missionaries. Within Latin America, churchmen have evidenced concern by opposing the concentration of power in nar-

---

30. See Efraín Zuluaga, S.J., "La humildad cristiana," *Ecclesiástica Xaveriana* 2 (1952).

18

row elite groups, finding that the Church can not confine its influence to the traditional elite. Father Caramuru de Barros in Brazil declares that economic relationships such as those of latifundia landholding have produced rigid social stratification, a great barrier to upward mobility, and a class system composed of an elite, a mass of common people, and a tiny, "insignificant" middle class. Adopting the oligarchical interpretation of Latin American politics that so many reformers have used as a justification for their programs, Father de Barros decries but unquestioningly accepts the assumption that political power lies in the hands of "a small aristocracy" of landowners.[31] Whether or not the Papal Volunteers are effective and whether or not de Barros' viewpoint is accurate, they both reflect the concern about popular disaffection that has spurred the new Catholic activism. Since this concern is likely to continue, the progressivism of Latin American Catholicism is likely to continue as well.

JUSTIFYING CHANGE

One of the greatest problems in Latin American politics is the justification of increasing economic productivity, a more equal distribution of wealth, and a wider sense of participation in political decision-making. These aspects of social change now require legitimation, because powerful middle- and lower-class groups have come not only to desire them but to be willing to battle against the upper class and against one another to implement their own conceptions of how such change should be achieved. Since a key function of religion is justification of social ethics and relationships, Catholicism can play a major role in this respect. To be most effective, Catholicism should not merely convince wealthy conservatives or militant radicals of the importance of productivity, income distribution, and political participation, but it should also encourage each segment of society to work more constructively together and to make sacrifices for the attainment of these goals. This role of legitimation has become so crucial that the future strength of Catholicism

31. Raimundo Caramuru de Barros, *Perspectivas pastorais para o Brasil de hoje* (Rio de Janeiro: Livraria Dom Bosco Editôra, 1964), p. 13.

in Latin America will probably depend on the degree to which it can perform this integrating function.

The new trends of Catholic thought in Latin America work in this direction. Priestly criticisms of existing social structures have won considerable support from Latin American students, as Catholic activism provides a non-Marxist outlet for idealism and youthful rebellion against tradition and authority. In times of social crisis, such as the present, the example of such critical clergymen may prove decisive for the maintenance of religious loyalties. Dutch historians have related the maintenance of Catholic "enclaves" during the rise of Dutch Protestantism in the sixteenth and seventeenth centuries to the presence of "worthy" priests in particular parishes and regions.[32] In Latin America, priests seem increasingly worthy to many of their parishioners as they identify with popular aspirations for change and reform.

One priest who has gained increasing recognition and influence by enunciating an ethic of social responsibility is a Brazilian Jesuit, Father Henrique C. de Lima Vaz. He believes that Christians should develop a personal consciousness of the evolution of history and then go on to reshape that evolution through their appreciation of its processes.[33] His thought combines a vivid sense of the possibilities of change with recognition that, in order to promote beneficial types of change, men must maintain both initiative and a willingness to adapt their programs to the exigencies of their social situation. The originality of his concept of "historical consciousness" calls attention to his ideas, and the major tenets of his thought gain support from the exceptional erudition and wide familiarity with theological trends in other countries with which he surrounds them.[34] Besides the intellectual excitement of his ideas, their clear implications for social innovation add to their appeal.

32. J. E. Ellemers, "The Revolt of the Netherlands: The Part Played by Religion in the Process of Nation-Building," *Social Compass* 14, no. 2 (1967): 101.

33. One of the best summaries of his thought is Henrique C. de Lima Vaz, S.J., "Cristianismo e história," *Vozes* 59, no. 11 (novembro, 1965). I am indebted to Thomas Sanders for first calling my attention to the importance of the thought of Father Vaz.

34. To appreciate how Father Vaz works out his theory in relation to traditional as well as contemporary philosophy, see Henrique C. de Lima Vaz, S.J., "Situação do tomismo," *Vozes* 59, no. 12 (dezembro, 1965).

Father Vaz sees all social thought of the present period as being ideologically conditioned and impossible to verify theoretically. Instead of supporting discussions of abstract theory, he suggests that the validity of ideas can only be seen in practice, in the degree to which men shape their actions according to humanism, Christian ethics, and the "concrete historical conditions of ongoing socialization."[35] Man must be seen "as the *center* of the active processes which modify 'nature' and give it a human significance."[36] Father Vaz develops a concept of "Christian anthropology," which he claims to be incomparable to human doctrines and ideologies.[37] To validate historical existence and live in a manner that is consistent with the principles of Christian anthropology, the individual should apply principles of Christian charity and love for his neighbor to the situation in which he finds himself.[38]

The rise and growth of "moral consciousness" is, for Vaz, a "dynamic" factor that can decisively change the course of historical development. A sense of common existence and man's historical responsibility for it should be prime elements of ethics.[39] In order to make his actions affect the "vital rhythm" of historical development, the Christian needs to develop a sense of "historical humanism," an ethical responsibility in his relations with other men. Historical humanism is a more rigorous and consequential doctrine than concepts based on predestination, because it assumes that men have "freedom . . . of decision, of historical responsibility."[40]

Although Father Vaz sets up no specific, programmatic approach to social change, he clearly sees the concept of historical responsibility as justifying major change and contrasting with other programs for change such as that of Marx. He finds that the "historical

35. Henrique C. de Lima Vaz, S.J., "Ideologia e verdade," *Vozes* 60, no. 1 (janeiro, 1966) : 44.
36. Henrique Cláudio de Lima Vaz, S.J., "Antropologia filosófica" (manuscript published for limited distribution by the Departamento de Filosofia, Faculdade de Filosofia da Universidade de Minas Gerais, 1966), p. 11. Father Vaz's italics.
37. Vaz, "Cristianismo e história," p. 284.
38. Henrique de Lima Vaz, S.J., "Nota histórica sôbre o problema filosófico do outro," *Kriterion* 16, no. 63 (1963) : 63–64.
39. *Ibid.,* pp. 71, 75–76.
40. Henrique C. de Lima Vaz, S.J., "Cristianismo e consciência histórica," *Síntese* 3, no. 9 (janeiro-março, 1961) : 41–42, 45. On liberty in Christian ethics, see also Vaz, "Antropologia filosófica," pp. 48–49.

imperative" of the present epoch is to surmount the social structures whose "alienating and dehumanizing character" we have now come to perceive.[41] He frequently discusses Marx, and his thought is superficially similar to Marxism in terms of its emphasis on the need to appreciate historical tendencies and to coordinate one's actions with selected aspects of those tendencies. He stresses, however, that his view of man's liberty and ethical duty to reshape his destiny sharply differentiates his Christian viewpoint from Marx's historical determinism.[42]

Like the doctrine of Father Vaz, the ideas spread so effectively in Chile by Father Roger Vekemans stress human awareness and effort. Vekemans complains that the republicanism of Latin American independence movements only masked absolute tyrannies, and that only the rule of aristocratic or populist oligarchies has replaced those tyrannies. He cites the Mexican, Bolivian, and Cuban revolutions as the only genuine revolutions in the area,[43] but aspects of even these revolutions make their solutions unacceptable to many Christian reformers. To answer problems of Latin American society and government, Vekemans suggests instead a conscious striving for "liberty," a kind of liberty that he defines as "man's essential liberty of self-realization," his freedom to realize his own goals. In contrast to many traditional churchmen, Vekemans finds that perfection can come only through "solidarity," through an integration of human efforts and a common striving for the Common Welfare, the *Bien Común*.[44] The Common Welfare, which takes on almost divine qualities, differs from more traditional concepts of deity in that it encompasses coordinated human efforts to achieve human ends.

Vekemans' emphasis upon cooperation coincides with the thinking of both solidarists and nationalists in the Latin American Church. Following the teaching of Heinrich Pesch, solidarists see moral bonds creating unity and solidarity among individuals and

---

41. Henrique C. de Lima Vaz, S.J., "A grande mensagen de S. S. João XXIII," *Síntese* 5, no. 18 (abril-junho, 1963): 32.

42. Vaz, "Ideologia e verdade," pp. 52–53.

43. Roger Vekemans, "Tesis fundamentales," in Roger Vekemans, S.J., and others, *América Latina y desarrollo social*, 2 vols. (Barcelona: Centro para el Desarrollo Económico y Social de América Latina, 1966), 1: 50.

44. *Ibid.*, pp. 53–68, 91–92.

22

groups. Society is not simply a collection of individuals, and its unity is not imposed simply because unity and common action benefit the members of society. Instead, society is bound together in moral terms and its members must therefore work for the common good. In this sense, solidarism seems largely a justification for common effort.

A similar opposition to individualism combines with opposition to Protestantism in numerous calls for unity and cohesion. Downgrading individualism seems, to some churchmen, to be required by Catholic tradition as well as by the need for community action. Father Peter Richards, a leader of the Movimiento Familiar Cristiano, complains that *"individualism*—the Protestant influences brought to Latin America through the doctrines of the French Revolution have put the emphasis on the person, leaving aside the community."[45] Disregarding the conflicts that have raged in such countries as Mexico between clerical and anticlerical factions, both claiming to be Catholic, conservatives praise Catholicism as a unifying force in their nations. Combining Catholic nationalism with a fierce denunciation of Protestantism, Eduardo Ospina writes that "Protestantism has never produced anywhere anything good. . . . Protestantism, with its inavoidable [*sic*] and increasing destruction is a social disease, it is a senile debility which finds a way through [the] religious life of a nation, and a nation whose religious life is weakened, advances towards its decrepitude."[46]

In addition to working for unity against "alien" Protestantism, contemporary Catholicism works at other times as a broader and more genuinely cohesive force on the behalf of Latin American nationalism. Illustrating the manner in which Catholic teachings can serve the particular political needs of individual Latin American countries, Manuel Moledo in Argentina notes the same dangers in the fractionalized nature of the Argentine polity that K. H. Silvert has described. Moledo postulates that progressive Catholicism

45. Quoted in Russell J. Huff, C.S.C., "The Family Crisis in Latin America," *Ave Maria* 95, no. 1 (Jan. 6, 1962) : 5. Father Richards' italics.
46. Eduardo Ospina, S.J., *The Protestant Denominations in Colombia: A Historical Sketch with a Particular Study of the So Called "Religious Persecution"* (Bogotá: National Press, 1954), pp. 201–2. This is a rough translation of the Spanish version, which is entitled *Las sectas protestantes en Colombia.*

can help to bring unity to the diverse segments of the Argentine national community, justifying his hopes in part through the analogy of Christ coming to earth "in order to bring unity to the divided sons of God."[47] Similarly, in a type of pastoral letter that has become increasingly common in Latin America, the assistant bishop of Quito recently called for greater "national integration." He said that what Ecuador and the rest of Latin America need is greater collaboration among social classes and groups, a sense of social integration that will create "a new mentality and a new social sensibility."[48] In promoting such measures as broader education, economic integration, and gradual agrarian reform as well as this spirit of national cohesiveness, churchmen such as Monsignor Muñoz Vega act to promote what they call "social peace." Even if their stand is motivated more by fear of social strife than by an intellectual appreciation of the potential force of contemporary nationalism, their actions nonetheless add to the potency of nationalism and work to shape it in a cohesive and pacific direction.

As an ethic legitimizing cohesion and evolutionary change, Catholicism is not the primary force underlying such change. Frequently, religion does not establish political tendencies; it justifies them. When a man derives his political outlook and his religious beliefs from his family and the social needs of his environment, political outlook and religion regularly reinforce one another. This does not mean that one set of beliefs gave rise to the other, however, even though religious persons continually justify their political views by saying that their religion has inspired them. Although religion is often more an element of reinforcement than the initial cause of new social attitudes, it remains a crucial instrument supporting constructive patterns of change.

47. Manuel Moledo, 'Los católicos argentinos," *Criterio* 39, no. 1515–16 (19 enero, 1967): 12–13. For analysis of the factional basis of Argentine politics, see K. H. Silvert, ed., *Expectant Peoples: Nationalism and Development* (New York: Random House, 1963), pp. 347–72. A balanced interpretation of contemporary Latin American nationalism, from the perspective of Argentine Catholicism, is "El nuevo nacionalismo latinoamericano," *Criterio* 43, no. 1593 (9 abril, 1970).

48. Pablo Muñoz Vega, S.J. (Obispo Coadjutor Sedi Datus de Quito), *Carta pastoral sobre las obligaciones morales de promover el desarrollo dentro de la integración nacional y latinoamericana,* Nov. 8, 1966 (Quito: Editorial "Vida Católica," 1966), esp. pp. 4–5.

24

PATTERNS OF POLITICAL ACTION

Increasing Catholic faith in man's ability to find solutions to political problems has probably, although not certainly, enhanced the likelihood of finding those solutions. Formerly, emphasis on the doctrine of original sin with its strong connotations of human imperfection undermined reliance on the political institutions created by man. The failure in Latin America of constitutional principles borrowed indiscriminately from the United States strengthened the view that formal institutions would not operate in the prescribed manner. Although some Latin American legalists have continued to rely on legal formulations and although institutions such as the Chilean legislature or the Uruguayan collegiate executive have operated as prescribed for certain periods of time, the majority of Latin American political leaders have worked outside legally provided channels to gain power. Now, however, with the Church's tacit acceptance of such institutional arrangements as the interest group collaboration within Mexico's dominant party or the collaboration of Chilean Christian Democrats with other reform-oriented groups, human achievement through political organization seems more possible. The new emphasis on human progress thus encourages constructive political activity, and neglects the older concern for original sin and human imperfection.

Easy optimism and a tendency to seek solutions in broad generalizations impede the efforts of Catholic leaders to establish effective patterns of reform. Some Catholic spokesmen evince a rather naïve optimism, which assumes an ease of fraternal cooperation and discounts the real barriers that the natural primacy of self-interest among groups and individuals imposes on Latin American political development. With the ring of an introductory civics textbook, the bishops of Peru in their 1963 annual statement declared that "a *sure way* to promote economic and social development is the exercise of political activity which presupposes interest in public affairs and the fulfillment of a citizen's duties."[49] The optimism with

49. "Peruvian Bishops' Pastoral Letter on Politics and Social Reform," in *Recent Church Documents from Latin America,* Center for Intercultural Formation Mono-

which Christian Democrats approach Latin American integration is manifest in Rafael Caldera's assumption that "we shall cease to be small, poor and relegated countries as soon as we unite and act as a single force."[50]

In approaching more concrete and realistic answers in Latin American politics, the basic stance of contemporary Catholics is to reject what they define as the two extremes. Church spokesmen castigate Marxism and laissez faire capitalism in the same terms, finding that both of them elevate money and economic gain to be the supreme value and so encourage human ambition and egotism above more altruistic sentiments.[51] Mario Zañartu rejects the extremes of both self-interested individualism and the "tyrannical collectivism" that would turn men into automatons. Taking a middle position instead, he supports the right of individual diversity in thought and action and the integration of individuals into society in a manner that allows them to work effectively for both personal and communal development.[52] In more specific political terms, many Catholics consciously disassociate themselves from both the traditional right and left in Latin American politics, finding as does Ángel Aparicio Laurencio that both leftists and rightists offer only sterile formulas and in practice oppress the working class. These Catholics claim that the epithet of "atheist" that rightists use against leftists is as meaningless as the "fascist" epithet that the left uses against the right, since both groups regularly seek dictatorships of the bourgeois or the proletarian variety.[53]

As part of the opposition to political extremes, most progressives as well as rightists and moderates reject violence as a political

---

graphs, no. 2 (Cuernavaca, Mor.: CIDOC, 1963), p. 46. This pastoral message was distributed just over a month before the election of President Fernando Belaúnde Terry on June 9, 1963. My italics.

50. Rafael Caldera, "Christian Democracy and Social Reality," in John J. Considine, M.M., ed., *Social Revolution in the New Latin America: A Catholic Appraisal* (Notre Dame, Ind.: Fides Publishers, 1965), p. 72.

51. Eduardo Boza Masvidal, *Revolución cristiana en Latinoamérica* (Santiago de Chile: Editorial del Pacífico, 1963), pp. 40–41.

52. Mario Zañartu, *Religión y desarrollo*, Secretariado Social Mexicano, Colección Desarrollo Integral, no. 9 (n.p.: n.d.), p. 6.

53. Ángel Aparicio Laurencio, "Prólogo," in Boza Masvidal, *Revolución cristiana en Latinoamérica*, p. 7.

instrument. Catholics publish numerous articles supporting the pope's call for peace in international relations,[54] and in domestic politics they take a similar stand. One of the most famous opponents of violence is Luis Cardinal Concha, the archbishop of Bogotá, whose opposition to Father Camilo Torres gained wide publicity. In his public statements Cardinal Concha readily admits that social institutions must change with the times and that a great many evils exist in Colombian society which have to be remedied. What he opposes is mass violence as a solution. Partly from a personal repulsion that he felt toward *la violencia* in Colombia while he was the bishop of Manizales,[55] he declares that those who affirm an ideal world through revolution provide only "illusory promises." "In exchange for a legal regime which has deficiencies," the mass revolution will most likely give the people only "domination by an absolute ruler or a tyrannical oligarchy which smothers their most justified protests."[56] Despite the continuing appeal of mass revolution to some activists, this interpretation is reinforced by the authoritarianism and the return of prerevolutionary conditions that have followed revolutions as massive as those of France in 1789, Russia in 1917, or Turkey in 1922.

One of the best-known orientations in Catholic politics, which has tried to reject naïve optimism and to demonstrate the possibility of nonviolent change, has been that of former Chilean President Eduardo Frei. Frei himself acquired a deep sense of humanism from his religion and from his personal appreciation for the painting of the Italian Renaissance and for the work of such writers as Dickens, Toynbee, Balzac, and Maupassant. His knowledge of Italian art is so considerable that once, when he was showing two friends around an Italian museum, a group of other visitors joined the party, mistook him for a guide, and tried to pay him at the end

54. See Pedro José Frías, "Los problemas de la paz, hoy, en el mundo," *Criterio* 39, no. 1515–16 (19 enero, 1967). Dr. Frías wrote this article as the Argentine ambassador to the Holy See.

55. On Luis Concha's personal concern for the excesses of *la violencia* in Colombia, see Luis Concha (Obispo de Manizales), *Carta pastoral sobre el precepto de la caridad* (n.p.: Editorial Lumen Christi, 1949), esp. pp. 10–11.

56. *El Espectador*, Aug. 15, 1965, as reprinted in Germán Guzmán Campos, *Camilo: presencia y destino* (Bogotá: Editores Publicidad, Servicios Especiales de Prensa, 1967), pp. 113–14.

of the tour.[57] Illustrating the Christian concern that pervades his thought, Frei summed up his attitude toward social reform in a speech at the Punta del Este summit conference in the spring of 1967. He defined Latin American problems as "primarily political, human, social, and moral in nature" and proposed that the basic question facing Latin America was "whether, in the next few years—and I emphasize 'few'—not in the next century, those who love freedom and believe in the dignity of man and his essential rights, those who think that man is an end and not a means, will be capable of bringing about at one and the same time economic development and social development, fulfilling the just aspirations of vast multitudes."[58]

While Frei's concept of political alternatives improves upon the most simplistic view of Latin American politics, it is still too simplified. As Luigi Einaudi neatly sums up the *freista* position, it tries to "reconcile primitive Marxism, nationalism and revolution with opposition to Communist as well as Yankee imperialism."[59] Instead of the stereotyped alternatives of conservative stagnation or a violent leftist revolution, Frei postulated that there were only three roads Chile could follow: those of capitalism, communism, or his own middle-ground solution. However, resources in Chile and most of Latin America actually allow many degrees and combinations of authoritarianism, economic freedom, incentives, and public ownership. Frei's party won votes in 1964 by saying that Chileans must support his program in order to avoid either of the two extremes, but in reality the positions taken by his government represented only some of the theoretical alternatives. What Frei is correct in showing is that only through agreement on one set of these alternatives can the middle—in terms of practical politics—counteract the force of the extreme right and left.

Frei won considerable support for his middle position through an ethic of governmental reform. Bringing a humanist sentiment to

57. Alejandro Magnet, "Semblanza de Eduardo Frei," in Eduardo Frei Montalva, *Sentido y forma de una política* (Santiago de Chile: Editorial del Pacífico, 1951), p. 49.
58. Quoted in *Christian Science Monitor,* May 5, 1967.
59. Luigi Einaudi, *Changing Contexts of Revolution in Latin America* (Santa Monica, Calif.: Rand Corporation, 1966), p. 34.

the reform of government itself, Frei derides the allegedly dehumanizing aspects of increasing government bureaucracy. The bribes that grease the workings of Latin American business and government are not the result of official dishonesty, he says, but rather of a bureaucratic system that imposes a paralyzing network of decrees, regulations, and formalities. One might suppose that Frei would conclude that, since the phenomenon of bureaucracy rather than specific personnel is responsible for this situation, a political party can do comparatively little about it. Instead, however, he concludes that the best way to make government more responsible to human needs is to elect the Christian Democrats, who will show initiative, responsibility, and a sense of justice.[60]

During his six years in office from 1964 to 1970, President Frei made solid and, in some areas, outstanding progress in implementing his program of nonviolent reform. His government bought out 51 per cent of the holdings of the major United States copper companies in Chile under a plan whereby the companies agreed to reinvest the funds received from the government in order to increase the production of Chilean copper. With the high world price for copper during the late 1960's, this policy of "chileanization" brought the companies under government control and also resulted in large profits and reinvestment. In the Chilean economy as a whole, growth was manifest in many ways. The international reserves of the Central Bank went from a deficit of $164 million in 1964 to a surplus of more than $211 million in 1969, while electric power capacity rose from 1.3 million kilowatts to 2.1 million kilowatts during the same period. In addition to impressive results from the highly publicized government investments in housing, the fishing industry, which gains comparatively little notice outside Chile, increased its catch from 1.4 thousand tons in 1964 to 11.7 thousand tons in 1969. Automobile production rose from 7,803 vehicles in 1964, of which only 26 per cent of the parts were made in Chile, to 22,069 vehicles in 1969, of which 58 per cent of the parts were Chilean. The number of students in school increased from 1.8 million in 1964 to 2.6 million in 1970, and university

60. Frei, *Sentido y forma de una política,* p. 174.

enrollment grew during these six years from 35 thousand to more than 82 thousand.[61]

In light of these significant accomplishments, the electoral defeat of the Christian Democrats on September 4, 1970, did not indicate a basic disaffection from most programs of the Frei administration. Public opinion polls indicated that, if Chilean law had not prevented Frei from running for a successive term as president, a majority of the Chilean people would have voted for him just as they had done in 1964. In the actual election, however, Radomiro Tomic Romero, the Christian Democratic candidate, ran a poor third behind Dr. Salvador Allende Gossens, who won 36.2 per cent of the vote, and Jorge Alessandri Rodríguez, who gained 34.9 per cent. The Tomic campaign was erratic and, in making particularly strong efforts to win votes from the left, Tomic was unable to put together the coalition that had brought Frei to victory six years earlier.

The electoral defeat of the Christian Democrats in 1970 also indicated that the Frei administration had raised reformist hopes to a level that even its solid performance could not justify. This was particularly true in regard to agrarian reform. Before the election, Jacques Chonchol, who had led President Frei's institute for agrarian development, left the Christian Democratic party and, with a number of supporters, worked for Allende's Popular Unity coalition. Frei's agrarian program increased agricultural production and efficiency, but it redistributed only a small amount of land. Agricultural credit rose from 569 million escudos in 1964 to 2,093 million escudos in 1969; the number of farm workers in trade unions increased from 1,658 to 104,666 during the same period.[62] But the rural vote went heavily to Dr. Allende after he promised to turn all large farms into peasant cooperatives.

Allende welcomed Christian Democratic support, not only from former members of the party like Chonchol but also from those Christian Democrats whose votes in Congress allowed congressional

61. *Sexto mensaje del Presidente de la República de Chile, don Eduardo Frei Montalva, al inaugurar el período de Sesiones Ordinarias del Congreso Nacional* (Santiago de Chile: Dirección de Informaciones y Radiodifusión de la Presidencia de la República, 1970), pp. 99, 102–3, 111, 132, 137, 142, 150–53.

62. *Ibid.,* pp. 119, 158.

confirmation of his narrow victory in the popular election. Although a Freemason, a founder of Chile's Socialist party, and a candidate backed in successive elections by Chile's strong Communist party, Allende did not allow these ties to prejudice his view of the Chilean Catholic Church. In an interview after his election, he declared, "The Catholic Church has changed fundamentally. . . . The church will not be a factor against the Popular Unity government. On the contrary, they are going to be a factor in our favor, because we are going to try to make a reality out of Christian thought."[63]

In the aftermath of Allende's victory, conservatives voiced an old fear with new fervor: the notion, summarized in the title of a conservative attack on Frei, that he was a Chilean Kerenski.[64] Had his administration, like that of Kerenski in Russia, set the stage for a Marxist or Communist victory? The notion seems most unlikely from the standpoint of Chilean electoral history. Allende, who defeated Alessandri by some 39 thousand votes in 1970, had lost to Alessandri by only 30 thousand votes in the presidential elections of 1958. These two opponents already had strong, dedicated followings before the upsurge in electoral support for the Christian Democrats during the 1960's.

63. Quoted in *New York Times,* Oct. 4, 1970.
64. Fabio Vidigal Xavier da Silveira, *Frei, o Kerensky chileno* (São Paulo: Editôra Vera Cruz, 1967). For other, contrasting studies of Chilean Christian Democracy, see Giles Wayland-Smith, *The Christian Democratic Party in Chile* (Cuernavaca, Mor.: CIDOC, 1969); Leonard Gross, *The Last, Best Hope: Eduardo Frei & Chilean Democracy* (New York: Random House, 1967); James Petras, *Chilean Christian Democracy: Politics and Social Forces* (Berkeley, Calif.: Institute of International Studies, University of California, 1967); Ricardo Boizard B., *La democracia cristiana en Chile* (Santiago de Chile: Editorial Orbe, 1963); Jaime Castillo Velasco, *Las fuentes de la democracia cristiana,* 2d ed. (Santiago de Chile: Editorial del Pacífico, 1968); Gerardo Mello Mourão, *Frei y la revolución en América Latina,* trans. Jorge Mellado (Santiago de Chile: Editorial del Pacífico, 1966); Arpad von Lazar and Luis Quiros Varela, "Chilean Christian Democracy: Lessons in the Politics of Reform Management," in Arpad von Lazar and Robert R. Kaufman, eds., *Reform and Revolution: Readings in Latin American Politics* (Boston: Allyn and Bacon, 1969); Sandra Powell, "Political Change in the Chilean Electorate, 1952–1964," *Western Political Quarterly* 23, no. 2 (June, 1970); Paul E. Sigmund, "Christian Democracy in Chile," *Journal of International Affairs* 20, no. 2 (1966); Roger P. Hamburg, "Soviet Foreign Policy: The Church, the Christian Democrats, and Chile," *Journal of Inter-American Studies* 11, no. 4 (Oct., 1969); and Alan Angell, "Christian Democracy in Chile," *Current History* 58, no. 342 (Feb., 1970).

Despite the inappropriateness of the Kerenski analogy, the *freista* orientation has appealed to many Latin Americans as an "unbrutalized" form of Marxism. In works such as that of Rodolfo Mondolfo, which have been translated into Spanish and published in Latin America, Marx is seen as a humanist who championed the liberty of the workingman. Supporting Erich Fromm's interpretation of Marx, Mondolfo stresses the "irreconcilable opposition" between genuine Marxist doctrine and the Soviet practice of totalitarianism.[65] Jean-Yves Calvez, a French Jesuit whose writing on Marx has been translated and widely distributed in Latin America, has shaped the attitudes of numerous Latin American churchmen. Calvez argues that what he calls "Marxist humanism" takes into account human brutality and alienation. He sees Marxism not as a simple antithesis of Christianity but as containing reformulations of such Christian doctrines as original sin and the perfect society. Calvez suggests that reconciliation with God will provide the force that Marxists call for, the force that will eliminate human alienation and allow man's reconciliation with nature and society.[66] On this basis, the Latin American approach of Catholic humanism is designed to capture the appeals of Marxism while pointing out its pitfalls. Churchmen agree that, unless humanism maintains its base in Christianity and its sense of a higher law, it can easily turn into brutal and self-seeking forms of conduct.

For many Catholics, a form of more genuinely representative government is a part of this alternative to Marxism. They decry "false" democracy and agree increasingly with the 1938 sentiment of C. J. Eustace that "the democracy that we know is nothing but a monstrous exploitation—commercial, artistic, philosophic, and religious—of the underprivileged by the privileged."[67] Social critics have seen through the cobwebs of constitutional democracy that shroud Latin American political reality. Pedro Velázquez H. stresses

---

65. Rodolfo Mondolfo, *El humanismo de Marx,* trans. Oberdan Caletti (México: Fondo de Cultura Económica, 1964), pp. 55, 60, 97.

66. Jean-Yves Calvez, *El pensamiento de Carlos Marx,* trans. Florentino Trapero (Madrid: Taurus, 1962), pp. 616, 676–77.

67. *Catholicism, Communism and Dictatorship: A Short Study of the Problems Confronting Catholics under Totalitarian Forms of Government* (New York: Benziger Brothers, 1938), p. 119.

that *"it is not laws but appropriate customs that make a people free."*[68] Granting that government in the Latin American republics has traditionally been more democratic in name than in fact, such Christian Democrats as Rafael Caldera aver that the redeeming virtue of a more genuinely representative system is that it allows profound social change to go on without mass violence and repression.[69]

The Christian concept of equality before God serves some Latin American reformers as a handy justification for political democracy, although it has by no means always done so. Now, as in the past, this doctrine of equality, like the other doctrines of the Church, is interpreted in whatever sense seems to benefit the Church and conform to existing or desired social forms. The doctrine of equality had no real weight in the contrasting environment of Visigothic Spain, where parishes, bishoprics, and monasteries possessed large numbers of slaves and where Church fathers upheld slavery as a necessary consequence of the fall of man.[70]

For an organization which evolved from this Spanish Church and which is still as hierarchically structured as is the contemporary Latin American Church, Catholic opposition to elitism has become surprisingly pronounced. Such influential laymen as Carlos Acedo Mendoza denounce dictatorship and the rule of narrow political elites. Acedo Mendoza distinguishes four types of Latin American dictatorship, and he criticizes each of them in turn. He opposes reactionary conservative regimes that seek to create "feudal peace in traditional societies," the professionally demagogic regimes that rely for support on mass emotionalism rather than effective programs, and the military regimes of the Stroessner or Somoza type that he optimistically feels to be doomed to extinction in the twentieth century. Acedo Mendoza similarly condemns the leftist extremism that is supported by well-educated "salon Marxists" who are as repelled by democracy as their wealthy and conservative par-

68. *Dimensión social de la caridad* (México: Secretariado Social Mexicano, 1962), p. 148. Velázquez' italics.
69. Rafael Caldera, *El bloque latinoamericano* (Santiago de Chile: Editorial del Pacífico, 1961), p. 112.
70. Aloysius K. Ziegler, "Church and State in Visigothic Spain" (S.T.D. diss., Catholic University of America, 1930), pp. 169–70, 179–85.

ents were and who try to install Communist regimes in order to associate themselves with the masses without giving up their own positions of special power and privilege. With an aversion to Fidel Castro characteristic of the Venezuelan "democratic left," Acedo Mendoza compares Castro directly to Dr. José Gaspar Rodríguez de Francia, the nineteenth-century dictator of Paraguay, and argues that Marxist rhetoric has not essentially changed the use of traditional dictatorial techniques by the ruling Communist elites of Castro's Cuba, Stalin's Russia, or Mao's China.[71]

The statements and actions of the Church hierarchy and the most respected Catholic laymen similarly oppose contrasting types of elitism. In Cuba, Monsignor Eduardo Boza Masvidal, the auxiliary bishop of Havana whom Castro forced out of the country in September, 1961, interprets the Church's conflict with Castro so as to show the Church's support for political liberty. Agreeing with North American interpretations of the Castro revolution such as that of Theodore Draper, Monsignor Boza Masvidal points out that Castro betrayed his early promises of democracy. The Church, which had supported improved living conditions as well as liberty, naturally turned against Castro after his betrayal and his open opposition to the Church.[72] In Brazil, Alceu Amoroso Lima has used his position as the country's best-known Catholic layman to oppose the curtailments of civil liberties that have accompanied the Brazilian revolution of 1964. In a classic manner that befits his stature as the senior spokesman for Brazilian Catholicism, Amoroso Lima argues that "it is not restricting liberty that avoids its abuse, but on the contrary continually guaranteeing more its exercise. Authority is more respected, the more it respects liberty."[73]

71. Carlos Acedo Mendoza, *Venezuela: Ruta y destino,* 2 vols. (Barcelona: Ediciones Ariel, 1966), 2: 247–51. Although Acedo Mendoza is directly related to four of the most powerful and conservative families in Venezuela, he has developed a profound social consciousness and become one of the leading progressive laymen in his country. The conservative members of his own family have denounced him as a Communist, but he actually represents a new kind of capitalist with a deep social concern.
72. Boza Masvidal, *Revolución cristiana en Latinoamérica,* pp. 67–71.
73. Quoted in Thomas G. Sanders to Richard H. Nolte, Oct. 14, 1967 (TGS-5 in series of field reports distributed by the Institute of Current World Affairs), p. 8. These excellent reports have been collected and published in Thomas G. Sanders, *Catholic Innovation in a Changing Latin America* (Cuernavaca, Mor.: CIDOC, 1969).

In Haiti, the Church excommunicated President François Duvalier for expelling the bishop of Port-au-Prince and the papal nuncio. Duvalier nevertheless published a picture of himself with God's hand on his shoulder and the caption "I have chosen him," and he had a yearly Te Deum said in Port-au-Prince to celebrate his own election for life to the presidency of Haiti. Despite such linkings of the Church to his own power position, however, the Church worked to maintain its antiauthoritarian image by refusing to cooperate with him until 1966.[74] In that year, a new concordat between Haiti and the Holy See entrusted control of the Haitian Church to five native bishops, thus replacing the foreign hierarchy to which Duvalier had strenuously objected. In return for this nationalization of the hierarchy and for a discreet silence from churchmen on violations of civil liberties, Duvalier has hung a photograph of the Pope in his office, designated a street in Port-au-Prince as "Paul VI Avenue," and presented such sumptuous gifts as American automobiles to his Haitian bishops.[75] Although official relations have thus been smoothed over, foreign priests have continued to be expelled and Catholic criticism of Duvalier is still regularly voiced from outside Haiti.

Going beyond mere opposition to authoritarians, Catholics have denounced the demagogic propaganda that encourages violence by pushing popular expectations and demands to levels that simply cannot be realized. In an attempt to provide constructive attitudes as well as constructive reforms, twenty-four Chilean bishops declared in 1962 that "prevailing conditions are so intolerable for many people that it is a growing temptation to promise immediate and total solutions in election speeches and propaganda. It is immoral to promise things with no intention of carrying them out, or things that cannot be achieved."[76] In cases like those of João Goulart in Brazil or Perón and Arturo Frondizi in Argentina,

74. For the Catholic side of the dispute with Duvalier, see David Finley, "Haiti: The Devil's Paradise," *The Sign* 44, no. 11 (June, 1965); Eric Fouchard, "The Haitian Church and Dictatorship," *CIF Reports* 5, no. 8 (April 16, 1966); and the Haitian Church publication, *Haïti Chérie!*.

75. Eduardo Gueydan, Bruno René Bazín, y Felix Lacambre, "Haiti: Una Iglesia en crisis," *Nadoc*, no. 125 (28 enero, 1970), pp. 1, 2.

76. "Social and Political Duties in the Present Time," in *Recent Church Documents from Latin America*, CIF Monographs, no. 2, p. 30.

where this clerical advice has been most flagrantly neglected, the frustration of inflated popular expectations has encouraged coups and military regimes. Despite the more moderate promises of such regimes, the old demagogic appeals leave a residue of frustration and hostility that impedes cooperative efforts. In this context, clerical warnings against demagogues seem most appropriate.

Many Catholics have begun to work for the realization of their new political ideals through party activity. As Richard Shaull and other North Americans have pointed out, liberal democracy has seemed an inadequate solution in Latin America because most political parties have represented only narrow elites. Since traditional parties and leaders are generally unable to meet rising popular demands for economic and social change, the need is for strong governments and parties that can direct such change, control foreign and domestic capital, and educate the people in a "new nationalism."[77] Like many other professors in Latin America, Ricardo Chartier, a professor of Christian social ethics in Buenos Aires, feels that the Church has an obligation to support the transformation of society. In order to effect this transformation, Chartier realistically finds that Christians must work through contemporary channels of power such as parties, trade unions, and cooperatives.[78] In addition to their efforts in "social transformation," the opposition of Christian Democrats to authoritarianism is well known. *Peronistas* and Perón himself interpreted the creation of a Christian Democratic party in Argentina as a clear sign of Church opposition,[79] and since 1961 the Christian Democratic party in Argentina has actively tried to incorporate *peronistas* within its ranks. In this context, insistence on "confessional" parties is dead as a genuine issue, as the Christian Democratic parties of the present are dedicated to social goals with a broadly representative system rather than to political influence for the Church per se.

The Christian Democratic parties in Latin America call for vig-

77. Richard Shaull, "Recientes estudios sobre el desarrollo político en Asia, Africa y América Latina," *Cristianismo y Sociedad* 1, no. 2 (1963): 45.
78. "Modos de relación entre la Iglesia y la sociedad," *Cristianismo y Sociedad* 1, no. 2 (1963): 13.
79. Pedro Badanelli, *Perón, la Iglesia y un cura*, 4th ed. (Buenos Aires: Editorial Tartessos, 1960), pp. 31–32.

orous presidential initiative, the direct representation of occupational groups in strengthened legislatures, and increased judicial authority, as well as such reforms as a career civil service and an end to literacy qualifications for voting.[80] Calling for stronger legislatures and judiciaries along with vigorous executive leadership is not really inconsistent; it is an attempt to make Latin American governments work more in accord with the constitutional theory underlying them. In other respects, Christian Democracy is also not as unique as its leaders sometimes claim. Other reformers promote the civil service and the broadened franchise, and the idea of occupational representation in legislatures merely revives the basic tenets of corporatism.

Sincerity rather than originality similarly underlies a current emphasis on electoral participation. Latin American prelates try to tone down the divisiveness of electoral battles by reiterating in pastoral letters that citizens' prime loyalty should be to their nation-state rather than to a particular political party.[81] They allege that all Catholics have political duties, but that those duties vary according to the aptitudes and role in society of the individual Catholic. According to Santiago Santa Cruz Cánepa, Catholics must not only fulfill such commonly accepted civic duties as exercising suffrage and accepting legal restraints but also go so far as to govern their conduct not by personal interests but by civic spirit and considerations of community welfare.[82] Backing up this orientation in a thoroughly North American way, a pamphlet in Spanish distributed by the Christophers on "Fifteen Ways to Improve Your Government" tells Latin Americans the importance of political participation with such admonitions as "Bad politicians are elected by those who don't vote" and with a description of how to increase voter turnout through personal persuasion and telephone campaigns. Although the pamphlet maintains a limited, North Ameri-

80. Edward J. Williams, *Latin American Christian Democratic Parties* (Knoxville, Tenn.: University of Tennessee Press, 1967), pp. 108–11.

81. See Mariano Rossell Arellano (Arzobispo de Guatemala), *Mensaje al pueblo de Guatemala en vísperas de elecciones presidenciales y de diputados al Congreso de la República*, Oct. 15, 1957 (Guatemala: Imprenta San Antonio, 1957), p. 16.

82. Santiago Santa Cruz Cánepa, "Deberes cívicos del católico," in Julián Rentería Uralde, ed., *La Iglesia y la política* (Santiago de Chile: Ediciones Paulinas, 1963), pp. 42–43.

can concept of political participation through its exclusive concentration on voting, it throws the authority of the Church behind citizen participation with frequent quotations of biblical passages as well as of Plato and William Penn.[83]

An ethic of honesty and dedication in government service is designed to balance and justify this concern for electoral participation. Without specifying much in the way of implementing techniques except the familiar bar to presidential reelection, Catholics have championed electoral reforms which encourage campaigns that emphasize ideas more than personalities.[84] Pastoral letters have stressed that government officials must avoid all forms of bribery and nepotism.[85] Among laymen, one of Christian Democracy's major contributions to Latin American politics is its projection of what political leaders should be. Christian Democrats see themselves as required to bring politically marginal citizens into an active political awareness and to infuse a humanistic and nonviolent dedication to economic and social change in the population as a whole. Furthermore, they stress an ethic of public service as opposed to personal self-interest for politicians themselves. As Rafael Caldera writes, "Politics demands the presence of men capable of working for ideals, with honesty and devotion."[86]

This stance on the part of such leaders as President Caldera underlines the importance of their early spiritual and social formation and incidentally indicates the influence of the priests who worked to shape their values. Sometimes this influence has even motivated the decision for a political career. In Caldera's case, for example, his original entry into politics stemmed largely from contact with Father Manuel Aguirre Elorriaga, the Basque Jesuit who since the 1930's has been responsible for bringing the social-Christian viewpoint to a whole generation of COPEI leaders.

83. *15 maneras de mejorar tu gobierno* (New York: The Christophers, n.d.). For a more general discussion of this topic, see José Carlos Aleixo, *The Catholic Church and Elections: A Study of the Catholic Thought on the Moral Obligation of Voting* (Cuernavaca, Mor.: CIDOC, 1969).
84. Laurencio, "Prólogo," in Boza Masvidal, *Revolución cristiana en Latinoamérica,* p. 19.
85. "Peruvian Bishops' Pastoral Letter on Politics and Social Reform," in *Recent Church Documents from Latin America,* CIF Monographs, no. 2, p. 43.
86. "Christian Democracy and Social Reality," p. 67.

Caldera had at first recognized that, with his legal training and natural abilities, he might become a millionaire by selling his talents to the oil companies. He decided to enter politics and work for social reform instead because, as Father Aguirre puts it, he came to see "that to become a politician is the highest profession except for that of a priest."[87] Father Aguirre clearly believes in this dual preeminence of the priestly and the political vocations, and he has convinced a generation of Venezuelan Christian Democrats to believe in it also. The doctrine would probably be inapplicable in the United States, where public opinion surveys have regularly shown that physicians and bankers win higher prestige than priests or politicians. But, in the Catholic cultures of Latin America, Father Aguirre's values stem logically and naturally from the traditional concept of two spheres of influence, one secular and the other religious, where the leaders of one sphere complement those of the other. Although Venezuela has come to enjoy the separation of Church and State, priests there and elsewhere have succeeded in maintaining the ideal of the nobility of public service and a political vocation.

A peculiarly intense dedication to service has characterized Eduardo Frei's approach to government. As he made clear in a statement of his program long before he became president, the realization of his goals requires a conscientious government service because "a government is not only one person but a group of men animated by a single spirit, inspired by common desires and with concrete plans to realize."[88] The sense of personal self-sacrifice that Frei's example brought out in some associates provided an appealing asset in his electoral campaign, but—as the intransigence of the Chilean civil service during Frei's six years in office also proved—self-sacrifice is a quality that Latin American governments still all too often lack. Although revolutionary leftists and even enlightened military men have also at times exemplified this quality, the necessary dedication derives most naturally

87. Interview with Manuel Aguirre Elorriaga, S.J., and Rafael Baquedano, S.J., at the Centro Gumilla in Caracas, Venezuela, June 14, 1968.
88. Eduardo Frei Montalva, *La verdad tiene su hora* (Santiago de Chile: Editorial del Pacífico, 1955), p. 100.

from the Christian impetus of *freista* programs. In the context of the self-interest, graft, and genial nepotism that have characterized the Latin American caudillo tradition, the governmental ethic of the Christian Democrats at least tries to provide a meaningful alternative.

This emphasis on honest government adds to the electoral strength that Catholic parties enjoy for such other reasons as the issue of atheism that still weighs significantly in the electoral politics of Latin America. Just as strong religious affiliations hurt a politician's standing in the Soviet Union, so militant atheism is a serious bar to office in Latin America. In the Chilean election of 1964, for example, even the earnest, evangelical Protestant sects chose overwhelmingly to support a popular Catholic spokesman, Eduardo Frei, against what then appeared to be the atheistic and potentially alien regime of Salvador Allende. Open and close affiliation with the Church hurts a politician's chances in a country like Mexico, where anticlericalism has been strong and where many politicians have been Freemasons as well as Catholics, but even in Mexico political leaders remain at least nominal Catholics and win votes by doing so. Even where, as in Mexico, Catholic parties have virtually no chance of taking power, their new orientation wins favor among formerly anticlerical groups and so allows their ideas and personnel more influence on government policy.

CATHOLIC DIVERSITY

The contemporary role of religion in Latin American politics does not fit easily into categories derived from other contexts. It does not fit the conflict of Church and State values that Max Weber described where a minority religious group believes in divine restoration of its social standing, nor the various situations of accommodation that Weber defined in the religious wars of Islam, the magical religion of Confucianism, the Calvinist justification for rule by religious leaders, or Buddhism's full retreat from politics and the world.[89] Instead of these relationships of conflict or ac-

89. Max Weber, *The Sociology of Religion*, trans. Ephraim Fischoff (London: Methuen & Co., 1965), pp. 227–28.

commodation, which presuppose a single line of activity in both religion and politics, alternative lines of both Catholic thought and political action intermingle and conflict in contemporary Latin America. Politicians and clergymen have always used religion to justify opposing policies, but the lines of Catholic politics emerging in Latin America are distinctive in their number, their internal consistency, and the degree of their mutual opposition. Although new middle positions in Catholic politics have appeared, they are still in a period of transition, simultaneously challenged and molded by more traditional and more radical Catholic viewpoints.

Latin American Catholics have come increasingly to recognize that beneath their common terminology lies a great diversity of orientations toward secular politics. Just as major conflicts arose in the colonial period among the different religious orders and between peninsular and Creole churchmen, so churchmen now recognize the splits among groups that in effect take diametrically opposed positions on the desirability and implementation of social reform. All Catholics proclaim that they desire such goals as "the triumph of the Church" or the "salvation of humanity," but, as Juan Luis Segundo points out, these common phrases cover extraordinary discrepancies in the ends and means actually promoted.[90] As an American Peace Corps volunteer told Jordan Bishop, Catholicism in Latin America is like a tent because "it covers everything."[91] The spectrum of Catholic thought is extremely broad; laymen and clerics who identify their social and political ideas as Catholic range from archdefenders of the status quo and the corporatist state to men who work actively to achieve Socialist goals through violent revolution. Critics of Catholic thought and the role of the Church in Latin America have too often focused on only a narrow part of that thought, and in doing so they have missed not only its comprehensiveness but also its gradual, overall movement to the left.

It is false to talk of the unity of Catholic thought in Latin America in other than a strictly religious sense, therefore, because

---

90. *Función de la Iglesia en la realidad rioplatense* (Montevideo: Barreiro y Ramos, S.A., 1962), p. 5.
91. Jordan Bishop to Frederick C. Turner, Cochabamba, Bolivia, June 4, 1967.

the social and political implications derived from Church doctrines have been so disparate. They vary on at least three spectrums: between the pole of reform and the pole of the status quo, between the pole of strict allegiance and the pole of indifference, and between the pole of intellectual understanding and the pole of abject reverence for Christian forms. Some Catholics support reform in the name of charity and Christian equality, while others oppose it in the name of a natural hierarchy and God-given rights. Like members of other religious groups, nominal Catholics in their actual indifference to religious teaching and its political implications provide a sharp contrast to the strict allegiance that other Catholics give to the teachings and the pastors of the Church. Finally, while some Catholics actively question the meaning of their faith, others merely draw psychological satisfaction from it by accepting its outward formulas and rituals with an unquestioning devotion.

Catholic thought varies in a "quantitative" sense in terms of the degree to which it actually affects the actions of the citizens who profess to believe in it. Although over 90 per cent of the citizens of most Latin American countries identify their religious affiliation as Catholic, the proportion of Catholics attending mass at least weekly in the cities and in rural areas where priests are available is just under 20 per cent.[92] The absence of priests in many villages makes the actual proportion still lower than these figures suggest, and the ritualistic significance of church attendance calls into question the degree to which even regular attendance at mass can be said to alter patterns of interpersonal relations in the secular world. As a United States Catholic magazine pointed out in 1964, nine out of ten Latin American children are Catholics "but unless things change, only one in ten is likely to practice the faith when grown up."[93] Catholic pronouncements have their widest impact, therefore, on a large group of "nominal"

92. For an excellent discussion of the degree to which weekly attendance at mass measures religious sentiment, and comparative statistics on the percentage of citizens attending mass at least weekly in the different Latin American countries, see Émile Pin, S.J., *Elementos para una sociología del catolicismo latinoamericano* (Bogotá: FERES, 1963), pp. 14–18.
93. "Latin America's Future Faces," *The Sign* 43, no. 6 (Jan., 1964) : 39.

42

Catholics, on that numerical majority of Latin Americans who call themselves Catholic yet fail notably in matters of religious observance. In terms of influencing new courses of individual action, this impact on nominal Catholics is not necessarily either deep or meaningful.

Catholic thought also varies "qualitatively" in terms of the secular patterns of action to which it relates. In this sense, Father Hoornaert of the Regional Seminary of the Northeast in Brazil recently commented that unity is the major problem of the Brazilian Church. Besides the different political orientations of Brazilian Catholics, the "neo-Christian" patterns of Indian and African Brazilians create a divisive pluralism in Brazilian Catholicism.[94] Localism further complicates effective unity of action. The degree to which the Church has accommodated itself to regionalism and local loyalties appears decisively in the tendency of Latin American Marians to associate the Virgin Mary with their special region, locality, or group.[95]

Peasant contexts—even those as ethnically and linguistically distinct as the Volga-Deutsch settlements in northern Argentina and the Indian and *ladino* communities of Guatemala—seem to contain a particularly inward-looking form of Catholicism. In his important empirical study of migration in rural Argentina, Richard Wilkie finds that those men with higher rates of confidence in priests tend to move shorter distances than those who do not share the same confidence. Those descendants of Volga-Deutsch settlers who draw their explanations of life from such authorities as priests tend to fear contact with the outside world, to fail to understand it, and therefore not to be very venturesome in exploring it.[96] Similarly, Nathan Whetten finds in the case of Guatemala that the prayers, myths, legends, and formulas used for appeasing the gods vary greatly even among neighboring *munici-*

94. Eduardo Hoornaert, "O Concílio Vaticano II e a Igreja no Brasil," *Revista Eclesiástica Brasileira* 27, fasc. 1 (março, 1967): 49–50.

95. For extensive descriptions of the regional attachments to Mary, see Rubén Vargas Ugarte, S.J., *Historia del culto de María en Hispanoamérica y de sus imágenes y santuarios mas celebrados* (Lima: Imprenta "La Providencia," 1931).

96. Richard Waldo Wilkie, "On the Theory of Process in Human Geography: A Case Study of Migration in Rural Argentina" (Ph.D. diss., University of Washington, 1968), pp. 88, 109.

pios. Patron saints, who are the centers of religious devotion in each *municipio,* are thought to be special persons who "live" in the local church and are quite different from the saints of the same name worshipped in other *municipios.*[97] Among Latin Americans having a firm attachment to the Church, therefore, the group of progressives is surrounded not only by Catholic conservatives but also by Catholics who see little real connection between their religion and broad questions of national reform.

The actions of Catholic progressives must differ in Latin American countries, depending on the size of the progressive movement and the traditional position of the Church. As Emilio Portes Gil indicates, the former position of the Church in Mexico was very different from its position in other Latin American countries. The Church was so closely tied to a powerful and conservative political faction that it had to be forced to renounce secular power.[98] In order to keep from jeopardizing the position of the Church with the Mexican government, Mexican bishops now issue no regular circulars or pastoral letters dealing directly with politics.[99] Although the Church in Colombia, Ecuador, and Peru has had power comparable to that of the old Mexican Church, it has not exercised the same degree of political influence in other Latin American countries. In such countries as Chile and Brazil where the Church has not been so consistently renounced as an alien and conservative influence, progressives have tended more often to identify themselves as Catholics. Where Catholic progressives have become such outspoken advocates of change that they have alienated the government, as they have done with the military officers who have guided Brazilian politics since 1964, then the openness of the progressives is curtailed.

Significant factionalism and opposing attitudes appear even within the Christian Democratic movement in Latin America; it should not be viewed as a unified whole. Churchmen recognize

97. Nathan L. Whetten, *Guatemala: The Land and the People* (New Haven, Conn.: Yale University Press, 1961), pp. 287–88.
98. Emilio Portes Gil, *The Conflict between the Civil Power and the Clergy* (México: n.p., 1934), pp. 101–3.
99. Lino Aguirre (Obispo de Culiacán) to Frederick C. Turner, Nov. 13, 1967.

that a Catholic political party cannot represent the great diversity of interests held by practicing Catholics within a country,[100] but they quite naturally do not like to elaborate on the resulting factionalism. Multiparty systems like those of Chile or Venezuela encourage a narrower range of intraparty viewpoint than exists in two-party systems or in a single-party system like that of Mexico, but in general the opposition of viewpoints and factions in the Christian Democratic parties of Latin America has been underestimated and played down. Tad Szulc may well be correct in his judgment that the overall growth in Christian Democratic strength is the most important development in Latin American politics since the rise of Fidel Castro,[101] and the Christian Democratic movement in Latin America contains enough consensus on reform to place it considerably to the left of the Christian Democratic Union in West Germany. Within the Latin American parties, however, Christian Democrats divide sharply on what kinds of measures should implement reform and on what positions should be taken in relation to *fidelistas* and the United States.

Divisions are especially likely to grow and to come out in the open after a Christian Democratic party has won control of the government. The need for unity to gain power has then disappeared, and a particular faction can assume immediate leadership of the government by taking control of the party. Christian Democratic factionalism has become increasingly evident in Chile, as in a July, 1967, statement of the National Council of the party that embarrassed President Frei by favoring the free operation in Chile of the *fidelista*, Latin American "Solidarity Organization," and guerrilla warfare against "governments that ignore the people's rights and offer no electoral solutions."[102] When and if Christian

100. Cardinal Pacelli stated this position nicely in a letter of June 1, 1934, to Monsignor Héctor Felici. He wrote that "a political party, although it seems to be inspired by the doctrine of the Church and to defend the rights of the Church, can not pretend to represent all the faithful, since its specific program can never have an absolute worth for everyone, and since its actions in practice are subject to error." The letter is reprinted in Rentería Uralde, ed., *La Iglesia y la política*, pp. 81–92.

101. "Communists, Socialists, and Christian Democrats," *The Annals of the American Academy of Political and Social Science* 360 (July, 1965): 100.

102. Quoted in *New York Times*, July 18, 1967.

Democrats do come to wield more influence in Latin America as a whole, the divisions within the movement can be expected to become more pronounced.

The diversity and factionalism within Latin American Catholicism raise the issue of who can appropriately be said to speak for the Latin American Church. If there really is such an entity as "Latin American Catholic thought," then whose thought is involved? Since nine Latin Americans in ten are at least nominal Catholics, Catholic thought in the broadest sense could be interpreted simply as the political thought and attitudes of the overwhelming majority of Latin Americans. In a more restricted and appropriate sense, however, it refers only to those orientations to action which their adherents identify as being Catholic in origin and content. Although this view of Catholic thought does not substantially reduce the extreme variation of attitudes included under the rubric of Catholicism, it does severely restrict the number of Latin Americans whose political thinking can be meaningfully identified as Catholic.

Paradoxically, Latin American Catholic thought also encompasses the orientations of people who are not native Latin Americans. There are so many European and North American churchmen working in Latin America that, in terms of Catholic policies and viewpoints in the area, it would be misleading not to include their views. Not only has the foreign clergy influenced the thinking of Latin American Catholics, but the exogenous clergymen are in some countries so numerous and in such high positions that they provide a most important segment of what is usually considered "Latin American" Catholic thought. A study of Catholic attitudes in Latin America should not detail the views of Catholics in other parts of the world which have simply influenced Latin American viewpoints, but it should include the views of the foreign clergy and laymen actively working in the area.

From the standpoint of Church policies, the ideas that matter most are the ideas of the men in positions of authority. Toward society as a whole these men are the spokesmen for the Church, and toward churchmen under their jurisdiction they are the immediate if not the ultimate policy-makers. In an institutional and organizational sense, the Catholic Church resembles a national military organization or a private corporation. Men on the lower rungs of the organization must accept the final authority of their superiors, and they can influence the policies of the organization as a whole only to the extent that they are willing to work within the framework of the policies already laid down; directly condemning those policies rarely has the desired effect. The size of the decision-making elite in the Latin American Church is very limited. José Luis de Imaz, for example, notes that in Argentina bishops and archbishops represent only 1 per cent of the clergy, and that in earlier years when there were no more than twenty dioceses bishops and archbishops represented only 0.5 per cent of the clergy.[103] Parish priests and lay spokesmen do sometimes initiate projects or ideas that get thrust up to public attention, but the thinking of these individuals is influential in shaping Church policies only to the extent that it first affects the views of the narrow Church hierarchy.

Given the central significance of the thinking of the Latin American bishops, several recent trends in Catholic thought have assumed notable importance. First, extraordinary divergence has developed among the attitudes that individual bishops take toward social issues. A paradox of the present situation of the Church is that, although the Church works increasingly to legitimize constructive forms of social change, splits within its own leadership place it in a poorer position to perform the legitimizing and integrating functions. Second, some members of the lower clergy have become such outspoken advocates of social change and have become so frustrated over the slowness of the Church to implement this change that they have gone outside the Church to work for reform. Father Camilo Torres, the Colombian priest who finally took up the cause of violent revolution in order to achieve his social goals, showed how far impatient members of the clergy may go. Third, the attitudes of Catholic populations have on some issues run far ahead of the Church's official position, so that the thinking

103. José Luis de Imaz, *Los que mandan* (Buenos Aires: Editorial Universitaria de Buenos Aires, 1964), p. 170.

of more conservative Church leaders is brought into question by the new beliefs of their flock as well as by the objective situation that helped to determine those beliefs. New desires for family limitation in cramped urban environments, for example, have encouraged many Catholics to accept officially forbidden techniques to prevent conception. As the Church's position increasingly comes in conflict with the beliefs of practicing Catholics, ecclesiastical thinking must adapt rapidly to social change in order to allow the authority of the Church to remain intact.

So far, the broadest effect of the evolution of Church preachments has been the degree to which they have altered Catholic support for individual freedom. Older interpretations of the influence of the Church claimed that it encouraged liberty in the sense that "theocentric" conceptions of man's worth inhibited the exercise of the license and irresponsibility that are the antithesis of liberty,[104] but in the 1960's the Church went on to promote a much broader concept of liberty. The older theocentric ethic encouraged acceptance of authoritarianism and social stratification along with its depreciation of license and anarchy, but the new ethic strongly encourages political participation and an achievement-oriented society. In doing so, it provides new social and economic orientations as well as a new orientation to politics.

104. Julio Tobar Donoso, *La Iglesia, modeladora de la nacionalidad* (Quito: "La Prensa Católica," 1953), p. 283.

II ~

The Reorientation
of Catholic Goals

Within the past decade, an increasingly large group of Latin American Catholics has become painfully aware of the inadequacies of their traditional attitudes toward economics and society. An apolitical stance, pious support for altruism, and ambiguous enunciations of social justice once seemed the best way to strengthen the moral authority of the Church, but, in the opinion of Catholic progressives, the ineffectiveness of this older orientation now merely undermines that authority. As a result, Catholic spokesmen have come more and more to support economic development and a quasi-Protestant ethic of hard work, to reject paternalism as a solution, and to organize such activities as trade unions, cooperatives, and land redistribution. A new educational emphasis on "consciousness" and new doctrines of population control have received more qualified support. These orientations have gone so far that traditionalists criticize progressives for overstepping their authority and disregarding the proper separation of Church and State. Progressives have encountered further difficulties, moreover, in formulating and implementing their own orientations. Despite these difficulties, however, Catholic attitudes toward economics and social change have evolved so far that they can not be neglected or rejected. They can be modified, but at least in the short run their modifications are likely to extend even further the tendencies in Catholic thought that have already arisen.

Outsiders have long recognized the inadequacies of Catholic social thought in Latin America. That Latin American Catholics paid comparatively little attention to social theory before 1960 is reflected in the fact that although Latin Americans make up more than one-third of the Catholics in the world, no statements by Latin Americans appeared even in such massive compilations of Catholic thought as that edited by A. Robert Caponigri.[1] As J. Lloyd Mecham suggests, the traditional program of Catholic Action has not had great influence on most Latin American societies.[2] The general ineffectiveness of such traditional programs has led both Catholics and non-Catholics to make pessimistic assessments of the Church's ability to change. Summing up a prevalent North American interpretation, George Lane attacks optimistic statements of the "new" Catholic viewpoint with the claim that "despite renewal in parts of Latin America, the Church as a whole does not appear able to disassociate itself from the *ancien régime* whose demise it predicts with unerring accuracy."[3] Father Hoffman of the Catholic University of America goes so far as to call the contemporary Latin American Church "an outdated European importation" and the "relic of a bygone age."[4]

Although the very fact that Catholics can criticize the Church in this manner indicates the extent to which Catholic thought is shifting, trying to overcome its old inadequacy, one must also recognize the important function that the inadequacy itself has played. The concept of social justice is still used ambiguously in

1. *Modern Catholic Thinkers* (New York: Harper & Brothers, 1960).
2. *Church and State in Latin America: A History of Politico-Ecclesiastical Relations,* rev. ed. (Chapel Hill, N. C.: University of North Carolina Press, 1966), p. 427.
3. Review of John J. Considine, M.M., ed., *Social Revolution in the New Latin America: A Catholic Appraisal,* in the *Hispanic American Historical Review* 47, no. 2 (May, 1967): 248.
4. Ronan Hoffman, O.F.M., "Social Change in Latin America: The Mission of the Church," *CIF Reports* 6, no. 8 (April 16, 1967): 66.

50

the writing of most Church leaders specifically because it carries the impression of reform without any substantive commitments. This is important, since substantive commitment to precise reforms alienates the secular conservatives upon whose contributions many Church enterprises depend. Furthermore, explicit commitments open fissures of disagreement between status-quo and avant-garde churchmen themselves, and so endanger Catholic unity. Even when statements reach the level of advocating specific areas of reform, therefore, a concentration upon agreeable generalizations usually prevents detailed advocacy of proposals that would hurt a particular group.

With this need for ambiguity, Latin Americans have often skipped over economic and social problems through the theological rationale that, since both individual men and nation-states are the creatures of God, there should be no conflict between them. Rejecting the libertarian theories of the French Revolution and the totalitarian theories of Nazi Germany and Stalinist Russia, one line of Catholic reasoning claims that neither does the state exist for the individual nor does the individual exist to serve the state. Instead, both exist to serve God.[5] To the extent that Latin American Catholics did formulate an ethic in regard to economic affairs, it was often a simple wish that altruism should prevail and that the barriers between men should not exist. In an editorial in *Sic,* the Venezuelan Jesuit journal, Ganuza typically avers that an "absence of brotherhood" is the major world problem, and that a feeling of charity must overcome barriers of race, religion, and nationality.[6]

What is surprising is not that such traditionally pious sentiments continue to be voiced in Latin America, but rather that other Catholic leaders should have provided a diversity of far more concrete, detailed, and programmatic solutions to problems of secular social change. The traditional reasoning on peace and cooperation has not, of course, prevented conflict between individual

5. For a contemporary statement of this position, see Luis Ambrosio Cruz, S.J., "La participación por dependencia total en la solución de los problemas originados entre individuo y estado," *Ecclesiástica Xaveriana* 10 (1960).

6. Juan M. Ganuza, S.J., "Inaplazables exigencias de la encíclica," *Sic* 30, no. 295 (mayo, 1967): 218.

men, between revolutionaries and their nation-state, or at the international level between nation-states. It is in trying to modify this continuing process of conflict in Latin America that the newer Catholic teachings on social responsibility go much farther than the older rationale of harmony deriving from divine creation. To change the unflattering image that they have created of themselves and their society, increasing numbers of Catholics believe that they must change the reality of that society, and they perceive a variety of ways in which to do so.

ECONOMIC ORIENTATIONS

Priests and even bishops argue that political freedom is meaningless unless individuals are also free to improve their economic and social positions, and they have set up organizations to propagate this viewpoint among the present generation of Latin American churchmen. As Dom Hélder Câmara puts it, "Political freedom means nothing to a man who lives in subhuman conditions, without food, without health, without education, and without hope of improvement. What is his freedom? The freedom to live in misery. We must elevate his standards of living to the human level, before he can even begin to think about political freedom."[7] Education for priestly work has begun to encompass this primary concern with development at such institutions as the Regional Seminary of the Northeast in Brazil and the Center for Intercultural Documentation (CIDOC) in Cuernavaca, Mexico. In a special program to train North American priests, religious, and laymen for work in Latin America, a CIDOC instructor emphasized in 1962 that "the most important fact of life" that these Catholics would encounter in the area was economic development.[8] This orientation is important for what it does not say as well as for what it says. The

7. Quoted in David St. Clair, "The Battling Bishop of Brazil," *The Sign* 44, no. 4 (Nov., 1964) : 46.
8. Everett Reimer, *Social Consequences of Economic Development,* CIF Monographs, no. 1 (Cuernavaca, Mor.: CIDOC, 1963), p. 1. This monograph is a synthetic summary of Reimer's course at CIDOC during 1962 and of some of his earlier work on Puerto Rico.

52

most significant "fact of life" for Catholics is not—as Latin American churchmen have so often said—the menace of Protestantism, or the scarcity of vocations, or family life and morality. Instead, it is economic development.

In a manner reminiscent of the Protestant ethic, contemporary Catholic teachings advocate hard work and self-improvement to achieve the goal of development. Jesuits praise Max Weber's study of *The Protestant Ethic and the Spirit of Capitalism* for what Father Martínez Galdeano describes as its view of "true" capitalism as being "urged on by religious and benevolent or other personal motives to better serve one's country and one's people through a more efficient production."[9] Father Vekemans in Chile believes that a Latin American "cultural mutation" is required to achieve development, that "the characteristics of the ethical and religious orders have been unduly projected into the profane world," and that the new developmental ideology should incorporate "all the virtues of Anglo-Saxon pragmatism." With the process of "symbiosis and osmosis" between Latin America and the North Atlantic community that he advocates,[10] Latin Americans would lose their reliance on revelation and more readily accept a scientific, technological orientation. Implicitly, they might also make the conscience-directed actions of each individual the real test of salvation, and so get away from the old idea that the Latin American priestly class is necessary for salvation. Although the Society of Jesus was originally set up in part to counter the spread and the effects of the Protestant Reformation, the ideas of Father Vekemans and his fellow Jesuits are designed to stimulate individual initiative and responsibility and so, in a sense, to bring the values of the Protestant Reformation to Latin America.

Besides propagandizing these values among fellow priests, their supporters have produced materials to inculcate the values among

9. Fernando Martínez Galdeano, S.J., "La encíclica social de Paulo VI," *Sic* 30, no. 295 (mayo, 1967): 220.
10. See Roger E. Vekemans, S.J., "Economic Development, Social Change, and Cultural Mutation in Latin America," in William V. D'Antonio and Fredrick B. Pike, eds., *Religion, Revolution, and Reform: New Forces for Change in Latin America* (New York: Frederick A. Praeger, 1964), pp. 127–42, and the related discussion by Father Vekemans on pp. 233–38.

53

ordinary Catholic laymen. A primer on agricultural techniques distributed to peasants in Colombia by Monsignor José Joaquín Salcedo's Acción Cultural Popular (ACPO) begins by telling peasants that "to perfect oneself is to give glory to God. The dignity of man is realized when he progresses on the spiritual, cultural, social, economic, occupational, familial and individual levels."[11] Similarly, a collective pastoral that all the twenty-four bishops of Chile signed in 1962 has been reprinted as a popular, well-illustrated propaganda booklet. Beside a series of pictures of slum dwellers, manual laborers, and a voter thinking hard as he places his ballot in the box, the most pithy statements of the pastoral denounce communism and laissez faire capitalism, support increased production and administrative responsibility, and argue that Christian charity is an active ethic that requires specific actions in the contemporary world.[12]

In showing what kinds of action are required, Catholic leaders address themselves directly to such contemporary problems as flight capital, unemployment, and employer-employee relations. Bishops join economists to denounce flight capital, as when the bishops of Brazil in 1963 declared that "it is a grave fault against justice and a deeply unChristian act to hoard unproductive capital or to send it elsewhere for speculative ends."[13] Bishops likewise show a sharp sense of the personal indignity that unemployment causes. Along with a number of his fellow prelates, the bishop of Ambato, Ecuador, speaks out strongly against the unemployment caused by migration to cities where industrialization has not yet provided sufficient work.[14] Primary concern for the rights of workers is also evident in statements on their proper relations with

11. Carlos Vargas Vanegas, *Cartilla Agricola* (Bogotá: Acción Cultural Popular, 1964), p. 7.

12. *La tremenda realidad de Chile: Resumen de la pastoral colectiva "El deber social y político . . ."* (n.p.: Editorial Nueva Esperanza, n.d.).

13. "Brazilian Bishops' Pastoral Letter on Social Reform," in *Recent Church Documents from Latin America,* CIF Monographs, no. 2 (Cuernavaca, Mor.: CIDOC, 1963), p. 37.

14. See Bernardino Echeverría Ruiz, O.F.M. (Obispo de Ambato), *La doctrina social de Pío XII: Conferencia pronunciada en el acto académico del Teatro Lalama, con la concurrencia de todas las autoridades y de numeroso público,* March 2, 1956 (Ambato: Edit. "Pío XII," 1956), pp. 6–7.

their employers. A leader in Venezuelan Catholic organizations has declared that workers must be paid a just salary to meet their spiritual as well as their material needs; in addition, profit-sharing plans and joint management must also allow workers to share increasingly in the companies for which they work.[15]

One of the most significant Catholic positions is that on the sanctity and use of private property. Congregations of Latin American bishops have gone on record as finding social progress to be more important than the maintenance of private property, as when a 1966 meeting of 200 bishops in Mar del Plata, Argentina, declared officially that "the fundamental right of all to the use of the material goods on earth precedes the right to private property."[16] Catholic moderates are unlike both Marxists and doctrinaire liberals in their view of private property; they find that individual ownership is an inherent human right but not an absolute or unlimited one. The pragmatism of the moderates becomes clear in the fact that they feel that the use to which land is put is the major criterion for determining the desirability of private property. Private ownership is seen not only as just but as a prime source of initiative and progress when the land is used productively, but both private property and communal ownership are decried when they detract from optimum productivity.[17]

Catholic pronouncements extend beyond economic policies to encompass a wide variety of social programs. Manuel Larraín, the late, influential bishop of Talca, likened social reform to missionary endeavor. In his view, Christians had two essential tasks: the Christianization of the world in a religious sense, and work through "social action" designed "to construct a humane world."[18] Characteristic of the older and more paternalistic implementation of this second task was the founding of the Associação Litoral de

15. Carlos Acedo Mendoza, *Venezuela: Ruta y destino,* 2 vols. (Barcelona: Ediciones Ariel, 1966), 2: 296.

16. *New York Times,* June 4, 1967.

17. See the moderate position on private property presented in Pedro Jamet Flores, "Actitud económico-social del católico," in Julián Rentería Uralde, ed., *La Iglesia y la política* (Santiago de Chile: Ediciones Paulinas, 1963), pp. 153–55.

18. Manuel Larraín Errázuriz (Obispo de Talca, Asesor General de la A. C. Chilena), *La hora de la Acción Católica* (Santiago de Chile: Editorial del Pacífico, S.A., 1956), p. 26.

Anchieta by Bishop Paulo de Tarso Campos in the early 1940's. Located in Santos, Brazil, the association recruited girls over the age of fifteen from slum sections along the wharves and beaches and gave them an intensive course in such domestic skills as sewing, home nursing, and child care.[19]

Another means readily available to churchmen has been the moral pronouncement, especially the pronouncement on evolving social practices and attitudes. In addition to customary denunciations of fornication, a recent Catholic campaign in northern Mexico has also opposed the use of drugs, the amount of money spent on cosmetics, and the tendency to prize a new and expensive automobile as a status symbol.[20] Such pronouncements add contemporary issues to the older list of moral concerns but, like the Associação Litoral de Anchieta, they reflect an essentially traditional Catholic approach.

Although many social pronouncements and programs naturally continue to reflect concern for traditional morality or for Catholic charities, the growth of Catholic programs has been toward a more wide-ranging and cooperative approach. This covers such diverse questions as race, health, and the worldwide distribution of income. As spokesmen for the Church outside Latin America have proclaimed racism and Catholicism to be fundamentally incompatible,[21] prelates have taken a new stand on the question of race and Indian incorporation within Latin America. In contrast to the colonial and nineteenth-century situation where churchmen saw themselves as the special protectors of the Indians, they now say that they should simply work along with other groups and institutions to integrate the Indian into the mainstream of Latin American culture.[22] Besides trying to strengthen Catholic religious ideals within their own families, members of the Christian Family

19. Mary Frederick Lochemes, O.S.F., and Mary Patrice McNamara, O.S.F., *The Church in Latin America* (Wichita, Kansas: Catholic Action Bookshop, 1945), p. 44.

20. Manuel Talamás Camandari (Obispo de Ciudad Juárez), *Cruzada de moderación y caridad cristiana* (n.p.: n.p., Feb. 2, 1963), pp. 10–11.

21. See Yves M.-J. Congar, O.P., *The Catholic Church and the Race Question* (Paris: UNESCO, 1961).

22. See Bernardino Echeverría R. (Obispo de Ambato), *La Iglesia católica y el problema del indio: Disertación que fue leída como ponencia en la Conferencia Episcopal de Río de Janeiro* (n.p.: Editorial "Pío XII," 1956), pp. 19–21.

Movement in Latin America have similarly given active support to improvements in living standards through such means as better nutrition and public health measures. Although it was initiated by upper- and upper middle-class couples, the Movimiento Familiar Cristiano has worked to win membership and support from all social strata. On the issue of the disparity in income between rich and poor countries, Christian Democrats have shown particular concern. In 1951 Eduardo Frei prophetically declared that his party even then found that the division between the industrialized and developing nations was even more important than the split between the United States and Russia that disturbed everyone so much at that time.[23]

Along with these concerns has come the demand to implement them partly through new Church financing and facilities. By 1970, the Vatican was spending about $400 million a year in direct aid to the Third World, and it had decided to concentrate most of this assistance in Latin America. The finances of the Holy See are so dispersed and so shrouded in mystery that even most churchmen have no precise idea of the real amounts involved, but it is clear that Vatican investments provide a considerable sum in disposable income. It has been alleged that the Vatican has continued to maintain interests in armaments manufacture and in a Danish firm producing contraceptives; unquestionably, the Holy See controls large real estate and stock market investments in the United States and has even been able to profit from revaluations of the German mark.[24] The fact that this income is being channeled to public service projects and investments in Latin America testifies—in a most concrete way—to the concern of the worldwide Church for Latin American development.

In the region itself, new Church facilities and a new concept of the roles of religious personnel have also evolved. The archdiocese of Cali, Colombia, has planned and constructed new parish centers that combine in one complex of buildings a medical

23. Eduardo Frei Montalva, *Sentido y forma de una política* (Santiago de Chile: Editorial del Pacífico, 1951), p. 181.
24. For an enlightened appraisal of the Vatican's wealth and investments, see Simon Spivac, "The Vatican As a World Power," *Atlas* 19, no. 5 (May, 1970).

dispensary, a store with staple foods at low prices, a social center, and schools for boys and girls, as well as a church and living quarters for religious personnel.[25] Like Church leaders from the sixteenth to the nineteenth centuries who saw themselves as protectors of the Indians, many twentieth-century leaders have defined themselves as the natural defenders of the poor. They no longer see themselves as the exclusive defenders, however, and many have now decided that such defense requires community mobilization rather than paternalistic protection. New kinds of training will naturally be required for community leadership. As Nazario has suggested in an issue of *CIF Reports,* the modern priest ought not to be a scholastic theologian, the employee of a bishop, or a celibate monk. Instead, "in order that a priest may be said to be 'raised up . . . from the midst of the faithful,' it is required that he grow under the influence of the community—become an adult in it—and that he show evidence through his community life of his qualities of understanding, leadership and charity which his testimony as president of a community requires. Obviously, this cannot be realized through a seminary."[26] Some evidence indicates that a majority of Catholics now wants priests to be able to undertake this new type of leadership. Nicolás Rosato, a priest trained in sociology, has conducted a survey in Argentina to determine what Catholics expect of their priests. While 45 per cent of the respondents still said that the priest should restrict his endeavor to specifically spiritual activities, the remaining 55 per cent declared that priests should also promote community development projects.[27]

Such community leaders—whether priests or laymen—could have a marked effect on the social development of Latin America, and in some cases it is clear that they already have. In Brazil, a segment of the clergy is one of the most influential groups calling

25. See *Parroquias vivas* . . . (n.p.: Carvajal & Cía., n.d.). This is a large and well-illustrated booklet showing the centers in operation and describing the ideas behind them.
26. Victor M. Nazario, "Training for the Priesthood," *CIF Reports* 6, no. 5 (March 1, 1967): 35.
27. *Latin America Calls!* 4, no. 4 (Nov., 1967), p. 3. For a more extensive discussion of the Rosato findings, see "¿Que espera la gente de los sacerdotes?" *Confirmado* 3, no. 107 (6 julio, 1967).

for reform. Three years after the Brazilian revolution of 1964, an American who spent much of that time observing politics in Brazil found peasants and slum dwellers apathetic and student groups more concerned with opposing United States influence than with cooperating with the Brazilian government in bringing reform. In this context, she commented, "The one articulate group whose voice continues to carry loud and far is that of the bishops of the Northeast."[28] In Chile, churchmen have tried to stimulate community development by citing the shocking statistics that have become their stock-in-trade. They decry the national situation of the early 1960's when one-third of all Chilean children were leaving school after the first year, one-tenth of the population was receiving half of the national income, and workers were consuming an average of only half as much meat between 1957 and 1959 as they had between 1945 and 1947.[29]

It is no disparagement of the new Catholic approach to note that it has arisen in response to the kinds of pressures that these statistics reveal. Representatives of the Latin American middle class have long criticized the Church for its failure to respond. In the late 1930's *Hechos e Ideas,* the journal of the Radical party in Argentina, violently attacked the Church's stance in relation to political and economic advancement, as when Abelardo J. Coimil wrote in 1937 that Argentina's historic Revolution of May was "fought against the God that Franco and his sympathizers in our country are defending today: a God of class. The God of privilege . . . that God of misery, submission and slavery . . . of the privileged minorities of our world."[30] More recently, active Catholic laymen have come to call for the reorientation of Church resources for the benefit of the mass of citizens. Professor Arias Calderón of the University of Panama complains that the human and economic resources of the Church have continued to propa-

28. Frances M. Foland to Richard H. Nolte, Nov. 4, 1967 (FMF-9 in series of field reports distributed by the Institute of Current World Affairs), p. 19.
29. Raúl Silva Henríquez (Cardenal Arzobispo de Santiago) and others, *Los obispos de Chile hablan: El deber social y político en la hora presente,* Sept. 18, 1962 (Santiago de Chile: Editorial Universidad Católica, 1962), pp. 10–11.
30. Abelardo J. Coimil, "El dogma de 'Dios, Patria y Hogar' y la U.C.R.," *Hechos e Ideas* 3, no. 24 (agosto, 1937): 290–91.

gate the faith "mainly among a select, minority group, socially above average and predominantly traditional in its outlook."[31] As the Latin American middle class has grown in strength and become critical of the older Catholicism, it is only natural that the great majority of the clergy, who were born into the middle class or who rose into it, should also become more critical and work for reform.

If the new lines of Catholic thought are responding to middle-class criticisms, they are also in a wider sense adapting to the new value patterns of Latin American citizens. Catholic thought has traditionally downgraded the importance of material goods, but with material goods increasingly abundant in the twentieth century this has come to seem anachronistic. As Ivan Vallier points out, Latin Americans are now far more concerned with chances for employment and advancement, with social status, and with material goods than they are with salvation. Since most Latin Americans do not see religion as helping them to obtain these goals,[32] churchmen are reformulating a Catholic ethic to deal with them. Besides concentrating more directly on the goals, the reformulation questions the traditional methods of paternalism.

THE REJECTION OF PATERNALISM

Some Catholic programs continue to be frankly paternalistic in outlook and operation. In order to awaken the wealthier citizens of Latin America to the real exigencies of hunger and poverty, they have encouraged voluntary contributions and abstinence. As the archbishop of Caracas reminded the Women's Union of Venezuelan Catholic Action when they arranged a day of partial abstinence in 1964, the money saved by refraining from a sandwich, a package of cigarettes, or a trip to the cinema would make only a

31. Ricardo Arias Calderón, "The Intellectual Challenge to Religion in Latin America," in John J. Considine, M.M., ed., *The Religious Dimension in the New Latin America* (Notre Dame, Ind.: Fides Publishers, 1966), p. 60. Before returning to teach philosophy in Panama, Professor Arias Calderón graduated *summa cum laude* from Yale University and did graduate work at the Sorbonne.
32. Ivan Vallier, "Catholicism: From Church to 'Sect'?" *CIF Reports* 3, no. 3 (May 15–31, 1964) : 4.

tiny contribution to the Campaign against Hunger. Individual contributions would make a meaningful sum when added together,[33] however, and the small effort served to ease the consciences of wealthy Venezuelan ladies. Although the decision to give up one treat on a single day does not give the well-to-do the same degree of sympathy for the poor that Moslems have traditionally inculcated through longer fasts, it is at least designed to stir social awareness and to manifest a concern that it is hoped will grow.

Actually, such programs salve the consciences of the rich far more than they alleviate the poverty of the poor. This traditional concept of charity has entailed the giving of a particular sum or gift from the rich to the poor; it has not been considered a real requirement but rather something that generosity might motivate. It has emphasized rather than shortened the gulf between rich and poor. Now, however, with the poor more insistently demanding that the material advances of improving technology provide benefits for them as well, the Catholic view of charity has come increasingly to stress necessity rather than caprice on the part of the giver. The rich must not simply give the poor a tiny, conscience-consoling bit of what they have, but they must permit institutions that allow the poor to build for themselves.

The new spirit manifests itself in sharp denunciations of distributive charity. Father del Corro upbraids such Catholic-sponsored programs as Caritas for having "ulterior" religious ends, for depriving the aid recipients of their "self-reliance," and for locking both recipients and givers into a system of perpetual handouts.[34] After specifically rejecting an exclusively redistributive orientation for Catholic programs, the Chilean hierarchy has affirmed that "a more appropriate distribution of opportunities, of production, of competences and of responsibilities can have a great influence on the increase of total production and therefore on the satisfac-

33. J. Humberto Cardenal Quintero, "Exhorta el Cardenal Quintero cumplir con el día ayuno en campaña contra el hambre," *Adsum* (Organo Oficial del Arzobispado de Caracas) 57, no. 268 (abril–mayo, 1964) : 548.

34. Alejandro del Corro, "TECHO and Urban Misery in Chile," *CIF Reports* 2, no. 1 (April, 1963) : 7.

tion of world needs."[35] Although Christian Democrats frequently cite the post-1945 social legislation of such countries as Italy, Belgium, and Germany as models for their own development,[36] the Latin American Christian Democratic movements have in fact lacked the social paternalism and the preoccupation with welfare legislation characteristic of the older tendencies of Christian Democracy in Europe.[37] The appropriateness of this overall stand appears in the fact that, when the Frei administration shifted the distribution of national income to favor the lowest socioeconomic groups who had a high propensity to consume, the increased level of national consumption seriously reduced savings and raised the demand for foodstuffs in a country with only modest agricultural productivity.[38]

The rejection of paternalism also encourages Catholics to take an antistatist position. Refusing to see the state as the automatic representative of all the people, Professor Comblin argues that the state has no special revelation of what the common good really is. Instead, the common good encompasses the diverse objectives of all citizens, and the state must consider this range of objectives rather than work for the desires of particular individuals or social groups.[39] Other Catholics denounce state control of economic life on the grounds that it is really an extension of control by a private oligarchy. Tiseyra sums up this antistatist viewpoint when he writes that "the Christian position does not admit the propriety of the means of production [being] in the hands of a few capitalists, nor in the hands of a *single Patron State*." By advocating that the means of production should be controlled by all those who work in the enterprise in question,[40] Tiseyra rejects the Cuban, Russian, and Chinese patterns of socialism.

35. Silva Henríquez and others, *Los obispos de Chile hablan*, p. 16.

36. See Eduardo Frei Montalva, *La verdad tiene su hora* (Santiago de Chile: Editorial del Pacífico, 1955), pp. 96–98.

37. For a comparison of the Latin American and the European movements, see Peter Molt, "La democracia cristiana latinoamericana vista desde Europa," *Sic* 30, no. 294 (abril, 1967), esp. 194–95.

38. *The Economist* (edición para América Latina) 1, no. 3 (16 junio, 1967): 12.

39. José Comblin, "La Iglesia y el poder en la sociedad pluralista," *Teología y Vida* 4, no. 4 (octubre–diciembre, 1963): 263.

40. Óscar Tiseyra, *Cuba marxista vista por un católico* (Buenos Aires: Jorge Álvarez, 1964), p. 178. Tiseyra's italics.

A spreading ideal of human equality underlies this opposition to charitable or statist paternalism. Even the clergy has become more egalitarian, as many priests have come to see themselves more as fellow workers with their parishioners than as special persons ordained to positions of superiority. Dr. Horacio Terra expresses this egalitarian thrust when he advises Catholics to "work with others shoulder to shoulder, brother to brother; fraternalism breeds love, paternalism exasperates."[41] Catholic social commentators such as Pedro Velázquez H. go further in setting out a new basis of equality for relations between workers and employers. Paternalism must cease in all its forms: the paternalism of political control, the "familial" paternalism of providing a worker's house and his whole environment, and the "utilitarian" paternalism that keeps the worker fed and housed only so that he can perform for his master. "The working class has grown up," Velázquez asserts, and workers must be treated as individual men rather than as parts of a paternalistic machine.[42] While some Catholics in every period since the Spanish Conquest have derived a sense of egalitarianism from Christian ethics, this emphasis upon it has now become more widespread and immediately relevant. It has also led to new Catholic concern for trade unions, cooperatives, and agrarian reform.

In the area of trade unionism, Catholic attitudes have been far from uniformly progressive. By advocating resignation among the poor and discouraging strikes and trade union activity, such nineteenth-century churchmen as Archbishop Mariano Casanova of Santiago de Chile regularly took attitudes that Church leaders now admit caused considerable popular disaffection. At times, as in the case of the Unión de Trabajadores Colombianos (UTC), Church-supported trade unionism has also appeared as a rightist counterweight to more centrist and radical tendencies in the labor movement. In contrast to other Colombian unions that supported union autonomy and *peronista* principles during the early

41. Quoted in John J. Considine, *New Horizons in Latin America* (New York: Dodd, Mead & Company, 1958), p. 218.
42. *Dimensión social de la caridad* (México: Secretariado Social Mexicano, 1962), pp. 129–32.

1950's, the UTC received major backing from the Church and was openly accused of really favoring the interests of industrialists and the Colombian oligarchy.[43]

Despite some disavowals of unionism or this favoring of "company" unions, many churchmen have come to promote actively labor reforms and effective trade unionism. The Centro para el Desarrollo Económico y Social de América Latina (DESAL) devotes an entire section of its two-volume program of social reform to the labor question. It calls for the actual application of minimum-wage laws, an end to child labor, equal pay for equal work, increased protection for working women, more technical training, and industrial hygiene.[44] Many priests have also come to work for union organization at the local level. To take only two examples out of many, Father Paulo Crespo and Father Antônio Melo have continued to organize the trade union movement in the Brazilian state of Pernambuco even after the military coup of April, 1964. Father Melo believes that the peasants must be made to fight and take land for themselves, while Father Crespo assumes that more can be accomplished by working with the government, but the government has allowed both priests to continue their leadership and their organizing of rural unions.[45]

Another area in which priests have become especially active is the establishment of credit unions and cooperatives. From the time of the early credit union founded by Maryknoll fathers in Puno, Peru, in 1955, priests have begun them as a practical application of the new approach to social welfare. While credit unions have encouraged saving and enterprise among *campesinos,* cooperative stores have reduced prices for them. Cooperatives

43. Vernon Lee Fluharty, *Dance of the Millions: Military Rule and the Social Revolution in Colombia, 1930–1956* (Pittsburgh, Pa.: University of Pittsburgh Press, 1966), pp. 125–26, 245–48.
44. Raúl Valdivia, "Condiciones de trabajo," in Roger Vekemans, S.J. and others, *América Latina y desarrollo social,* 2 vols. (Barcelona: Centro para el Desarrollo Económico y Social de América Latina, 1966), 2: 45–68.
45. For a discussion of the activity of these priests and the contrasts in their approach, see Fanny Mitchell to Richard H. Nolte, Nov. 9, 1967 (FM-17 in the series of field reports distributed by the Institute of Current World Affairs). A more comprehensive view of Catholic unionism in Brazil is Howard J. Wiarda, *The Brazilian Catholic Labor Movement: The Dilemmas of National Development* (Amherst, Mass.: Labor Relations and Research Center, University of Massachusetts, 1969).

have run into the problem of obtaining enough members to allow substantial reductions in price, but despite this they have shown noticeable results in many parts of Latin America. An objective evaluation of a large cooperative in the capital of the Department of Boyacá, Colombia, for example, gives great credit to the clergy involved in the enterprise, finding that it has been the clergy who have persuaded *campesinos* to work with the cooperative.[46] The Church has even formed its own cooperatives to finance care for priests and religious during sickness and old age.[47] In departing from the older system of care for religious personnel by their orders and in Catholic hospitals, this rise of cooperatives for religious marks a striking adaptation to the secular world. If the movement should be considerably expanded, it could even allow priests greater financial independence from local landowners and so increase the priests' tendencies to speak out for social reform.

The Church has encouraged the formation of cooperatives by the use of propaganda, and in doing so it has fostered the wider ideal of self-help as well as the cooperative movement. One of the most effective pieces of propaganda has been a handbill entitled "Principios internacionales del cooperativismo" distributed by Papal Volunteers in Mexico. It describes the savings of cooperative purchases, advocates mass education, and even supports the principle of "one man, one vote." On the back, the handbill illustrates its central message with a cartoon story. Two donkeys tied together at first pull in opposite directions in trying to reach stacks of hay on opposite sides of the handbill, but, after sitting down together and thinking things over, the donkeys move together to eat one pile of hay after another. This illustration of the mutual advantages of cooperation comes across with force

46. Emanuel Martínez Palacios, "Estudio de las posibilidades de desarrollo de Boyacá," in *CPC: Informes y balance, presentados a la Asamblea General de Delegados, reunida el 27 de octubre de 1967* (n.p.: n.p., 1967). This is a report on the Caja Popular Cooperativa, which was founded in Tunja, Colombia, in 1949.

47. For a statement of the origins, benefits, and laws of the model religious cooperative formed in Tunja, Colombia, in 1965, see *Régimen de la Cooperativa Interdiocesana de Previsión y Seguridad Social, Ltda. ("CIPRESES")* (Bogotá: Editorial Andres, 1965).

not only to readers but also to the numerous illiterates among whom Papal Volunteers do much of their work.

As in this use of cartoon advertising, Catholic spokesmen have taken an increasingly insightful approach to questions of agrarian reform. Rather than neglecting agriculture or merely calling for reform, they have supported methods, including expropriation, designed to increase agricultural productivity. In 1963 the National Conference of the Bishops of Brazil championed expropriation of land as a vital part of agrarian reform and suggested that partial indemnification through money or government notes would provide adequate compensation for former landowners.[48] In a commencement address to agricultural students in December, 1964, Dom Hélder Câmara pointed up the other side of the productivity issue by urging "agricultural industrialization."[49] Reflecting attitudes also commonly expressed in Chile and Peru, a 1963 pastoral of the bishops of Ecuador called in detail for the redistribution of land, the industrialization of agriculture, and the creation of cooperatives to buy tools and to give peasant farmers a sense of solidarity and an appreciation of savings.[50] In 1967 the Ecuadorean bishops went on to denounce the "selfish" agrarian interests that oppose land reform and thus seriously endanger social peace.[51] This viewpoint has become more pervasive in Latin America; it is worth noting that it has even spread in the Spain of Francisco Franco, where members of the Spanish clergy call for an immediate end to "oligarchical predominance" and latifundia in Spanish agriculture, for such innovations as agricultural cooperatives and heavy capital investment in agriculture, and for far stronger support for agrarian reform from Catholic leaders. Claiming that to abandon leadership in agrarian reform to anti-Christian ideologies would be a "criminal desertion" and a "sui-

48. "Brazilian Bishops' Pastoral Letter on Social Reform," in *Recent Church Documents from Latin America*, p. 36.

49. The address is reprinted in *CIF Reports* 4, no. 10 (May 16, 1965) : 74–79.

50. Carlos María de la Torre (Cardenal Arzobispo de Quito) and others, *Carta pastoral del episcopado ecuatoriana al pueblo del Ecuador sobre el problema agrario*, April 23, 1963 (Quito: Editorial "La Unión," 1963), pp. 11–15, 20–21.

51. *Declaración programática de la Conferencia Episcopal para la Iglesia en el Ecuador*, June 1, 1967 (Quito: Editorial "Don Bosco," 1967), p. 52.

cidal attitude," Father Alfonso Gándara Feijóo echoes *freista* phrases in declaring that the most pressing duty of Spanish Christians is to create a more just and a more humane society.[52]

The reasoning behind Church proposals for land reform extends well beyond the endangering of "social peace" or the creation of a "humane society." Although supported by some as a means to halt communism, land reform has received backing from other Catholics because it appears to encourage specific social trends. An old justification for it came out at the Third Inter-American Week of Catholic Action held at Chimbote, Peru, in 1955, when the delegates resolved that agrarian reform was necessary in order to fight Communist influence.[53] Although numerous Catholic meetings have made similar declarations since then, fear of communism does not automatically produce calls for reform. Such fear has led some Catholics to support reform, but the most outspoken anti-Communists have loudly opposed all expropriation in the name of private property. The backers of reform and expropriation justify them as being humanistically sound, as more likely to benefit those who obtain the land than harm those who lose it. The reformers tie their programs to the assumption that wider benefits will result for the national community as a whole. A joint pastoral of the bishops of the Dominican Republic joins the concept of reform to an exhortation that Dominican *campesinos* form "professional" associations. When these associations teach young people to love farming and the rural life, the young people will supposedly not migrate in massive numbers to the cities and urban overcrowding can be reduced.[54] The late Bishop Manuel Larraín, after frankly admitting that he was neither an economist nor a sociologist, argued for agricultural reforms on the basis that they would increase peasant incomes and so provide the broader

52. A. Gándara Feijóo, O.F.M., "La elevación social del campo," *Verdad y Vida* 21, nos. 81–84 (enero-diciembre, 1963) : 358–65, 392–94.

53. *La IIIe Semaine Inter-Americaine d'A.C.* (*Chimbote—Pérou, 18–25 octobre 1953*): *Rapport de la Délégation Canadienne* (Montréal: Secrétariat National de l'A.C.C., 1954), p. 36. The first two meetings in this series were held in Santiago in 1945 and in Havana in 1949.

54. Octavio A. Beras (Arzobispo Metropolitano de Santo Domingo) and others, *Situación campesina en la República Dominicana: Declaración conjunta del episcopado dominicano sobre la situación campesina,* July 30, 1967 (n.p.: Editorial Petrus, 1967).

67

consumer market needed for increased industrialization.[55] Although the contented rural life and consumer-financed industrialization may be more illusory than these approaches assume, they certainly deserve what support they can get.

One of the most direct ways in which the Church can support them is in the distribution of its own land. The distribution of Church land to peasants has been widely publicized in Chile, but it has also occurred in other countries and even in Colombia, the Latin American state ordinarily considered to be the most conservative in its Catholic orientation. In July, 1967, Bishop Giulio Franco Arango gave 800 acres of land owned by his diocese to the Colombian government for distribution to peasants, citing as he did so the statement in the *Populorum Progressio* encyclical that "private property is not an absolute and unconditional right for anyone when others are in need."[56] Although the comparatively small size of contemporary Church landholdings in Colombia and the other Latin American countries limits the direct value of such donations for land-reform programs, the donations are designed to prompt secular landowners to do likewise.

This visible evidence of the Church's support for peasants is particularly significant in the context of Latin American Catholicism, because the Church has traditionally centered a large part of its resources and personnel in the cities. Even in Paraguay, where urbanization has progressed less rapidly than in the rest of Latin America, churchmen have congregated in the capital. Of the ninety priests estimated to have served the Paraguayan population of 900,000 in 1932, about half lived in Asunción while fewer than fifty ministered to the 800,000 Paraguayans in the countryside.[57] In 1957 when the proportion of Latin Americans living in large cities was still far smaller than it is today, the proportion of priests in urban areas was surprisingly high. In Uruguay 419 priests out of a total of 662 in the country resided in Montevideo, while 891 out of 2,197 Chilean

55. Manuel Larraín Errázuriz (Obispo de Talca), "El problema del agro y del campesinado en América Latina," in Larraín E., *Escritos sociales* (Santiago de Chile: Editorial del Pacífico, S.A., 1963), pp. 258, 263.

56. *New York Times,* July 17, 1967.

57. Edwin Ryan, *The Church in the South American Republics* (New York: Bruce Publishing Company, 1932), p. 50.

68

priests worked in Santiago and 148 out of 309 Paraguayan priests worked in Asunción.[58] With priests becoming even more scarce in relation to Latin America's burgeoning population, there continue to be far too few for pastoral duties in the countryside. Catholic progressives have met this problem partly through support for peasant-oriented programs of land reform, but also through special programs of education designed to stir peasants into activity of their own.

EDUCATION FOR "CONSCIOUSNESS"

A great deal of thought, discussion, and writing on Catholic education in Latin America still concentrates on the old issues of freedom for Church schools, government subsidization of them, and the teaching of religion in public schools. The Church continues to wield considerable power through education even in the most progressive Latin American republics. In Costa Rica, for example, when Archbishop Víctor Manuel Sanabria y Martínez objected adamantly to a proposed article in the 1949 constitution providing that education be a function of the state, the constitutional article was dropped.[59] While not discounting the amount of effort that Catholic leaders put into such issues, one should recognize that they matter very little from the standpoint of social and political development. What matters is the amount and type of education dispensed, not whether the schools are private or public. Religious education relates to political development only to the extent that it may take time away from substantive courses of study, or communicate an ethic for or against particular types of change, or provide a moral outlook sanctioning the fundamental goal of social change. Rather than looking at jurisdictional conflicts in education between clerical and secular leaders, therefore, it is more important to consider the changing emphases of Catholic education itself.

A comparatively small group of Catholic educators has tried to

58. William J. Gibbons, S.J. and others, *Basic Ecclesiastical Statistics for Latin America 1958* (Maryknoll, N. Y.: World Horizon Reports, 1958), pp. 14–24.
59. Fredrick B. Pike, ed., *The Conflict Between Church and State in Latin America* (New York: Alfred A. Knopf, 1964), p. 3.

give peasants and workers a sense of their deprived social status, while their educational systems as a whole have come increasingly to stress the social responsibilities of all citizens. Catholics have pressed for the expansion of public as well as private education, and they have urged and implemented new programs in sociology, political science, and the natural sciences. Since the great majority of Church leaders and activists are themselves the products of Catholic education, the changes now taking place in that education will significantly shape the role of the Church during the decades ahead. Although the results of the new activities have not always been what Catholic educators have expected, the activities require attention both as they demonstrate contemporary reorientations within Latin American Catholicism and as they indicate some of the probable lines of its future development.

"Participation" and "consciousness" are two key concepts in the newer Catholic education. For many progressives, they sum up a desire to see Latin Americans contribute more to their societies and win more benefits from them. As a DESAL pamphlet tells Chileans, the "marginality" against which the Latin American must fight is made up of a "LACK OF CONTRIBUTIVE PARTICIPATION, in which he has no chance to influence collective decisions, and [a] LACK OF RECEPTIVE PARTICIPATION, in which he remains excluded from the benefits that the world society distributes."[60] In 1963 the annual statement of the National Conference of the Bishops of Peru discussed the rise of "a genuine social consciousness" in Latin America and declared that the Church was and should be helping to form this consciousness.[61] A new attitude in Church teachings is thus evident in various Latin American countries; its variety can be seen in three quite different movements: the Instituto de Formación Demócrata Cristiana (IFEDEC) in Venezuela, Acción Cultural Popular (ACPO) in Colombia, and the Movimento de Educação de Base (MEB) in Brazil.

A particularly interesting training ground for middle-level Chris-

60. *Una estrategia contra la miseria* (Santiago de Chile: DESAL, 1966). DESAL's capitalization.
61. "Peruvian Bishops' Pastoral Letter on Politics and Social Reform," in *Recent Church Documents from Latin America,* p. 41.

tian Democratic leaders has been IFEDEC, an organization offering special courses in a suburb of Caracas. Started in 1962, IFEDEC has given one-month courses on such subjects as community development, the political participation of women, and the latest strategies of electoral behavior and campaigning. IFEDEC is not widely known outside Latin America, partly because of its reluctance to allow publicity that could endanger the Christian Democratic leaders it trains. Since it attracts participants and Christian Democratic support from all over Latin America, too much public exposure might aid its electoral opponents in their reiterated charge that the Christian Democrats represent an international conspiracy rather than a truly national movement in each country.[62] IFEDEC students in each course try to experience as well as study the "communitarian" principles of their social Christian movement, as they wash their own dishes, make their own beds, and even elect course leaders who jocularly receive the authoritarian titles of *comandante* and *teniente*. This center has worked quietly and effectively to give programmatic training in the democratic process to a new generation of political activists.

In terms of mass rather than elite education, one of the best-known formulators of the new Catholic approach has been Monsignor José Joaquín Salcedo, the leader of ACPO and its special Radiophonic School program that was initiated in Sutatenza, Colombia. Through shortwave radio programs with an estimated audience of 2.5 million and special books designed to be read along with the radio programs, he has since 1947 been giving peasants lessons in literacy, self-improvement, health, mathematics, and basic economics as well as in Christian morality. Putting Catholic social doctrine into action, ACPO declares that its objective is to develop "literacy, community development, and the change of social attitudes."[63] For the special classrooms that receive the radio broadcasts, ACPO supplies

62. Interview with Gerardo Hudon, at IFEDEC, in Los Chorros, Venezuela, June 17, 1968.

63. ACPO, Department of Sociology, *What Is, What Are the Objectives of, What Does Acción Cultural Popular?* (Bogotá: Editorial Andes, 1965), p. 43. This illustrated booklet, which ACPO issues in English, contains a wealth of data and background material. The statistics that follow, however, were taken from a letter of Hernando Bernal Alarcón, the director of ACPO's Planning and Programming Department, to Frederick C. Turner, Dec. 9, 1970.

71

chalk, paint for a blackboard, and even two hoops and a basketball for groups of students who construct their own playing field. ACPO gives each student free notebooks, pencils, and copies of five copiously illustrated primers entitled *Reading and Writing, Health, I Believe in God, Numbers,* and *Land.*

The social ethic of the ACPO movement is clear in its attitude toward agrarian reform and in its leadership training programs. In support of a government project in 1961, the radio program "Social Justice and Peace" carried special programs on agrarian reform themes. *El Campesino,* the weekly ACPO newspaper, coordinated a special page of agrarian reform information with the radio appeals for 51 weeks. ACPO even made two recordings on which agrarian reform was discussed against a background of Colombian music. At its own expense, ACPO also provides room, board, and instruction for its students in rural leadership programs at Sutatenza. Between 1954 and the end of 1969 the men's institute at Sutatenza trained 2,663 leaders; the women's institute trained 3,401 women between 1956 and 1969. Requiring candidates to have roughly a third-grade education and selecting persons between the ages of eighteen and twenty-six, the leadership programs train promising individuals in community action and then send them back to their villages. In addition to training in such fields as child care, recreation, and rural economics, the leadership programs inculcate the message of progressive Catholicism by teaching special units on such themes as the "crusading spirit and social leadership," the "obligations and privileges of the *campesino*," and "recognizing the need for cultural transformation in rural areas."

The Movimento de Educação de Base in Brazil similarly brought literacy and self-awareness education to an estimated 180,000 pupils before the 1964 revolution. The government of João Goulart underwrote this educational program, but it was set up and supervised by a council of bishops and actually run by a group of Catholic laymen, many of whom came out of the Catholic youth movement. Operating in 120 Brazilian dioceses, MEB worked through 25 radio stations and 7,353 radio schools to bring Brazilian peasants a message that Miss Marina Bandeira, the executive director of the radio schools, summed up in the ethic, "Love thy neighbor and be just unto thyself."[64] As she frankly admitted, MEB was not merely to bring literacy education but also to make the Brazilian worker conscious of his rights, "including the right to fight for a fair and just solution to his problems."[65] The leaders of the April, 1964, revolution in Brazil defined MEB as subversive and reoriented it. Even before the April revolution, Carlos Lacerda, the governor of Guanabara, had confiscated the allegedly subversive primer of MEB, *Viver é Lutar,* "To Live Is to Struggle."[66] Although the Brazilian government since 1964 has rejected the approach of MEB, the approach vividly demonstrates how far Catholic progressives still want to go in fundamental political education.

Although this militant MEB project has been greatly reduced in size, the Church has been more successful in expanding other programs, in encouraging wider educational efforts by Latin American governments, and in suggesting that both public and private systems of education should fit the needs of society. The Church has long been able to obtain money from the rich for Catholic education. Even in the early 1940's Father Miguel Giraldo Salazar, the pastor of the wealthiest parish in Medellín, Colombia, collected enough money from parishioners to found and endow more than thirty schools to provide basic education, religious training, and even hot lunches for the children of the district.[67] Many Catholics have come to recognize that expanding the number of Catholic schools is not enough, however; they see that national governments will also have to do far more. Alfredo Zareástegui, a leading Bolivian Catholic, asks that between 30 and 40 per cent of the Bolivian budget be spent on education. Although a hint of self-interest appears in his desire that part of this money finance Catholic schools, he also advocates a system of progressive taxation by which the costs of education would be paid in direct proportion to the annual income

64. Section by Marina Bandeira in John J. Considine, M.M., ed., *The Church in the New Latin America* (Notre Dame, Ind.: Fides Publishers, 1964), p. 81. The best single study of the MEB is Emanuel de Kadt, *Catholic Radicals in Brazil* (London: Oxford University Press, 1970).

65. *CIF Reports* 3, no. 1 (April 16–30, 1964): 1, 6.

66. See Emanuel de Kadt, "Religion, the Church, and Social Change in Brazil," in Claudio Veliz, ed., *The Politics of Conformity in Latin America* (New York: Oxford University Press, 1967), pp. 216–18.

67. Lochemes and McNamara, *The Church in Latin America,* p. 40.

of each Bolivian.[68] The advocates of wider education also recognize that social work is not the exclusive prerogative of the Church. Rather than relying exclusively on religious missionaries or even on groups like the Papal Volunteers, Church leaders now demand that special personnel be trained to serve the needs of culturally isolated individuals. A 1967 meeting of bishops and provincials in Goiânia, Brazil, made recommendations on missionary matters, but it also proposed that university faculties in medicine and social service offer special courses for young people wanting to work in interior Brazil.[69]

Catholic leaders also recognize the need for greatly expanded programs of scientific and technical education in Latin America, and they have begun work to implement such programs. They have established special vocational schools to train boys for jobs that can increase productivity in industry and agriculture.[70] The implications of humanistic and economic thinking coincide, as Catholic economists contend that the quality of workers must be sharply raised through such programs of technical training in order to raise per capita income.[71] As in other areas, Catholic leaders have worked to spread this idea among laymen as well as among themselves. Along with all of its other information on what Catholics should do in regard to baptism, confession, and marriage, the Catholic directory of Ciudad Juárez, Mexico, tells Mexican fathers that they should provide their sons with "a technical and scientific knowledge to supply the economic and social needs of the present and the future."[72]

Besides calling for more education in science and technology, Catholic spokesmen advocate the creation of institutes where human affairs can be studied from the objective standpoint of contemporary

68. Alfredo Zareástegui, "The Catholic University in Bolivia," *CIF Reports* 6, no. 1 (Jan. 1, 1967) : 7.

69. "Conclusões da 15a. Reunião Ordinária dos Bispos da Província Eclesiástica de Goiânia com padres e madres provinciais," *Revista da Arquidiocese* (Goiânia, Goiás) 10, no. 10 (octubro, 1967) : 753.

70. For a good description of a vocational training program set up in Panama by the Benedictines, see Rafael Matas, "La escuela vocacional agricola-industrial," *Dominical*, Oct. 2, 1966.

71. Mario Zañartu, S.J., "Investment in Human Beings: An Economist's Approach," in Arthur McCormack, ed., *Christian Responsibility and World Poverty* (London: Burns & Oates, 1963), pp. 250–51.

72. *Directorio de servicios católicos, Diocesis de Ciudad Juárez, décimo anniversario,* Sept. 7, 1967, p. 62.

social science.[73] Nearly all the Catholic universities of Latin America have established new schools of political and social studies, and these schools have both spread the social doctrines of the Church and developed more sophisticated techniques in social science research.[74] In 1967 a joint declaration of the Ecuadorean episcopacy even recommended the creation of institutes of advanced political science at all universities under their control.[75] Bernardino Piñera C., the bishop of Temuco, Chile, points up a reason for such actions when he says that too wide a gulf still exists between science and the Church, that Latin American professors are too often outside or hostile to the Church. Instead of asking that scientific investigations be adapted to the instrumentalities of the Church, however, he asks that within the Church "the presentation of morals, particularly sexual and social morals, be made with knowledge of present planning and terminology." Study of the findings of anthropology, sociology, and psychology should come to have a major impact on Catholic teachings.[76]

The discipline of "religious sociology" has come increasingly to the fore in Latin America, and in doing so it mirrors changes in both Catholicism and sociology. Religionists found sociology acceptable when it dropped its early antireligious tendencies and became an empirical science.[77] Catholic sociologists now make a sharp distinction between Church mysteries that are best studied by theology and the temporal community of Church members that is best studied by modern social science.[78] With the twentieth-century

73. See José Comblin, "El problema de las universidades católicas," *Teología y Vida* 5, no. 4 (octubre–diciembre, 1964) : 282.

74. Rodolfo Stavenhagen, "Behavioral Science in Latin America: An Overview," in Robin F. Badgley, ed., *Behavioral Science and Medical Education in Latin America,* Milbank Memorial Fund Quarterly 44, no. 2 (April, 1966) : Pt. 2, p. 20.

75. *Declaración programática de la Conferencia Episcopal para la Iglesia en el Ecuador,* June 1, 1967, p. 58.

76. Bernardino Piñera C., *Chile, hoy; Exposición de hechos: Sugerencias apostólicas* (Santiago de Chile: Ediciones Paulinas, 1967), pp. 120–21, 131.

77. See Antonio O. Donini, *Sociología y religión* (Buenos Aires: Editorial Sudamericana, 1961), p. 59.

78. Alain Birou, *Sociologie et Religion* (Paris: Économie et Humanisme, Les Éditions Ouvrières, 1959), p. 55. For recent studies in the sociology of religion, see especially Roland Robertson, *The Sociological Interpretation of Religion* (Oxford: Basil Blackwell, 1970); Norman Birnbaum and Gertrud Lenzer, eds., *Sociology and Religion: A Book of Readings* (Englewood Cliffs, N. J.: Prentice-Hall, 1969); Joan Brothers, ed., *Readings in the Sociology of Religion* (Oxford: Pergamon Press, 1967);

shifts toward increasing empiricism in sociology and increasing Catholic concern for temporal human welfare, Church leaders find sociology a useful method to study patterns of human deprivation and their remedies. As early as 1958, the National Conference of the Bishops of Brazil resolved to encourage work with sociologists at the diocesan level in order to create a group within the Church having professional competence in regard to issues of social change.[79] The impact of sociology on Catholicism should not be exaggerated, of course. As the secretary of the Catholic Center for Religious Sociology in Paris commented in 1960, it is still bishops rather than sociologists who govern the Church.[80] The priest-sociologists of Latin America have not yet worked up into positions of command in the Church hierarchy. Their influence has been felt, however, by bishops as well as by other priests and laymen.

Study of contemporary social science has caused some Latin American churchmen to withdraw from the Church. In a case where such study went particularly far, the refusal by Father Gregoire Lemercier and his fellow Benedictine monks to give up the practice of psychoanalysis led in 1967 to their withdrawal from the priesthood and the closing of their monastery in Cuernavaca, Mexico. Father Lemercier, a former Belgian who assumed Mexican nationality after living in Mexico since World War II, underwent psychoanalysis six years before he left the priesthood. He became so convinced of its usefulness in the monastic life that he suggested it for all other monks and postulants at his monastery. His experience was so successful that twenty of the twenty-four Benedictines at the monastery decided to join him and become laymen rather than comply with a Vatican order to give up the practice.[81]

Charles Y. Glock and Rodney Stark, *Religion and Society in Tension* (Chicago: Rand McNally & Company, 1965); and Talcott Parsons and others, *Sociología de la religión y la moral* (Buenos Aires: Editorial Paidós, 1968).

79. "Conclusões gerais da IV Reunião Ordinária da C.N.B.B. realizada em Goiânia," *Revista da Arquidiocese* (Goiânia, Goiás) 2, no. 7 (julho, 1958): 8.

80. F. Malley, O.P., "Sociologia e religião," *Revista Eclesiástica Brasileira* 20, fasc. 2 (junho, 1960): 355.

81. *New York Times,* Sept. 6, 1967. For an objective discussion of Father Lemercier's program on the eve of his withdrawal from the Church, see Thomas G. Sanders to Richard H. Nolte, June 1, 1967 (TGS-1 in series of field reports distributed by the Institute of Current World Affairs), pp. 2–6. For a statement of Father Lemercier's

Another unforeseen consequence of the present tendencies in Catholic education may be the tacit encouragement of violence. In sharp contrast to the Church's older position as a supporter of the status quo, Catholic educators now reiterate the new theme that massive social change is possible. A Mexican primer of the progressive movement teaches, "In the first place, get rid of the idea that our society has no remedy, that it must be as it is—full of violent injustices."[82] This kind of teaching reinforces the popular desires for change evident throughout much of Latin America. In doing so, however, it also raises hopes which if frustrated may turn for recourse to the revolutionary means of social reform that the Church is now working to prevent. By stating categorically that earthly society is unjust and that it can and must be remedied, Catholic leaders raise expectations and encourage an insistence upon action which cannot be quelled by the protestation that the meek will inherit the earth. Progressive Catholics may be thwarted in attempts at peaceful social revolution, and change in parts of Latin America may follow unbridled violence. If so, the current Catholic protests will be seen in retrospect as having helped to create the postrevolutionary situation by raising hopes that had to be satisfied.

BIRTH CONTROL

Fewer progressive churchmen have supported concepts of population limitation than have supported the ethic of educational "consciousness." The present growth in Latin American populations makes the Church's traditional opposition to birth control appear outdated to many laymen; at the same time, the ponderous rise in parishioners has made it very difficult for the Church, even with new foreign missionaries, to increase the proportion of priests in Latin America. Even though population limitation would seem to be in the interest of the Church as an institution as well as in the interest of economic development and the welfare of individual fami-

---

viewpoint, see Lemercier, "A Benedictine Monastery and Psychoanalysis," *CIF Reports* 4, no. 20 (Oct. 16, 1965).

82. Velázquez H., *Dimensión social de la caridad,* p. 41.

lies, churchmen have been most reluctant to change their position. Showing an unconcern for population growth that is traceable in part to the present position of the Church, Latin American states have opposed assistance for population limitation in the United Nations.[83] Only in individual cases have priestly attitudes toward birth control begun to change. They have done so in response to the increasingly evident use of contraceptives by Catholic laymen, the ineffectiveness of prohibitions against specific contraceptive techniques, and new realization of the importance of population limitation for the social goals of the Church. Joining lay exponents of new attitudes on population issues, the small coterie of Latin American churchmen who have changed their views may nevertheless point the direction of future thought for the Catholic Church.

Although many Church spokesmen still resort to the old argument that Latin America is an empty continent in terms of population, others have come to recognize the imminent danger of a national population that rises faster than living standards can be raised. Father Beni dos Santos presents Brazilian readers with the arguments of Dr. John Rock as well as with Cardinal Cushing's objections to them. Father Santos concludes that the communion of love is as valid a basis for conjugal union as procreation, and that the ideal family is neither large nor small but rather of whatever size individual parents can educate and care for.[84] The Chilean founders of the Centro Latinoamericano de Población y Familia (CELAP) in 1964 recognized that population growth was outstripping economic growth in many parts of the world and that, under these conditions, concentration on increasing economic growth by

83. See J. Mayone Stycos, "Demography and the Study of Population Problems in Latin America," in Stycos and Jorge Arias, eds. *Population Dilemma in Latin America* (Washington, D. C.: Potomac Books, 1966), p. 228. On the Vatican's emphatic instructions to papal nuncios to oppose support by the United Nations and the government of the United States for policies of population limitation, see "Vatican Attacks U. S. on Birth Curb: U. N. Is Also Criticized for Favoring Contraception," *New York Times,* Jan. 27, 1971.
84. B. Beni dos Santos, "Contrôle dos nascimentos e uso dos contraceptivos," *Revista Eclesiástica Brasileira* 27, fasc. 1 (março, 1967): 89, 93. For the official United States Catholic position on birth control, see the statement made by North American bishops in 1959, in Peter H. Odegard, ed., *Religion and Politics* (n.p.: Oceana Publications, 1960), pp. 195–200.

itself was insufficient.[85] Nearly all of the Chilean bishops whom Thomas Sanders interviewed on this point indicated their openness to newer methods of family planning.[86] The Frei government, which in 1967 hosted the first World Planned Parenthood Assembly ever held in Latin America, actively encouraged the distribution of birth control information and devices.[87] In stark contrast to the position of the Puerto Rican Church during the long governorship of Luis Muñoz Marín, even the bishops of that island in 1970 signed a statement favorably endorsing the government's program of birth control.[88]

More indirectly, a Mexican Church publication features the picture of a poor, worn-out-looking mother and father and their fourteen children with a caption reading, "The increase in population was not in proportion to the increase in sources of work."[89] Summing up this questioning of the official Church position, Father Gustavo Pérez argues that God gave man the intelligence and the will necessary to take part in the creative process, and that the common good should be the cause for man's intervening in natural processes. Since, even physiologically, there is no necessary connection between sex and procreation, he argues that sexual relations between partners in marriage naturally have a psychological importance that goes beyond procreation.[90]

85. For a statement of this position and a discussion of the activities of CELAP in promoting it, see "CELAP: Hacia una solución global," *Reportaje DESAL* 1, no. 2 (abril, 1967) : 7.

86. An assessment of the Chilean hierarchy's attitude toward birth control, based on interviews with twenty-three of the twenty-nine Chilean bishops, appears in Thomas G. Sanders, *The Chilean Episcopate: An Institution in Transition,* American University Field Staff Reports, West Coast South America Series 15, no. 3 (Aug., 1968) : 16. This report, together with the important newsletters that Sanders wrote for the Institute of Current World Affairs, is reprinted in Thomas G. Sanders, *Catholic Innovation in a Changing Latin America* (Cuernavaca, Mor.: CIDOC, 1969).

87. See James Nelson Goodsell, "Population Spiral," *Christian Science Monitor,* May 27, 1967.

88. For a copy of their statement, see "Apoyo del episcopado de Puerto Rico al programa estatal de planificación familiar," *Nadoc,* no. 130 (25 febrero, 1970).

89. *Investigación regional para la planeación pastoral* (México: Impresos Offsali-G, S. de R.L., 1966), p. 82.

90. Gustavo Pérez, "La planificación familiar y la problemática latinoamericana. Perspectivas en la Iglesia católica en 1965," in *Iglesia, población y familia* (Santiago de Chile: DESAL–CELAP, 1967), pp. 207–10. This article was first published in *Revista Concilium* (Madrid) in Dec., 1965.

With this questioning of the Church's position on family limitation, the 1968 encyclical upholding the traditional position met a mixed reaction in Latin America. The cardinal-archbishop of Santiago, Chile, issued a public statement emphasizing all of the important points in the encyclical except the rejection of "artificial" techniques and stressing that the Church would never turn away from conscientious Catholics who obeyed the dictates of their conscience. When asked about the encyclical, Cardinal Silva Henríquez said, in a hopeful tone of voice, that he felt the encyclical would not cause many Catholics to turn away from the Church, because they would find a way to live with it.[91] Chilean priests have been especially concerned with problems caused by the frequent ineffectiveness of family planning through the rhythm method and with the psychological problems sometimes caused in a marriage through enforced abstinence. In the aftermath of the encyclical, some of them openly counseled Catholic couples to follow their consciences and accepted the fact that couples already using contraceptive devices could not realistically be expected to revert to the rhythm method.

The reaction of Luis Cardinal Concha of Bogotá, Colombia, stands in sharp contrast to that of the more open Chilean priests. Before Pope Paul VI issued "On Human Life," the cardinal had already sent a pastoral letter on the subject taking the same stand as the encyclical. When asked about it, he reiterated that there are some parts of the Christian message which simply cannot change, that the apostles and spiritual leaders of the Church were given the task of preserving Christ's message rather than adapting it, and that sacrifice is demanded of all the followers of Christ. Self-denial would be necessary in order for couples to abstain from sexual relations during the woman's fertile period, but certainly Christian laymen could be expected to show this degree of self-sacrifice when their clergy was undergoing the much more stringent sacrifice of total, lifetime abstinence from sexual relations.[92] Critics of this traditional

91. Interview with Cardinal-Archbishop Raúl Silva Henríquez, in Santiago, Chile, Aug. 6, 1968.
92. Interview with Cardinal-Archbishop Luis Concha Córdoba, in Bogotá, Colombia, Aug. 15, 1968.

position claim that the intimacy of sexual relations in marriage creates a bond whose complexities a celibate priest can easily fail to understand, but—from the priest's or bishop's viewpoint—it similarly seems difficult to understand why laymen who profess the same faith cannot practice abstinence for short periods of time.

A strong argument against this traditional position on birth control is the fact that Catholic moral teaching in this area has been notably ineffective. With common-law marriages still frequent among the lower classes, virginity before marriage is rare among the majority of Latin Americans. A Belgian priest working in Bolivia reports sadly that in over one thousand marriages that he performed, only three of the couples did not have children either born or on the way.[93] Prohibitions against divorce are sometimes so trying as to make a Colombian priest, Father Martín Amaya Martínez, declare that divorce is "more Christian" than the "living hell of an unhappy marriage."[94] In the area of birth control itself, Catholic prohibitions have not been able to stem the widespread sale, advertisement, and use of forbidden contraceptive devices. In Guatemala even in the 1940's, Mary P. Holleran found all kinds of birth control devices openly advertised in the leading newspapers.[95]

The Venezuelan survey research of Frank Bonilla and José A. Silva Michelena points up a surprising continuity in attitudes toward birth control. Among the five of their twenty-four sample groups that were completely rural, for example, only between 43.2 and 49.2 per cent of all five groups accepted the statement, "Birth control should never be practiced or only when the Church permits."[96] The rural groups differed widely in such matters as regular church attendance, with 38.5 per cent of the farm owners attending church at least once a week and only 6.6 per cent of the traditional *campesinos* doing so, but this difference did not significantly alter their at-

93. Vicente O. Vetrano, "La Iglesia en Bolivia," *Criterio* 39, no. 1515–16 (19 enero, 1967): 15.

94. Quoted in John Gunther, *Inside South America* (New York: Harper & Row, 1966), p. 458.

95. Mary P. Holleran, *Church and State in Guatemala* (New York: Columbia University Press, 1949), p. 253.

96. John R. Mathiason, "The Venezuelan Campesino: Perspectives on Change," in Frank Bonilla and José A. Silva Michelena, eds., *A Strategy for Research on Social Policy* (Cambridge, Mass.: M.I.T. Press, 1967), pp. 132–34.

titudes toward birth control. Although physical inaccessibility prevents many subsistence farmers from regular attendance at mass, these *campesinos* remain as tied to Church doctrine on this point as do the wealthier Venezuelan owners of ranches and farms. Significantly, however, over half of the members of each of these rural groups has come to reject the notion that the Church can make binding pronouncements on the birth control issue. Even in the rural context, Venezuelans appear to be more alienated from the Church's position on birth control than they are from its position on such matters as divorce or the importance of religion in daily life. The religious attitudes of these five groups are given in Table 2.

Confirming the widespread use of contraceptives among practicing Catholics, surveys of urban groups have also indicated that no correlation exists between regular attendance at mass and the use of contraceptives. Sometimes the use of contraceptives is even greater among women who attend mass regularly. In Caracas, Venezuela, a survey has shown that 56.7 per cent of the women who claimed to attend mass once or more per week used contraceptives, whereas only 54.8 per cent of the women who never attended mass used them. In Panama, 59.3 per cent of the women surveyed who attended mass at least once a week used contraceptives, whereas only 50 per cent of those never attending mass used them.[97] Such findings suggest that contraceptives are used by women who can afford them, whether or not the religious sentiments of those women are strong enough to make them participate regularly in the rituals of the Church.

On the basis of thorough research into the problems of population control in Latin America, J. Mayone Stycos also rejects the simplistic notion that Catholicism prevents rational population control. While his survey research indicates that Church teachings in this area have had comparatively little influence,[98] many Latin Americans have become indifferent or hostile to birth control for other reasons. Latin

97. See tables 2 and 3 in Pérez, "La planificación familiar y la problemática latino-americana," pp. 202–3.
98. See J. Mayone Stycos, "Survey Research and Population Control in Latin America," *Public Opinion Quarterly* 28, no. 3 (Fall, 1964); and J. Mayone Stycos, *Family and Fertility in Puerto Rico: A Study of the Lower Income Group* (New York: Columbia University Press, 1955), esp. chap. 8.

Table 2: *Religious Attitudes of Rural Groups in Venezuela*

Responses to Questions	Campesinos			Owners	
	Land Reform Farmers (N = 191) %	Subsistence Farmers (N = 183) %	Agricultural Laborers (N = 166) %	Owners of Farms (N = 171) %	Owners of Ranches (N = 175) %
Religion is very important in daily life	57.6	51.9	75.4	63.8	60.7
Attend church at least once a week	6.8	6.6	24.2	38.5	32.0
Birth control should never be praticed or only when Church permits	49.2	48.6	43.2	46.6	44.4
Divorce should always be granted	29.3	28.4	37.9	23.0	32.0

SOURCE: This table is adapted from that in John R. Mathiason, "The Venezuelan Campesino: Perspectives on Change," in *A Strategy for Research on Social Policy*, ed. Frank Bonilla and José A. Silva Michelena, by permission of the M.I.T. Press, Cambridge, Massachusetts. For a detailed analysis of the sample groups, see Appendix 2A to chap. 2 in the Bonilla and Silva study.

American intellectuals have praised population growth on the grounds that it is necessary to exploit natural resources, to provide a domestic market for industrial goods, or to allow sufficient development of intellectual talent. To the extent that population growth does cause suffering, some leaders have postulated that suffering will force the pace of social and economic innovation. Opposition to birth control has arisen from the assumption that it was a trick of Yankee imperialists to reduce the strength of Latin America, and from the assumption that education and urbanization would automatically check population increases. Communists and nationalists have further claimed that United States companies make exorbitant profits on the sale of contraceptives. Just as Catholic teaching on birth control is not the major barrier to its implementation, so liberalization of the Catholic position is only one force working in the direction of population limitation. Working along with it are such other forces as the research and grants of North American foundations and universities, the slum-crowding of rapid urbanization in Latin America, and the growth of general economic planning by Latin American governments.[99]

The Catholic position on abortion indicates another logical reason for change in the position on contraceptives. Churchmen generally agree with the bishop of Ciudad Juárez, Mexico, who has said that nothing, absolutely nothing, can justify a premeditated and voluntary abortion. Obstetricians have no moral right to perform an abortion, he asserts, and, even when the health of the expectant mother is in danger, a pregnant woman should voluntarily accept her own death rather than destroy her unborn child.[100] This adamant stance has not prevented the widespread practice of abortion in Latin America, however. With common-law marriages frequent outside the middle and upper classes, women usually resort to abortions because of the economic inconvenience of having another child rather than because of fear of having a child out of formal wedlock. In a survey of 500 families in central Chile carried on under Church sponsorship in the summer of 1957, 60 per cent of the men questioned favored

99. See J. Mayone Stycos, "Opinions of Latin American Intellectuals on Population Problems and Birth Control," *The Annals of the American Academy of Political and Social Science* 360 (July, 1965): 15–25.

100. Manuel Talamás Camandari (Primer Obispo de Ciudad Juárez), *III carta pastoral sobre la inmoralidad del aborto*, April 2, 1961, pp. 2–6.

abortion. Local opinion held that no soul entered the body of a fetus until four months after conception, so that abortion seemed to be morally permissible up to this time.[101] Leaders of the Movimiento Familiar Cristiano (MFC) such as Father Peter Richards readily admit that abortions nearly equal births in parts of Latin America. Instead of advocating the use of newer birth control techniques to make abortion unnecessary, however, MFC leaders generally hope to prevent abortion through their regular program to strengthen Catholic loyalties in the family. Like Father Richards, many MFC leaders have outspokenly condemned what he calls the "sterilization pills" promoted by former Governor Luis Muñoz Marín of Puerto Rico.[102] While Catholics may stand for some time behind this dual condemnation of abortion and contraception, the effects of another doubling in Latin America's population should encourage them to change their minds. As they do, they are likely to opt for contraception rather than abortion.

In the meantime, outsiders will find it difficult to work for change in Latin America when they seem to be opposing the moral authority of the Church. Catholics still shy away from many reforms of the Scandinavian countries, and the example of change abroad is not enough to produce it in Latin America. Instead of taking up the argument that illegitimate children should have equal rights and opportunities, for example, Latin American pastorals on the subject still stress the sanctity of marriage, the moral dangers of improvident unions, and the chance of contracting diseases when illegitimate children are conceived.[103] Catholic support for the traditional features of morality also hampers foreign attempts to aid Latin American efforts in population control. In 1967 when reports came from a sparsely settled region of central Brazil that a program of birth control and the experimental use of contraceptives had been started by Protestant missionaries including several North Americans, the Bishop of Belém and other Catholic clergymen violently denounced the program. As the Brazilian press gave wide coverage to the de-

101. Considine, *New Horizons in Latin America,* p. 140.
102. For a detailed statement of Father Richards' views based on an interview with him, see Russell J. Huff, C.S.C., "The Family Crisis in Latin America," *Ave Maria* 95, no. 1 (Jan. 6, 1962).
103. See Francisco José Castro y Ramírez (Obispo de Santiago de María), *Décima cuarta carta pastoral: Los hijos sin padres,* July 6, 1967.

nunciations, part of it reacted xenophobically by running such headlines as "Foreigners Keep Brazilians from Being Born."[104]

Given the need for population control to implement the social and economic goals of the new Catholic thought, it would be most helpful if the Church rather than laymen or foreigners should take the lead in this area also. The 1968 encyclical "On Human Life" did not alter the Church's opposition to techniques of family planning other than the rhythm method, however, even though Latin American newspapers have often stressed that—as Pope Paul himself has pointed out—the encyclical "is in no way against responsible limitation of the number of children, nor the scientific investigation of the problem, nor truly responsible parenthood."[105] With the great reluctance of the papacy to further liberalize its position, however, the alternative appears to be for Catholics to practice birth control as their consciences permit and for Church doctrine to catch up later. Resorting to abortion or to mechanical devices of birth control does not force Latin Americans to reject other tenets of their Catholic faith. Like the alcoholic, unchaste, but devoutly believing Mexican priest in Graham Greene's novel of *The Power and the Glory,* they can believe themselves to be under God's jurisdiction and still violate his rules. Just as the Church's old prohibition against usury is no longer enforced, so the birth control issue could be resolved simply through neglect to uphold the prohibition against contraceptive devices. Since individual churchmen as well as laymen have come to question the doctrine on contraception, however, it should not be too long before the majority of Church leaders does so also.

THE CHANGING ISSUE OF CHURCH AND STATE

For centuries the conflict for political power between Church and State was the most pressing religious issue in Latin American

104. *Christian Science Monitor,* June 5, 1967.
105. "Comentario del Papa Ante Oposición a la Encíclica," *El Mercurio* (Santiago de Chile), Aug. 5, 1968. For contrast, see the harder-line papal statement in "Paulo VI Reitera Objeciones al Control Artificial de Natalidad," *El Mercurio,* Feb. 13, 1969, which claims that ecclesiastical guidance on such issues as birth control is especially necessary "because human reason is weak, insecure, and predisposed to errors."

politics, but in the old sense this conflict is now a dead issue. Some contemporary Catholics still speak out on the old issues, as in arguments that while civil marriage ceremonies are permissible for persons never baptized in the Church, exclusive jurisdiction for marrying Catholics must rest with the Church. This argument tries to appear entirely fair by claiming that it merely renders to God what is God's and to Caesar what is Caesar's,[106] but its pretense of relying on Church-State separation is only a sham. If generally applied, it would greatly restrict civil ceremonies, since most Latin Americans are at least baptized by the Church. The more general reconciliation between Church and State is not a sham, however, because the Latin American Church has lost so much of its old political and economic power in the temporal sphere.[107] The rejection of temporal power has gone so far that advocates of reform now even call for the Church to become a totally selfless institution, for it to orient all its actions toward the benefit of the world community rather than toward its own benefit.[108] As Church leaders have correspondingly become far less concerned with their own direct intervention in politics, they have come to compete with governments less directly and so been able to cooperate effectively with the ideological descendants of anticlerical liberalism. Parts of the Church leadership have become so deeply concerned with problems of social development that the new question of paramount importance has become how Church and State can best reinforce one another's efforts in producing the kinds of social development that progressive leaders in each group desire.

In each of the Latin American countries, the Church has retreated during the twentieth century to a safe avowal of Church-State separation. Early sensing that Catholic political activity was largely responsible for the anticlericalism that had restricted the Church in Ecuador, Archbishop Federico González Suárez in 1906 established

---

106. Alonso Arteaga Yepes, "La Ley Concha ante el derecho de la Iglesia," *Ecclesiástica Xaveriana* 6 (1956) : 197.

107. The standard work on the general issue of Church-State relations remains Mecham, *Church and State in Latin America.* Useful comparisons of Church-State relations in the different Latin American countries may also be found in the Jan., 1964, issue of *CIF Reports;* and in Carlos Oviedo Cavada, "Iglesia y estado en latinoamérica," *Teología y Vida* 3, no. 1 (enero-marzo, 1962).

108. See Ricardo Chartier, "Modos de relación entre la Iglesia y la sociedad," *Cristianismo y Sociedad* 1, no. 2 (1963) : 7.

what has now become a long-standing Ecuadorean prohibition against clerical support for any political party.[109] In the case of Mexico, reconciliation did not come until the 1930's, but a new compatibility since that time has allowed the "revolutionary" goals of Church and State significantly to reinforce one another.[110]

With the more recent rise of the Christian Democratic movements, the hierarchy in such countries as Venezuela has been careful not to compromise the Christian Democrats by making them appear to be pawns of the Church. In a collective pastoral letter written at the time of Vatican II, the Venezuelan hierarchy reaffirmed this policy by categorically refusing to try to influence party politics.[111] Although some bishops privately favor COPEI because of personal friendships with its Christian Democratic leaders, the Copeianos themselves have helped to maintain a firm separation between Church and State. They believe that no party should represent the Church, but rather that the Church's social doctrines should have influence among all parties. Unlike the Chilean election of Eduardo Frei in 1964, when funds from Miserior in Europe helped to finance his campaign, the successful campaign of Rafael Caldera in 1968 received no funds at all either from the Church or from European Christian Democrats.[112]

More broadly, an end to state financing of regular Church expenses has brought new freedom to the Church. As the apostolic administrator of Montevideo, Uruguay, told me, "Here we don't get any help from the state, and we like it that way. We are poor here, but it is happy to be poor. This gives us great freedom of action."[113] The elimination of state funding has thus curtailed one source of secular leverage and interference. Along with limiting Church

---

109. Robert W. Bialek, *Catholic Politics: A History Based on Ecuador* (New York: Vantage Press, 1963), pp. 77–78.

110. On the Mexican case, see Frederick C. Turner, "The Compatibility of Church and State in Mexico," *Journal of Inter-American Studies* 9, no. 4 (Oct., 1967).

111. *Carta pastoral colectiva del episcopado venezolano: Estadísticas de educación gratuita* (n.p.: Publicaciones del Secretariado Permanente del Episcopado Venezolano, n.d.), p. 8.

112. Interview with Dr. Valmore Acevedo, a prominent Copeiano and Venezuelan political scientist, in Caracas, Venezuela, June 17, 1968.

113. Interview with Carlos Parteli, the apostolic administrator of Montevideo, Uruguay, in Montevideo, July 9, 1968.

funds, the clergy's rejection of direct political involvement has reduced its sphere of activity and the costs that once went with the larger sphere; the Church now appears to be more pristinely Christian in its comparative poverty and its religious orientation.

The policy is also useful because it removes the necessity of unwanted attacks on contemporary regimes, while it does not prevent propagation of Catholic social ethics. After the 1966 coup of General Juan Carlos Onganía, Argentine bishops simply refrained from commenting on politics and cited the recent Vatican Council statement on the separation of Church and State to justify their position.[114] As Chileans point out, they are free to stress religious awareness as one element of their national ethic, so long as they also admit the secularity of the Chilean nation-state.[115]

The new stance on Church and State in one sense has prevented a more rapid deterioration in the institutional power of the Church. It was officially established in the last quarter of the nineteenth century, when Pope Leo XIII rejected the old Thomistic support for monarchy and formulated the doctrine that the Church is indifferent to particular forms of government so long as they respect the rights of the Church. This stance allows the Church to coexist with a great variety of different regimes. Even the Cuban regime of Fidel Castro, which has nationalized Catholic schools and colleges, proscribed political activity by the Church, and limited Catholic social work and Catholic Action, has also cooperated with the Church's stance to the extent of allowing regular Catholic activity in the strictly religious sphere.[116] Under most regimes, the Church further safeguards its position by advocating national loyalty and support for the government in power. As the assistant bishop of Quito, Ecuador, pledged in a 1967 pastoral, the Church's educational system will not merely expand education but also provide that training in patriotism which

114. See Alberto Devoto (Obispo de Goya), untitled pastoral letter, July 28, 1966. The council statement that Devoto cites said in part that "the political community and the Church are independent and autonomous, each one in its own field. . . ."

115. Javier Lagarrigue Arlegui, "Pluralismo político chileno," *Teología y Vida* 4, no. 4 (octubre-diciembre, 1963): 247–48.

116. For a sympathetic interpretation of this new separation of Church and State in Cuba, see Yvan Labelle, "The Church in Socialist Cuba," *CIF Reports* 4, no. 7 (April 1, 1965).

will give citizens the motivation as well as the capacity for more active roles in national life.[117]

The separation of Church and State also works to ease the process of political modernization.[118] Besides removing the roadblock of Church support for the *ancien régime,* it benefits the Church's own position and so both allows and encourages that position to support modernization. Many Catholic progressives not only accept but welcome limitations on the Church's direct political activity. As a leading Brazilian layman said in 1965, "Today no one doubts that the loss of the Papal States was a blessing for the Holy See. But when it took place Christians did not know how to accept it. God had to use the force of non-Christians to free the Church from her manifestations of earthly power."[119] Father William Coleman, an astute observer of the Latin American Church, recognizes that separation of Church and State now benefits the Church there, because it allows the Church to disassociate itself from political regimes that fall and become discredited.[120] As recognized by the respondents in Joseph Fichter's study of Catholic activists in Santiago, the Church can work more effectively in promoting social change when it is not tied to a particular government.[121]

Some danger exists that the state will gain too direct control over individuals as this secular power of religion recedes further and further. Catholic concern for maintaining the family as a social institution derives initially from a vivid sense of the Church's institutional self-interest, but it also derives in part from a more general fear of the increasing power of the state if the family is dissolved or restructured. Church influence is maintained in the family; religious elders

117. Pablo Muñoz Vega, S.J. (Obispo Coadjutor Sedi Datus de Quito), *Carta pastoral sobre las grandes obligaciones de la hora presente,* Jan. 22, 1967 (Quito: Editorial "Vida Católica," 1967), p. 5.

118. See the discussion of this process by K. H. Silvert in Silvert, ed., *Churches and States: The Religious Institution and Modernization* (New York: American Universities Field Staff, 1967), esp. p. 218.

119. Luis Alberto Gómez de Souza, "Christians and Social Institutions," *CIF Reports* 4, no. 12 (June 16, 1965) : 91.

120. William J. Coleman, M.M., "The Need of a Lay Apostolate for Latin America," in Margaret Bates, ed., *The Lay Apostolate in Latin America Today* (Washington, D. C.: Catholic University of America Press, 1960), p. 5.

121. See Joseph H. Fichter, *Cambio social en Chile: Un estudio de actitudes* (Santiago de Chile: Editorial Universidad Católica, 1962), p. 39.

here try to imbue children with their own religious values. But when men think of themselves first as individuals rather than as members of a cohesive family unit, they may also be swept up more easily as in Nazi Germany into undivided loyalty to the secular nation-state.[122] Maintaining familial or religious loyalties does not automatically prevent the rise of totalitarianism. In specific cases such as Nazi Germany, Fascist Italy, or the early Perón regime in Argentina, the Church may fail to oppose authoritarianism or even collaborate with it on the national level in order to safeguard its own interests. As the Nazi and *peronista* cases also indicate, however, churchmen ought to recognize the opposition to religion that such movements keep veiled under the facade of religious tolerance. Liberal democrats naturally fear the curtailment of individual freedoms from the same totalitarian source. In a manner that would make some anticlerical, nineteenth-century liberals shudder, therefore, democrats may have a vested interest in maintaining a degree of Church influence on political values rather than seeing that influence disappear entirely.

As Catholic leaders have become less concerned about protecting the economic prerogatives of the Church as an institution, their calls for activity have taken on a new meaning. For some time Catholic intellectuals have called for "social power" for the Church, and by it they have meant something very different from the political intervention of the nineteenth century. When by 1900 the Church in Venezuela had lost the direct political power that it

122. The best study of the Church in Nazi Germany is Guenter Lewy, *The Catholic Church and Nazi Germany* (New York: McGraw-Hill Book Company, 1964). See also F. S. Betten, "The Catholic Church in Contemporary Germany," *Catholic Historical Review* 17 (1931–1932); George N. Shuster, *Like a Mighty Army: Hitler versus Established Religion* (New York: D. Appleton-Century Company, 1935); Nathaniel Micklem, *National Socialism and the Roman Catholic Church: Being an Account of the Conflict between the National Socialist Government of Germany and the Roman Catholic Church, 1933–1938* (London: Oxford University Press, 1939); Michael Power, *Religion in the Reich* (London: Longmans, Green, 1939); Hugh Martin, Douglas Newton, H. M. Waddams, and R. R. Williams, *Christian Counter-Attack: Europe's Churches Against Nazism* (London: Student Christian Movement Press, 1943); Camille M. Cianfarra, *The Vatican and the War* (New York: E. P. Dutton, 1944); Edmond Vermeil, *Hitler et le Christianisme* (Londres: Éditions Penguin, 1944); Andrew J. Krzeshinski, *Religion of Nazi Germany* (Boston: Bruce Humphries, 1945); and Saul Friedländer, *Pius XII and the Third Reich: A Documentation*, trans. Charles Fullman (New York: Alfred A. Knopf, 1966).

had exercised since the colonial period, Venezuelan intellectuals like Pedro Arcaya and Laureano Vallenilla Lanz advocated a return to "social power" for the Church. They wanted no more political intervention, but they thought that increased religious influence on social behavior would help to overcome such national problems as the high rate of illegitimate births.[123]

Many churchmen recognize, however, that such a "return" to power might be dangerous, allowing their secular opponents to restrict the religious ministry. In interviews bishops now frequently stress, as did Bishop Santos of Valdivia, Chile, that the future role of the Church should be entirely spiritual, rather than political in any sense. They fear that direct political or social intervention would —even if it tried to support progressive reforms—ultimately bring on a secular reaction which would prevent the Church from performing its central religious functions.[124]

Other contemporary priests reject Bishop Santos' concern for the primacy of the spiritual ministry. Father Roger Vekemans not only finds that the Church should concern itself with technological, economic, and social issues; he also finds that at certain times and in certain matters the hierarchy of the Church can intervene legitimately in specific political questions.[125] This attitude contrasts sharply with the ecclesiastical withdrawal from political issues occasioned by the failure of the Cristero movement in Mexico and other confrontations on the old issues of Church-State separation. In a sense, however, the withdrawal has allowed the new insistence on progressive political activity. In varying degrees the Latin American states have curtailed the economic power, the legal prerogatives, and thereby the primacy of institutional self-interest in the Church. Before this was done, although Catholic leaders often couched their appeals in terms of the people's welfare, their outcries for political action regularly were designed to promote the interests of the Church. Now, with the institutional ambitions of

123. Mary Watters, *A History of the Church in Venezuela, 1810–1930* (Chapel Hill, N. C.: University of North Carolina Press, 1933), p. 221.

124. Interview with Bishop José Manuel Santos Ascarza, in Valdivia, Chile, Aug. 3, 1968.

125. Roger Vekemans, *Doctrina, ideología y política,* Colección Desarrollo Integral, no. 9 (n.p.: Secretariado Social Mexicano, n.d.), p. 16.

the Church more circumscribed, the appeals for political activity are more genuinely designed to improve the general welfare.

The end of the old argument over Church intervention in politics has created the unexpected situation of Catholic progressives becoming the strongest champions of Catholic political involvement. When the Church as both doctrine and institution was a largely conservative force, its restriction to strictly spiritual ends supported the liberal policies that seemed progressive in the nineteenth and early twentieth centuries. As an ethic of democratic socialism has supplanted laissez-faire liberalism, the churchmen who espouse the new ethic are criticized as interventionists. Conservatives now regularly use the argument of the apolitical clergy to suppress activities of the Catholic left. As far as the new mainstream of Catholic social thought is concerned, therefore, the practical effects of the old insistence on political abstinence for the clergy has shifted from a progressive to an essentially regressive function.

Nevertheless, even the leftist opponents of the new Catholic activity denounce it as a mere revival of the old conflict between Church and State. Chilean Communists blame Father Vekemans for supporting the Alliance for Progress, for using the term "revolution" in the same nonviolent sense that John Kennedy used it, and for allegedly being a missionary for the profane enterprise of Yankee imperialism.[126] One of the most outspoken opponents of the new types of Catholic involvement is Yvan Labelle, a former Canadian priest who worked in Castro's Cuba. He says that a "new clericalism" as well as a new colonialism threatens Latin America, that "priests are ignoring the essential tasks of the priesthood. Latin America would not need more priests if those she has now would dedicate themselves to their real mission in life rather than to teaching mathematics and planning sociological interviews."[127] A nonbeliever might question what social utility there is to the purely sacramental functions of the priest, except as religious ob-

126. See "El pensamiento de Vekemans," an article first published in *El Siglo* on Oct. 30, 1963, which is reprinted in Orlando Millas, *Los comunistas, los católicos y la libertad* (Santiago de Chile: Editorial Austral, 1964), pp. 89–93.

127. Yvan Labelle, "To Live by the Sword," *CIF Reports* 4, no. 17 (Sept. 1, 1965): 128.

servance strengthens the very other-worldly orientation and the traditional neglect of inequalities that Labelle by no means seeks to strengthen. Critics of the new Catholic involvement should recognize that, in achieving a Church that could coexist with almost any regime, they would be leaving it entirely up to that regime or other groups actively to foster the social goals that a series of popes has now demanded.

If the new argument on Church and State is used to impede the evolution of Catholic programs, those programs face equal difficulties of quite different sorts. Instead of publicizing their activities and changing the image of the Church, churchmen often initiate efforts in the area of social reform without reporting on them in pastoral messages or even in the local press. Bishop Samuel Ruiz of Chiapas, Mexico, has typically worked for clinics, cooperatives, and agricultural schools, although his pastoral messages deal almost exclusively with religious subjects.[128] Christian Democratic parties face further problems in the diversity of groups within their own party organizations, their general failure to convert reformist ideals into practical programs, and their resultant inability to deal with rapidly changing questions of day-to-day politics.[129] In still another area, many Latin American bishops have a vivid sense of the problems facing different social classes and the limited effect that they themselves or the Church that they represent can have on these classes. In the words of Bishop Daniel Núñez of David, Panama, bishops often feel as if they are "between the sword and the wall." The self-centeredness of social classes is evident when Bishop Núñez describes how "on one side our directing and economically powerful class, in whose hands are the means to solve many problems, possess little social spirit and in some cases: none" while "on the other side the working class, workers and employees, the victims of so many injustices, in their salaries, often in hunger, surrender to all categories of vice, especially drunkenness, therefore not having the moral solvency to overcome their real needs."[130]

128. Samuel Ruiz (Obispo de San Cristobal de Las Casas) to Frederick C. Turner, Chiapas, Dec. 9, 1967.
129. See Edward J. Williams, *Latin American Christian Democratic Parties* (Knoxville, Tenn.: University of Tennessee Press, 1967), pp. 238–39.
130. Daniel E. Núñez to Frederick C. Turner, David, Nov. 13, 1967.

An ethic of cooperation and social responsibility appears to be a necessary part of the solution to these problems, but as Bishop Núñez and his fellow churchmen recognize, the Church has so far had only limited effect in propagating this ethic. A basic reason it has not been able to do so more effectively has been the fundamental barrier of division within the Church itself, a barrier created by the fact that besides Catholic progressives there are traditionalists and avant-garde militants with very different, antagonistic orientations.

III ~

Tradition and Reaction
within the Church

Because the Church is a source of at least tacit loyalty
for so many Latin Americans, groups with very different political
ideologies try to justify their position in terms of Church doctrine.
This is especially true of the conservatives who oppose all social
change, and a large part of the thought which is most self-consci-
ously and most vociferously "Catholic" in Latin America represents
nothing more than the attempt of right-wing ideologues to use the
Church in defense of the status quo. Catholic progressives, who try
to win legitimacy for their approaches to contemporary problems
by claiming that the approaches merely apply Christian humanism
to modern society, are continually thrown back by these conservatives and by the real weight of tradition in Latin American Catholicism. Traditionalists and reactionaries stand in positions of authority both inside and outside the Church, and the force of their
authority works to circumscribe the new Catholic orientations. As
Antonio de Castro Mayer, the bishop of Campos, Brazil, has defined
the situation, true Catholics must be continually on their guard

against the "modernists" who have "infiltrated" the Latin American Church since World War I.[1]

Differences within the conservative sector appear in the fundamental stances of its several segments. A basic distinction between groups that can be designated "traditionalist" and "reactionary," for example, is that the traditionalists simply have no positive attachment to the social reform goals of the new Catholic progressives, whereas the reactionaries actively denounce these goals and try to defeat their implementation. One must also differentiate among the segments of the Latin American Church that favor the status quo in governmental and in social terms. One group, in which papal nuncios figure prominently, supports the status quo in terms of backing the current government. If the government shifted from conservative to *fidelista,* then their official position would ordinarily shift to backing the new status quo of the *fidelistas,* because nuncios exist to carry on a dialogue with whatever government is in power. Other churchmen favor maintaining the status quo in terms of advocating economic and social stratification, and this group reacts violently against even the hint of *fidelismo.*

Even when supporters of existing governments are considered separately, the latter group of Church conservatives is strong indeed. The conservative movements in Argentina and Colombia are well known, and in Paraguay the Church long continued to uphold General Alfredo Stroessner. Even where a progressive movement appears to exist, one is frequently tempted to agree with Bialek's interpretation of Ecuadorean progressivism: that churchmen regularly only pay lip service to social problems and are fundamentally far more concerned with such other issues as battling Protestantism.[2] Furthermore, the Church has stood against a series of non-Communist, nationalist movements for reform, and by failing to side energetically with them, it has seriously lessened their chances

1. *Considerações a propósito da aplicação dos documentos promulgados pelo Concílio Ecumênico Vaticano II: Carta pastoral* (São Paulo: Editôra Vera Cruz, 1966), p. 23.
2. Robert W. Bialek, *Catholic Politics: A History Based on Ecuador* (New York: Vantage Press, 1963), p. 97.

for success. In contrast to the situation in Costa Rica where the clergy has worked successfully with reformist governments since the Figueres revolution of 1948, the Bolivian clergy stubbornly failed to collaborate with the process of change initiated by the Bolivian revolution of 1952. In the Dominican Republic, Juan Bosch divides religious personnel into three groups that allegedly differ only in the degree of their opposition to his reform program: the Social Christians who backed their own reformers, the old Dominican clergy who openly opposed him, and the small group of clergy who actively plotted to overthrow him.[3] In Puerto Rico the Church has weakened support for itself as well as for reform by adamantly opposing birth control and the social legislation proposed by former Governor Luis Muñoz Marín and his Partido Popular Democrático.

In Brazil the growth of the Catholic left has produced staunch resistance from reactionaries. Just as Teilhard de Chardin ran up against opposition from his Jesuit superiors in France, so Dom Hélder and other avant-garde churchmen have encountered strong opposition from Brazilian critics who claim that they are a greater danger than the Communists. Pressure by Catholic groups against President João Goulart and such anti-Goulart demonstrations as the "March of the Family with God for Liberty" in São Paulo on March 19, 1964, prepared the way for his overthrow in April, as they helped to convince the army and wavering political leaders that the President and his leftist policies lacked popular approval.[4] After the coup, conservative members of the Brazilian hierarchy were quick to voice their support. In the words of Dom Jaime de Barros Câmara, the late cardinal-archbishop of Rio de Janeiro, "When the guilty go unpunished there is neither peace nor order, and the guarantees of life, property, honor and dignity disappear. The armed forces were right when they required a clean-up not only of the Militant Communists but also of dishonest officials who

3. Juan Bosch, *The Unfinished Experiment: Democracy in the Dominican Republic* (New York: Frederick A. Praeger, 1965), pp. 126–27.
4. James W. Rowe, "Revolution or Counterrevolution in Brazil? Part I: The Diverse Background," *American Universities Field Staff Reports Service,* East Coast South America Series 11, no. 4 (Brazil), June, 1964, p. 12.

wronged the people. . . ."[5] Brazilian conservatism is also manifest in the Sociedade Brasileira de Defesa da Tradição, Família e Propriedade (TFP), a militantly anti-Communist organization, backed by rightist churchmen, which squarely opposes Catholic progressives. The society claims that it played a "decisive role" in the 1964 coup.[6] With headquarters in São Paulo and some 3,000 members drawn from various Brazilian cities, the society's leaders claim that its "ever-increasing action against Socialism, Progressivism, Leftism, etc." have made it "the most powerful support of the Christian Civilization in Brazil." Following the Brazilian society's example, similar societies with identical names have also arisen in Chile, Argentina,[7] and other Latin American countries.

As Catholic conservatives continue to support the tenets out of which the ideas of Catholic progressives have emerged, the conservatives stoutly oppose the evolving progressive doctrines. Edward Williams, a sympathetic observer of Latin American Christian Democracy, admits that the fundamental theory of the Christian Democrats "is essentially traditional, Catholic corporatism."[8] Despite the abstract similarity of this theory to many of their own assumptions, the Catholic conservatives oppose the whole range of specific, Christian Democratic programs from free trade unionism to agrarian reform. Instead of a "confiscatory" policy of land reform, for example, conservative Church leaders propose greater cooperation between the government and private landowners, with such policies as the stabilization of markets and prices, rural in-

5. *O Jornal,* April 18, 1964, as translated and reprinted in *CIF Reports* 3, no. 1 (April 16–30, 1964) : 7.
6. From a propaganda leaflet entitled "A Vigorous Effort of Modern Brazil against Communism: The Brazilian Society for Defense of Tradition, Family and Property (TFP)." Issuance of this leaflet in English indicates the society's concern to propagate its ideas outside Brazil. The leaflet details the work of the society, lists its various publications, and prints the translation of a letter from Cardinal Pizzardo praising the society's work.
7. Letter from Professor Fernando Furquim de Almeida, the vice-president of TFP, to Frederick C. Turner, São Paulo, Sept. 21, 1967. Copious information on the society's positions appears in its English-language press releases and in its journals: *Catolicismo,* published in Campos, Brazil, and *Fiducia,* published in Santiago de Chile.
8. Edward J. Williams, *Latin American Christian Democratic Parties* (Knoxville, Tenn.: University of Tennessee Press, 1967), p. 234.

dustrialization, better uses of fertilizers and insecticides, financial credit for landowners, and the opening of unpopulated government lands.[9] Naturally, this approach wins backing from *latifundistas* and wealthy laymen.

The national environments of Latin American Catholicism help to shape tendencies toward revolutionary and reactionary militancy, as they create different patterns of progressive-traditionalist interaction in the different republics. In Colombia and Brazil, where part of the hierarchy has been staunchly conservative, Catholic militants have come to demand radical forms of change. In Mexico and Chile, on the other hand, where the government and a major segment of the Church hierarchy promote progressive policies, Catholic militants work more easily within the established political framework rather than in opposition to it. In each Latin American state, however, there remain enough exponents of traditional Catholicism to make the spread of the newer Catholic viewpoints slow and difficult.

TRADITIONALIST VIEWPOINTS

Catholic conservatives advocate social justice and renovation just as do other Latin American churchmen, but in doing so they interpret the concepts in terms of the traditional goals and methods of Latin American Catholicism. As Professor Fredrick B. Pike of the University of Notre Dame puts it, they interpret "social justice" to mean "the expansion of charitable work within a society that will continue to be stratified and largely closed."[10] For conservatives, modernization means not so much the adaptation of Church policy and personnel to secular change and popular aspirations as it does

9. Geraldo de Proença Sigaud (Arcebispo de Diamantina), Antonio de Castro Mayer (Bispo de Campos), Plinio Corrêa de Oliveira, and Luiz Mendonça de Freitas, *Declaração do Morro Alto*, Sept. 8, 1964 (São Paulo: Editôra Vera Cruz, 1964), pp. 17–30. Coffee growers in the state of São Paulo have strongly supported this statement by Brazilian churchmen.

10. Fredrick B. Pike, "Catholicism in Latin America Since 1848," a manuscript to be published in *The Christian Centuries: A New History of the Catholic Church*, vol. 5, *The Church in a Secularized Society*, p. 60. In the United States, these volumes are being published by the McGraw-Hill Book Company.

the adaptation of popular aspirations to traditional Catholicism. "Renovation" is the newly effective propagation of the faith.

The innate traditionalism of many members of the Church hierarchy clearly appears in the position of José Humberto Quintero, the cardinal-archbishop of Caracas, Venezuela. When asked in an interview what were the major problems facing the Venezuelan Church, he significantly never mentioned—as a progressive churchman would have done—the poverty or lack of development of the common people. For him, the four greatest problems were the lack of adequate religious education, poor family life and the resulting number of illegitimate children, the low rate of priestly vocations, and Communist infiltration among the youth. These problems could be resolved, the cardinal believed, through energetic programs of religious education and retreats, special campaigns to increase vocations, the importation of foreign priests, and warnings to Venezuelan youth on the dangers of communism.[11] When specifically questioned on the issue of poverty, the cardinal was quite candid in implying that its extent had been overrated. As the German ambassador to Venezuela had recently told him, he said, even the dwellers in the shanty towns around Caracas could be seen to have television sets, and oil revenues had of course brought a great deal of money into the country.

Although the progressive wing of the Church is most disappointed in the failure of many prelates to share its deep concern for poverty and social development, the failure can be easily understood in the case of such men as Cardinal Quintero. Institutionally, Quintero's position still resembles that of a secular monarch in an earlier period, as he is the national head of a hierarchical organization and—from one standpoint—would seem to have earned the right to spend his time and energies as he pleases. Like many prelates, the cardinal has a deep love for books and also enjoys painting. Personally, he is a charming, rather shy man, and he has already adapted to some of the customs of an age which does not give all of the respect to his position that was given in earlier times. In an audience room which contained some twenty-five

11. Interview with José Humberto Cardinal Quintero, in Caracas, Venezuela, June 17, 1968.

chairs and a small throne on a raised dais, for example, he chose to conduct the interview by shaking my hand in a most comradely fashion and sitting in an ordinary chair rather than mounting his throne. He showed a professional pleasure in the good working relationship that Church and State had achieved in Venezuela before the COPEI victory of 1968, and his concern for the spiritual welfare of the Venezuelan people is incontestable. From his own perspective, it seems clear that his primary work should be in these traditional areas of archepiscopal service, rather than in turning the Church into an institution dedicated to secular change.

In contrast to the traditionalism of Cardinal Quintero stands the more reactionary position of Jorge Iván Hübner Gallo, a professor at the national university in Chile. He declares that the modern enemies of the faith are more surreptitious and dangerous than the older enemies who attacked the Church openly, because the new enemies claim that they are Catholic and work to destroy the Church from the inside. With a fitting use of the magisterial "we," Hübner Gallo concludes a denunciation of modern trends in Latin American Catholicism by saying that:

> All these tendencies, to a greater or lesser degree, have a dangerous element in common: the desire to reconcile the traditional and permanent doctrine of the Church with the errors of the modern world. . . .
>
> For our part, against the sad attempts to adapt Christianity to the modern world, we believe that we must fight to adapt the modern world to Christianity, manfully holding on high, against every tendency to yield, the incorruptible banner of an integral faith.[12]

Applying this principle to politics, he agrees with European Fascists that the best governments are not those which represent the greatest number of voters but rather those which work most effectively for the "Common Good."[13]

In its most extreme form, Catholic conservatism seeks this common good in a Church-directed society. Churchmen emphasize that there are some mysteries which surpass the capacity for intellectual

---

12. Jorge Iván Hübner Gallo, *Los católicos en la política* (Santiago de Chile: Zig-Zag, 1959), p. 11.
13. *Ibid.*, pp. 95–96.

understanding with which men were endowed,[14] and in doing so they continue to justify the position of the Church hierarchy as interpreters of what should happen as well as of what has happened on earth. The proper "adaptation" to the modern world is an "organic growth of the Church," and as Bishop Castro Mayer admits, the concept of this adaptation is simply "part of the Catholic tradition."[15] Some conservatives go so far as to tie belief in Church direction of society to opposition to all ideas not originally set out by the Church hierarchy. In a book ostensibly designed to prove why Protestant charges of Catholic intolerance in Colombia are unfounded, Eduardo Ospina fiercely denounces Protestantism and presents this traditional clerical prescription. He concludes that "to become a great and happy people, to have a radiant life, it is enough for Colombia to be submerged into the Blood of Christ Who is the youthful and eternal life of the Church."[16]

Traditionalists see a lack of respect for authority as the greatest sin of the modern world. To justify their own influence and hierarchical patterns of authority, they continue to reiterate in public statements that, just as the pope is the direct successor to Saint Peter, so they are the direct successors to the apostles. They pride themselves on the Church's being an antiegalitarian institution and list in detail the differing degrees of power which the various authorities in the Catholic Church possess.[17] Since they sincerely see themselves as the bearers of moral truth, the widespread absence of respect for religious authority naturally disturbs them. Like earlier clergymen they see Church and State as parallel institutions, so that, especially with the settlement of the old Church-State conflicts, they naturally desire the same respect for state authority

14. Antonio de Castro Mayer (Bispo de Campos), *Carta pastoral, por ocasião do 250.° aniversário do encontro da milagrosa imagem de Nossa Senhora da Conceição Aparecida e do 50.° aniversário das aparições de Nossa Senhora do Rosário em Fátima, sôbre a preservação da fé e dos bons costumes,* Feb. 2, 1967 (São Paulo: Editôra Vera Cruz, 1967), pp. 22–23.

15. Castro Mayer, *Considerações a propósito da aplicação dos documentos promulgados pelo Concílio Ecumênico Vaticano II,* p. 12.

16. Eduardo Ospina, S.J., *The Protestant Denominations in Colombia: A Historical Sketch with a Particular Study of the So Called "Religious Persecution"* (Bogotá: National Press, 1954), p. 202.

17. See Antonio de Castro Mayer (Bispo de Campos), *Instrução pastoral sôbre a Igreja,* March 2, 1965 (São Paulo: Editôra Vera Cruz, 1965), pp. 26–39.

that they wish for their own. Their assumption that the Church should dispense power and authority often leads them to exaggerate the extent to which it actually does so, as in the case of a ludicrously tragic bishop in Spanish America who began construction on a huge new church in the late 1960's, despite the fact that he had only thirteen priests in his entire diocese, and the building of a large new seminary, although he had no seminarians to fill it once it was completed.[18]

Conservatives loudly denounce the increasingly egalitarian tendencies of contemporary Catholicism. In attacking what he calls "absolute egalitarianism," Bishop Castro Mayer places it in the same category as such other doctrines as pantheism, naturalism, laicism, and evolution against which the Church must contend. The hierarchical orientation of Catholic traditionalists is clearly revealed in his contention that egalitarian doctrines contravene "all legitimate superiorities" in the political sphere, just as they undermine the distinction which Christ allegedly established between the Church hierarchy, the clergy, and the faithful.[19] Political and social inequalities are natural and "legitimate"; they do not result simply from oppression or a temporary human failure to organize resources most effectively for the realization of social goals. Consequently, the Church should not make common cause with the working class, oppose capitalism and private property, or support majoritarian democracy.[20] In finding that the Church should support all classes and recognize the benefits of aristocratic as well as majoritarian forms of government, Bishop Castro Mayer and his fellow conservatives use the ethic of Church abstention from political involvement to oppose the principal tendencies of Catholic progressivism.

Conservatives go on to attack political pluralism and the humanistic tendencies of religious thought. They criticize the activists who wish to make the satisfaction of human needs the primary

18. Based on personal observation and an interview in Spanish America in 1968. The names of the bishop and the country have been withheld at the request of the person who provided the original information.

19. A. de Castro Mayer (Évêque de Campos), *Catéchisme de Vérités opportunes qui s'opposent aux Erreurs contemporaines. Lettre pastorale sur les Problèmes de l'Apostolat moderne*, Jan. 6, 1953 (Québec: La Cité Catholique, 1962), p. 16.

20. *Ibid.*, pp. 87–98.

goal; they accuse these "modernists" of "sensuality," of wishing to use the Church like the rest of society to promote man's "pleasure."[21] In arguing for an integral social unity, the conservatives denounce pluralism as factionalism. They do not accept the fact of political pluralism; they battle against it. In appreciating this conservative rejection of pluralism, of course, one should not confuse traditionalism with frank and accurate appraisals of the difficulties of implementing particular techniques of democracy. When the bishop of David, Panama, says that honest and responsible elections are impossible in his country at the present time,[22] he is merely evaluating the political culture in which he lives. His own desire for a more broadly participant and responsive political culture lies in sharp contrast to the system that he observes and criticizes. There is a vast difference between a prelate who recognizes the need to find more effective means to deal with the growth of pluralism, however, and the churchmen who deny its existence or deal with it only through formulas of Church-centered unity.

When conservatives advocate a static pattern of human relationships, they tie such advocacy to odd combinations of contemporary rhetoric and divine commands which they allege to be unalterable. In a famous Brazilian denunciation of agrarian reform, Archbishop Proença Sigaud and others claim that the "fundamental principle" of private property derives "from the very nature of things," from God who is the "Author of nature."[23] They claim that agrarian reform requires abolition of both private property and the family, which will in turn create "totalitarianism."[24] Here they argue not from divine commands but from the Cold War invective of "to-

21. Castro Mayer, *Instrução pastoral sôbre a Igreja*, pp. 55–56.
22. Daniel E. Núñez to Frederick C. Turner, David, Nov. 13, 1967.
23. Geraldo de Proença Sigaud, S.V.D., Antonio de Castro Mayer, Plinio Corrêa de Oliveira, and Luis Mendonça de Freitas, *Reforma agrária, questão de consciência*, 4th ed. (São Paulo: Editôra Vera Cruz, 1962), p. 27. For an early statement of the central themes in this conservative volume, see Geraldo de Proença Sigaud, S.V.D., "Reforma agrária," *Verbum* 10, fasc. 3 (1953). On the archbishop's support for the 1970 agrarian reform program of the Brazilian government, which caused him to break with the TFP, see "Brasil: 'Familia, Tradición y Propiedad' responde a Dom Sigaud quien ha renunciado al grupo," *Informaciones Católicas Internacionales*, no. 373 (diciembre, 1970) : 18.
24. Proença Sigaud, Castro Mayer, Corrêa de Oliveira, and Mendonça de Freitas, *Reforma agrária*, p. 30.

talitarianism" to which social scientists have given respectability.[25] Their arguments justify rather than explain their positions, as they champion landowners and try to tar agrarian reformers with the brush of "totalitarian" oppression. Their opposition to their own particular straw man of totalitarianism gives credence in a Latin American context to the conclusion that the North American concept of totalitarianism has grown not as a valid intellectual construct but as a rhetorical weapon against the Nazis and the Soviets.[26]

In opposing violence and social strife, Catholic conservatives are hypothetically correct in thinking that strife would slacken if most Latin Americans accepted their traditional Catholic values. What the conservatives fail to recognize is the virtual impossibility of traditional Catholicism's becoming an internalized ethical system for the majority of Latin Americans. Citizens' apparent interests are too contradictory and the possibilities of secular change are too striking for them passively to accept the "social peace" of an inflexible, highly stratified society. In this context, the pleas for peace of conservative Catholicism are effectively inoperative, and the contrasting formulas for change of Catholic moderates and progressives take on increased meaning.

To the extent that the preachments of Catholic conservatives are effective, they clearly work in the interests of the possessing classes, so that it is no surprise that conservatives receive their greatest support among those classes. Industrialization encourages new attitudes, but in some cases it also leads businessmen into attempts to inculcate in their employees some form of traditional religiosity. In the state of Nuevo León in northern Mexico, Pablo González Casanova has found that factory owners still foment a paternalistic type of religiosity in order to tie workers into the factory system.[27]

25. The classic American analysis is Carl J. Friedrich and Zbigniew K. Brzezinski, *Totalitarian Dictatorship and Autocracy,* 2d ed. (New York: Frederick A. Praeger, 1965).

26. See Herbert J. Spiro and Benjamin R. Barber, "The Concept of 'Totalitarianism' as the Foundation of American Counter-Ideology in the Cold War," a paper delivered at the 1967 annual meeting of the American Political Science Association, Chicago, Sept., 1967.

27. *La democracia en México,* 2d ed. (México: Ediciones Era, S.A., 1967), p. 49.

Catholic progressives frequently complain of this orientation. Father Óscar Maldonado alleges that the Colombian Church hierarchy works consistently to maintain Colombia's rigid social structure and class stratification, reinforcing them with the deleterious ideal that the "difference among those classes should only be glossed over through mutual love between those on top and those on the bottom." He complains that Colombian bishops speak of social justice only in the most general terms to the wealthy, while to the poor they denounce violence precisely and explicitly.[28]

Despite such criticisms from progressives, the mutual support between secular and religious conservatives is most natural. The Church in Latin America has traditionally been associated with conservative forces because it is a source of power as well as a source of personal security and prestige, but the reason that conservatives have contributed to it is that it has used this power in their interests. Rural priests in Colombia still depend so heavily on wealthy landlords for their meager support that they find it difficult to reject the conservative policies that most of the landlords advocate.[29] Catholic educators have often taken neutral or conservative positions not out of conviction but out of necessity, recognizing that the financing for their parochial schools depends largely upon a wealthy and conservative clientele.

As Catholic educators take this position, however, it reinforces the very situation that limited their options in the first place. Despite the new orientations becoming evident in Catholic education, the education dispensed at Catholic institutions in Latin America has remained traditional in its overall doctrinal content. Fathers Houtart and Pin, two of the foreign priests who have studied the Latin American Church most carefully, admit that "Catholic education on the continent is one of the weakest sectors of Church action because of its conservatism, individualism and refusal to adapt." With a few notable exceptions, Catholic universities in

28. Óscar Maldonado, "Camilo Torres," *CIF Reports* 5, no. 6 (March 16, 1965): 45.
29. Pat M. Holt, *Colombia Today—And Tomorrow* (New York: Frederick A. Praeger, 1964), p. 178.

their words have only "an intellectual standing of second or third rank" and serve only "as centers of conservatism and social reaction."[30] Fashionable girls schools maintain rigid barriers of social and racial segregation, while they teach their students almost nothing about the range of social conditions around them. As a system of private education for the rich, parochial schools regularly feature classical culture and anti-Communist pronouncements. Seminaries, which one might hope to be the seedbeds of the new Catholicism, continue in many cases to produce priests who want a restoration of Catholic authority rather than the accommodation of the Church to the secular changes of the twentieth century.

As is shown in a 1961 survey of the attitudes of university students in Colombia, this pattern of education has encouraged pervasive support for the traditionalist viewpoint. Among the sample of 610 students from the different faculties of the national university, 23.8 per cent of the students said that a "more intense religious life" would provide a solution for the problems facing their country. Another 31.4 per cent of the students said that such a religious upsurge would "probably" solve the problems. While some of the students interpreted a "more intense religious life" to mean a new emphasis on moral values, others clearly interpreted it as devotion to traditionalism and Catholic ritual.[31] An overwhelming number of the students at the national university came from families who were wealthy enough to afford their education, and the Colombian Church has traditionally been so strong that one would expect its viewpoint to predominate even among contemporary students. The survey considered the spectrum of students at a secular university that archconservatives have characterized as a hotbed of radicalism, however, rather than the students at a more obviously devout Catholic institution. Thus, the students' tendency to relate questions of political development to an intensity of religious life indicates a striking inclination to interpret problem-solving in terms of the traditional values of Latin American Catholicism.

30. François Houtart and Émile Pin, *The Church and the Latin American Revolution,* trans. Gilbert Barth (New York: Sheed and Ward, 1965), pp. 220, 224–25.
31. Benjamín Edward Haddox, *Sociedad y religión en Colombia (estudio de las instituciones religosas colombianas),* trans. Jorge Zalamea (Bogotá: Ediciones Tercer Mundo, 1965), pp. 128–30.

ATTITUDES TOWARD DICTATORSHIP

Political scientists have commonly assumed that the authoritarian traditions and organization of the Church compel it to contribute to dictatorship or at least to retard the rise of democracy in Latin America.[32] Actually, the interconnections between authoritarianism and the Church are far more subtle than the usual questions of tradition or organization imply, and they involve sources of friction and antagonism as well as compatibility. With opposition to Juan Perón in 1955 the outward position of the Latin American Church shifted against dictatorship, but even this shift in policy has not been consistently upheld. Where churchmen have opposed dictatorship, the interests of the Church have figured prominently in their actions. Where they have continued to support dictators, a sense of public welfare and more recently a sense of nationalism have generally motivated the clerics as much as have traditions or their own patterns of organization.

Clerical attitudes toward Manuel Odría in Peru and Rafael Trujillo in the Dominican Republic illustrate the older Church position on dictatorship. Under the regime of President Odría, his picture figured prominently with that of General Francisco Franco of Spain in Church publications.[33] Although these men were thoroughly praised as defenders of the Church and although they still have partisan defenders within it, the autocratic tendencies of their regimes were to receive increasing criticism after 1955. Church support for Rafael Trujillo lasted right up to his assassination in 1961. Trujillo encouraged religious activity, as he let the number of diocesan and regular priests in the Dominican Republic rise steadily from 93 in 1944[34] to 310 in 1959. He supported many

32. See Russell H. Fitzgibbon, "Catholicism, Protestantism, and Politics in Latin America," *Hanover Forum* 2, no. 1 (Winter, 1956): 4.
33. See the pictures of Odría, Franco, and Catholic leaders opposite p. 24 in *¡Urubamba! Historia de la vida heroica de los misioneros dominicos españoles en las selvas del Perú* (n.p.: Extraordinario de Misiones Dominicanas, n.d.).
34. Isidoro Alonso and Gines Garrido, *La Iglesia en América Central y el Caribe: Estructuras eclesiásticas* (Bogotá: FERES, 1962), p. 121. Compare Alonso and Garrido's figures with those in Table 3 on p. 184.

Catholic institutions and even provided station wagons for nuns and newly ordained priests. Through material support similar to that provided by Mussolini and Hitler, Trujillo kept Church leaders from opposing his regime during the three decades of his rule. Although such Catholic critics as Father Nevins later came to accuse Trujillo of "buying" some members of the Church "for the price of a free gasoline ration each month,"[35] such criticisms scarcely touched the "Benefactor of the Church" during his lifetime.

The Church naturally supported regimes that treated it so well, but its support also rested on the assumption that dictators could bring order and stability to their countries. To the occasional prelate who thought in terms of economic growth before the mid-1950's, some dictators seemed able to bring this growth as well. Furthermore, as priests spoke out against the moral degeneracy that some "free enterprise" governments allowed to flourish, the moralistic tendencies of reform-oriented, Latin American autocracies also appealed to numerous clergymen. A striking, contemporary example of this process has been Catholic backing for Fidel Castro's program against vice. A Cuban priest told Óscar Tiseyra that, in moral terms, Cuba before Castro seemed the creature of its "decadent capitalist bourgeoisie." In discussing the famous nightclubs and houses of prostitution that attracted foreigners to Havana before Castro closed them, Tiseyra declares that Cuban cities were "infected by the moral virus of the tourist dollar."[36] While condemning Castro's antireligious policies or his betrayal of libertarian promises, many Catholics at least sympathize with his stand against prostitution and the moral laxity condoned or encouraged to win the money of Yankee tourists. As a dictator, he has ruled out the common pleasures to which Catholic doctrine also objects.

Although the Church has long had numerous reasons to back dictators, Catholic opposition to authoritarianism has also had a

35. Albert J. Nevins, M.M., "Hopes and Fears in the Dominican Republic," *The Sign* 43, no. 12 (July, 1964): 18. See also James A. Clark, *The Church and the Crisis in the Dominican Republic* (Westminster, Md.: Newman Press, 1967), pp. 46–47.

36. Óscar Tiseyra, *Cuba marxista vista por un católico* (Buenos Aires: Jorge Álvarez, 1964), p. 167.

long tradition in Latin America. As early as the 1790's, Father Toribio Rodríguez de Mendoza opposed authoritarian thinking in the Church as well as in Spain when he altered the curriculum of the Real Convictorio de San Carlos in Lima to stress popular sovereignty and the natural rights of man.[37] More recently papal support for right-wing autocrats has been far from lasting or complete. Catholic commentators are quick to point out that the kind of corporate state advocated by Pope Pius XI was very different from that of the European Fascists, and that the Church upheld these regimes only because of its fundamental tolerance for different forms of government.[38] Some clerical backing for Juan Perón, Gustavo Rojas Pinilla, and Marcos Pérez Jiménez did indeed resemble the support that a large Jesuit faction within the Vatican gave to Mussolini: a support not based on doctrinal similarities or personal liking but on the churchmen's belief that the interests of the Church could be best secured through negotiations with the paternalistic government under which they lived.[39] Church policy has changed as the likelihood of realizing this fundamental interest has seemed to change, as when Venezuelan bishops issued a strong pastoral attacking the dictatorship of Pérez Jiménez before his overthrow and so drew support from all of the opposition parties. This pastoral and its antidictatorial position significantly helped to usher in the period of warm relations between Church and State in Venezuela during the 1960's,[40] during which democratic parties remained in power and the Christian Democratic party finally won the presidency. Clerics have nevertheless continued to recognize that, while eventual and timely opposition to a Pérez Jiménez may invigorate Church activists, such opposition also creates the risk of repression by secular enemies and an unhappy martyrdom for the Church.

37. Pike, "Catholicism in Latin America Since 1848," p. 2. See also Fredrick B. Pike, *The Modern History of Peru* (New York: Frederick A. Praeger, 1967), pp. 38–39.

38. Melvin J. Williams, *Catholic Social Thought: Its Approach to Contemporary Problems* (New York: Ronald Press Company, 1950), p. 477.

39. On clerical support for the Italian Fascists, see Richard A. Webster, *The Cross and the Fasces: Christian Democracy and Fascism in Italy* (Stanford, Calif.: Stanford University Press, 1960), esp. pp. 122–23.

40. Interview with Valmore Acevedo, in Caracas, Venezuela, June 17, 1968.

111

The continuing ambiguity of the Church's position appears in the simultaneous backing and denunciations of rightist organizations in countries as widely separated as Bolivia and Guatemala. In Bolivia the Comunidad Demócrata Cristiana, which is an outgrowth of the old Falange Socialista Boliviana, has some Catholic backing and remains largely Fascist in orientation. In Guatemala, on the other hand, a bishops' statement on May 9, 1967, was the only organized protest to atrocities carried out against rebel groups by right-wing terrorists and especially by the White Hand, an anti-Communist vigilante group linked to the Movimiento de Liberación Nacional that with CIA aid in 1954 worked to oust the pro-Communist government of Jacobo Arbenz. Since both plantation owners and the Guatemalan army backed the right-wing terrorists and since the reform government of President Julio César Méndez Montenegro did not move decisively to curtail their activities even when members of the President's own Partido Revolucionario were murdered,[41] the bishops' message indicates a striking tendency to oppose rightist excess as well as genuine independence of action and the humanitarian commitment of the Guatemalan episcopate.

Catholic thinking as a whole has now developed to a point where many spokesmen admit that the Church should not support dictators merely in return for their support of the Church.[42] Priests talk about the "excesses" of dictators and suggest that they need to be opposed because their interests conflict with popular aspirations. Almost no churchmen go on to differentiate between dictators, however, to suggest that the Church should perhaps support those autocrats who are able to bring economic growth as well as stability, who encourage mass politicization through interest groups or party organization, and who are ultimately willing to leave office themselves. Although churchmen have backed autocratic chief executives for a variety of reasons, they do not regularly do so on such

41. *The Economist,* June 10, 1967, p. 1111.
42. See Renato Poblete, S.J., "The Phenomenon of Dictatorship," in John J. Considine, M.M., ed., *Social Revolution in the New Latin America: A Catholic Appraisal* (Notre Dame, Ind.: Fides Publishers, 1965), esp. pp. 49–51.

pragmatic grounds as the autocrat's abilities to promote growth or politicization. In this sense, the new Church opposition to dictators may not be as fully progressive as its exponents believe.

A useful test case in the development of this position is the Argentine regime of Colonel Juan Perón from 1945 to 1955, a regime that some observers have seen as the turning point in Catholic attitudes. Perón, although not known for religious devotion before his rise to power, tried hard to appease the Church during the first years of his rule. He said, "I have always wanted to be inspired by the teachings of Christ."[43] With a decree in December, 1943, requiring compulsory religious education in public schools, the Church hierarchy at first turned strongly behind the military regime that Perón came to dominate.[44] Perón went even further in abandoning the old separation of Church and State, as he encouraged priests to say a blessing at his labor rallies and allowed Catholic sound trucks to proselytize in the capital with sermons and hymns. He was rewarded with friendly decisions and policies from most of the national hierarchy and active collaboration by some priests in his policies to mobilize Argentine labor.

Given conservative strength within the Argentine Church, some opposition to Perón was inevitable despite official policies on both sides. Soon after the fall of Perón in 1955, Father John Considine questioned Argentines about the strength of the Church and its relation to politics in Argentina. He was told that, among the population as a whole, only about one-eighth of the population attended mass every Sunday, and that the great majority of these was women. Among the most conservative 15 per cent of the population in the central province of Buenos Aires, however, nearly all of the conservatives were devout Catholics, with most of the women and some of the men actively practicing their religion.[45] Since conservative laymen figured so prominently in the

---

43. Quoted in George I. Blanksten, *Perón's Argentina* (Chicago: University of Chicago Press, 1953), p. 236.

44. See Robert J. Alexander, *The Perón Era* (New York: Columbia University Press, 1951), chap. 11, "Church and State in Perón's Argentina."

45. John J. Considine, *New Horizons in Latin America* (New York: Dodd, Mead & Company, 1958), p. 97.

Church and since they generally opposed Perón, a tendency for Church opposition to him underlay the growth of his dispute with the hierarchy.

Perón refused to accede to Church opinion in all matters that the hierarchy wanted to control, and his programs alienated him from Catholic democrats and put him into competition with Catholic charities and reformers. His legalization of prostitution and the provision of regular health inspections in red light districts provoked a concerted attack from the hierarchy. Members of the hierarchy and a number of priests also worked against Perón on the grounds of his clear and increasing suppression of political freedoms and the guarantees of the old constitution. Rivalry in the field of social welfare, an area that Perón felt to be crucial in order to maintain the support of his *descamisados,* threw him into direct competition with the Church. With all of Eva Perón's work to mobilize feminists behind her husband's regime, the Peróns were never able to destroy the Federation of Catholic Societies of Employed Women, the strong welfare organization that has long provided recreational facilities and medical services as well as living quarters for Argentine women. Perón's spurious ideology of *justicialismo* disturbed many churchmen, just as the creation of a Christian Democratic party in turn disturbed Perón. As these sources of friction multiplied, they led to the final falling-out in which *peronista* mobs attacked and burned churches and official Church opposition helped to push Perón from office.[46]

Why has a vocal group of clergymen continued to support Perón and other authoritarians even after the Church's part in his overthrow and its subsequent denunciations of other dictatorships? Is it because they rightly reject the popular notion of the late 1950's that dictatorship is passing from the Latin American scene? Is it because, as has so often been claimed, they prefer authoritarian regimes since they have authoritarian personalities and work in a highly authoritarian Church structure? A detailed apologia for Perón that Father Pedro Badanelli wrote in 1955 shows other causes for such support of dictatorship. Father Badanelli's

46. On Perón's conflict with the Church, see Pablo Marsal S., *Perón y la Iglesia* (Buenos Aires: Ediciones Rex, 1955).

114

personal loyalty to Perón is revealed in the fact that, in the fourth edition of his study published five years after Perón's fall, he still maintained emphatically that "peronism without Perón" was as "ridiculously absurd" as trying to establish "Christianity without Christ." Badanelli claims that, far from persecuting the Church, Perón did more to aid it than any other leader of the Argentine government and that trouble arose only because the Church hierarchy required unconditional obedience in all matters from Perón. Badanelli finds that the Church fully supported Perón for eight years while his subsidies built sumptuous episcopal palaces, only to turn suddenly and completely against him when in legislation like that on divorce he tried to legislate "for all Argentineans" rather than for the special benefit of the Church hierarchy.[47]

A key to the backing given Perón by Father Badanelli and other *peronista* priests appears in their joint concern for the underprivileged. Perón built his power on giving dramatic wage increases and a sense of political participation to previously nonparticipant working groups, and the apparent concern for workers and for the poor that resulted from this policy seemed to his clerical supporters to bear the hallmark of traditional Christianity. In vehemently defending Perón against the charge that he promoted social justice only to secure his own power and glory, Father Badanelli points out that personal glory is also regularly assumed to be the motive behind Columbus' discovery of America and God's creation of the world.[48] Some priests clearly gained in prestige and power under Perón's early dispensations, and others certainly rallied behind him because they found in his authority the best way to maintain that civil order and opposition to communism in which they believed.

Far from supporting *peronismo* primarily because of personal gain or the authoritarian character of the regime, however, Badanelli and later priests like him seem to have done so most of all because of Perón's populist appeal. Fifteen years after the over-

47. *Perón, la Iglesia y un cura,* 4th ed. (Buenos Aires: Editorial Tartessos, 1960), pp. 16, 151.
48. *Ibid.,* p. 145. For Father Badanelli's interpretation of Perón's help for the poor, see *ibid.,* pp. 83–88.

throw of Perón, in the same month as the kidnapping and execution of anti-*peronista,* former President Pedro Aramburu, Argentine priests showed that the influence of the populist dictator was as lasting for the Church as for Argentine society as a whole. Reaffirming their "formal rejection of the capitalist system" and their advocacy of the "revolutionary process" of socializing the means of production, the Movement of Third World Priests declared that "in Argentina the Peronista experience and the great fidelity of the masses to the Peronista movement are a key to the incorporation of our people in this revolutionary process." This group, like the original *peronistas,* is populist in orientation, supposing that it defends "the mass of the oppressed in all the world."[49] Although dictatorships in Latin America have more recently tended to be run by military technocrats —like the Argentine leaders whom the Third World priests denounce—rather than by demagogues of the Perón variety, populist dictatorships may well return along with dictatorships that are more overtly moralistic, militaristic, or *fidelista.* As the various types of dictatorship persist, some clerics for their own reasons will continue to make peace and work with them.

The unsuccessful campaign of Father Ramón Talavera against General Alfredo Stroessner illustrates the dangers of failing to recognize this continuing likelihood for accommodation between Catholicism and dictatorship. The Catholic hierarchy long continued to uphold the established regime in Paraguay and, when Father Talavera came repeatedly to oppose it, his opposition led not to Stroessner's downfall but to Talavera's own exile and the curtailment of his priestly functions.

In 1958, at the age of twenty-eight, Father Talavera was a

49. "El Movimiento 'Tercer Mundo' de la Argentina y su opción por la liberación," *Nadoc,* no. 147 (3 junio, 1970): 8, 9. The original document was published on May 5, 1970. On the assassination of Aramburu, in connection with which two priests from the Third World Movement were arrested, see "Expose Macabre Alliance in Aramburu Plot," *Hemispherica* 19, no. 7 (Aug.–Sept., 1970); and "El caso Aramburu," *Siete Días Ilustrados* 4, no. 189 (28 diciembre, 1970 al 3 enero, 1971). For an extensive description and denunciation of the Movement of Third World Priests, see Carlos A. Sacheri, *La iglesia clandestina,* 2d ed. (Buenos Aires: Ediciones del Cruzamante, 1970), esp. chap. 13, "El Movimiento del Tercer Mundo en la Argentina."

parish priest near Asunción. Like many young priests working in Latin America, he developed a special concern for the poor and for the political system that seemed to hold them down. Talavera openly opposed the Stroessner regime in the 1958 election, when no other candidates were allowed to enter and the general had himself reelected to a five-year term. Police "detained" Talavera for several hours when he said in a public speech that all Paraguayans should support "active resistance against tyranny," that graft encumbered the army officers connected with Stroessner's Colorado party, and that the real duty of the Paraguayan army should be to "guarantee the rights of the citizens to govern themselves."[50] Police forcefully broke up a later rally at which Talavera exhorted a crowd of 2,000 persons to stand up for their freedom, and after the meeting unknown persons in a jeep showed their displeasure by stoning a church and shouting their loyalty to Stroessner.

Infused with the antidictatorial spirit of the late 1950's, members of the Paraguayan hierarchy apparently allowed Talavera to voice his sentiments and so associate the Church with democratic reform. Talavera's superiors gave him written permission to speak, and the vicar-general of Asunción, Monsignor Bartolomé Adorno, refused either to repudiate Talavera or to have a priest who was loyal to Stroessner publicly present the other viewpoint. Archbishop Aníbal Mena Porta even issued a pastoral letter on March 23, 1958, advocating that the government economize in the public interest, try to promote a healthy freedom of public opinion, and allow "a real and progressive participation of the people in political life."[51] When Stroessner remained in firm control of the government, however, Mena Porta responded in August to his demands that Talavera be disciplined. When the archbishop ordered Talavera not to make further public statements without permission,

50. *Hispanic American Report* 11, no. 2 (Feb., 1958): 108. A series of interviews that I conducted in Paraguay concerning Father Talavera indicated that some of the details in the *Hispanic American Report* were mistaken, even though this periodical provides the best general coverage of his activities. In such cases, I have followed the information provided and cross-checked in the interviews.

51. *Hispanic American Report* 11, no. 3 (March, 1958): 170.

the priest went on a nine-day fast before the presidential inaugura-
tion. Then, after drinking some orange juice at the request of
friends, he continued the fast for another six days.[52]

In November, 1958, the government moved directly against
Father Talavera by ordering the inhabitants of the parish of El
Carmen to leave so that new officers' quarters and a parade ground
could be built there. The homes of the parishioners were fired
upon and wrecked when he organized a resistance among them,
and he himself disappeared just before a mass rally that he planned
to hold in downtown Asunción. The crowd at the rally was dis-
persed by tear gas, and next day Father Talavera was found dazed,
barefoot, with his clothing ripped, some fifteen miles outside the
capital. The archbishop ordered him to take a tour outside the
country and, when he left for Uruguay, the government claimed
that he had become insane.[53] To demonstrate fealty to the government, the office of the archbishop issued a statement saying that
Talavera had gone to Montevideo to be treated by specialists for
"certain abnormalities" and that his statements had been merely
expressions of his personal opinion.[54]

Continuing efforts to unseat Stroessner in the following years
led only to personal frustration for Father Talavera. He went on
a long series of hunger strikes, tried repeatedly to reenter Paraguay,
and worked hard to stir intervention by other American states, but
his efforts brought no success. The Church officially rejected him
when, at the request of Archbishop Mena Porta, Cardinal Barbieri
of Montevideo prohibited him from saying mass.[55] When the government prevented his return to Paraguay in August, 1959,
Monsignor Aníbal Maricevich officially said that Father Talavera
was "psychologically ill."[56] In February, 1960, he was forced to
give up one of his hunger strikes after sixteen days when doctors
said that it was seriously endangering his health.[57] In April he
joined other exiles to represent his country at the Second Inter-

52. *Ibid.,* no. 8 (Aug., 1958): 462.
53. *Ibid.,* no. 11 (Nov., 1958): 635.
54. *Ibid.,* no. 12 (Dec., 1958): 696.
55. *Ibid.* 12, no. 2 (Feb., 1959): 116.
56. *Ibid.,* no. 8 (Aug., 1959): 460.
57. *Ibid.* 13, no. 2 (Feb., 1960): 134.

American Conference for Democracy and Freedom,[58] a meeting of Latin American democratic leaders in Venezuela that was to have little effect on the regimes in Nicaragua, Haiti, and Paraguay that it denounced.

After touring Venezuela, Panama, and Mexico, Father Talavera came to the United States in May, 1960. In July the Inter-American Peace Committee of the Organization of American States refused to give Talavera the hearing that it had earlier promised to him; he denounced the United States government for supporting the Paraguayan dictatorship and suppressing attempts to end it.[59] By 1961 Talavera was reduced to the position of a poor exile, undergoing yet another hunger strike in a cheap room in New York City in the hope that it might "influence Christians to ask Bishop Mena or Pope John XXIII to reinstate me in the Church."[60]

His activity since that time has hardly been such as to justify a reinstatement, however. Former student leaders, who knew Talavera during the 1950's when he advised the Catholic youth movement, report that he was quite popular then, but that he has since married and obtained a divorce.[61] In a 1966 service in Brazil, Talavera had himself named the first bishop of the Paraguayan Apostolic Catholic Church for which he claimed that he could obtain many converts if he returned to Paraguay.[62] His former friends among the Paraguayan clergy stress that they share his concern for the poor and his desire to manifest this attitude, but that they can not realistically follow the brand of activism that he practiced.[63]

A particularly interesting view of Talavera's role came to light in an interview with Archbishop Mena. The archbishop's progressivism appeared in the fact that, when asked what was the most pressing problem facing Paraguay, he replied that "the greatest problem

58. Ronald Hilton, "Commentary," in *ibid.,* no. 4 (April, 1960): 221.
59. *Ibid.,* no. 5 (May, 1960): 345; *ibid.,* no. 6 (June, 1960): 416–17; and *ibid.,* no. 7 (July, 1960): 483.
60. *Ibid.* 14, no. 1 (Jan., 1961): 78.
61. Interview with Domingo Rivarola, in Asunción, Paraguay, July 3, 1968.
62. "Cresce o movimento das igrejas nacionais da América Latina," *Diario da Noite,* June 27, 1966.
63. Interview with Father Pascual Páez, in Asunción, Paraguay, July 1, 1968.

is economic, because this is an underdeveloped country." In discussing Paraguayan politics, however, he commented—in the candid, open manner that he maintained throughout—"They say it is a dictatorship here, but you can work and study. You just can't make a revolution against the government." The archbishop clearly appreciated government financing for Catholic schools, and the fact that, as he said, his signature alone would allow the Church to import automobiles, motorcycles, refrigerators, and typewriters free of all duty.

His attitude did not seem to be "bought off" by these favors, however, or by the government's provision of his personal car and chauffeur. It was not determined by the medal that Stroessner had presented to him for all of his "service to the country," although, as a nationalist, recognition for this service had deeply pleased the archbishop. He simply rejected Talavera's overriding concern to overthrow the Stroessner government, by violence if necessary, and said that absolutely no other Paraguayan priest shared this particular approach to the country's problems. The archbishop supported efforts to aid the poor but also stressed that there was no need to alienate the government in doing so.[64]

The relationship of the Paraguayan Church and the Stroessner regime after Talavera's exile illustrates the same ambiguities in the Church's stance toward rightest authoritarians. Opposition by members of the lower clergy has been repeatedly voiced against such practices as the torture of Paraguayan political prisoners,[65] and some Catholic leaders have continued to provoke the government's anger with calls for reform. In a radio broadcast over a station owned by the Franciscan fathers in 1963, Luis Resck, a leader of the Movimiento Social Demócrata Cristiano, castigated the government's tight control of political parties, but Resck was promptly arrested for doing so.[66] In 1969, Christian Democratic leader Irala

---

64. Interview with Archbishop Juan José Aníbal Mena Porta, in Asunción, Paraguay, July 1, 1968. His nationalist attitudes appeared in the pride with which he identified both his father and mother as Paraguayans, and his comment that "Father X is Paraguayan and knows more about Paraguay than does Father Y, who is Spanish and a foreigner."

65. See the *Hispanic American Report* 12, no. 4 (April, 1959): 232.

66. *Ibid.* 16, no. 5 (May, 1963): 298.

Burgos declared that Stroessner would not allow Paraguay to go "beyond a mere democratic formalism."[67]

The government struck out at its critics, confiscating the official Church publication *Comunidad*[68] and, in October, 1969, abruptly exiling a Jesuit professor at the Catholic University in Asunción who had denounced Paraguayan press censorship while he was traveling in the United States.[69] Church statements criticized these actions, and Archbishop Mena went so far as to declare the excommunication of those who ordered physical attacks on priests and nuns. Church criticism never fell into broad opposition to the regime, however, or hinted at the need for attempts to overthrow it. Instead, episcopal messages categorically reaffirmed that "neither hatred nor violence are compatible with the Spirit of Christ,"[70] and that the Church "denounces efforts that try to identify it with political-party interests."[71] Sensing that Stroessner has not been likely to fall from power as did Perón or Rojas Pinilla, Paraguayan clergymen have been forced into a continuing, uneasy coexistence with him.

OPPOSITION TO COMMUNISM

One reason for the Church's refusal to oppose right-wing dictatorships more openly is their firm stand against communism. In discussing the conflict between communism and Christianity, Western scholars often stress the dangers of such inveterate anticommunism, since Christian adamancy only prevents diplomatic compromises and may even lead to a catastrophic war.[72] This counsel fits the

67. "Despertar democristiano en Paraguay," *The Economist* (edición para América Latina) 3, no. 3 (5 febrero, 1969) : 10–11.

68. "El movimiento estudiantil, la iglesia ye el gobierno paraguayo," *CIDOC Informa,* Document 69/200. This issue of *CIDOC Informa* also contains a number of other statements relating to the Church-State confrontation in Paraguay.

69. Gregorio Selser, "La iglesia rompe con Stroessner," *CIDOC Informa,* Document 69/192, p. 192/3.

70. "Comunicado de la Conferencia Episcopal Paraguaya a la opinión pública," *Nadoc,* no. 113 (3 diciembre, 1969) : 1.

71. "Mensaje del Arzobispo y Consejo presbiteral de Asunción," *ibid.,* p. 3.

72. See Herbert Butterfield, "Christianity and Politics," *Orbis* 10, no. 4 (Winter, 1967) : esp. p. 1245.

situational needs of British or North American Christians, but it fails to come to grips with the real issues of the Catholic-Communist confrontation in Latin America. Domestic development concerns Latin Americans far more than does the international confrontation with powerful Communist states. A related danger, the danger of anticommunism retarding the reform stance of Latin American Catholicism, is at least as great as the danger which militant Christianity poses in diplomatic terms for North Americans, however. The danger is that many Catholics will oppose social reform as being "communistic," that Catholics will become alienated from one another over the issue of reform, and that the resultant impasse in domestic politics will force the process of change to be one of a violent revolution from which no group can initially benefit.

Cuban experience demonstrates that the danger of uniform, undifferentiating anticommunism is probably as great for the Latin American Church as it is for the United States government. Leslie Dewart concludes that Cuban churchmen overreacted to the specter of communism, that they had neglected the social goals of Fidel Castro's revolution and turned against him largely because of his professions of communism. They defended United States policies against Castro and opposed Russian policies to support Castro, even though the Russian policies seemed to be the ones helping Cuba. Dewart's research indicates that many churchmen took this stand on the underlying assumption that in the Cold War the United States was defending Westernism and Christianity against Soviet atheism.[73] Cuban exiles with whom one talks similarly react strongly to the atheism of Castro's professed communism, as they decry anti-Catholic education in the schools, the turning of some churches into recreation centers where people allegedly play ping-pong, and the duplicity of Castro himself in wooing Catholics' support before the fall of Batista only to turn on them after the victory. Many laymen and churchmen fail to appreciate Castro's efforts to achieve such goals as the wider educational opportunities or the wider income distribution that progres-

73. Leslie Dewart, *Christianity and Revolution: The Lesson of Cuba* (New York: Herder and Herder, 1963), pp. 180, 309–10.

sive Catholics outside Cuba have been advocating. Like the United States government in Vietnam, they have failed to see that the force of nationalism and the sharpest advocacy of social improvement lie with a group calling itself Communist. In a situation where a *fidelista* regime effectively channels nationalist aspirations, tries consistently to promote social reform, and is willing to tolerate a nonreactionary Church, the long-term interests of the Church are probably best served through cooperation with the regime.

Nevertheless, opposition to communism has such a long history in the Latin American Church that its force continues to orient policies and attitudes in the other direction. Latin American clergymen have praised democracy throughout the twentieth century, but opposition to socialism or communism long slowed the evolution of the concept of democracy from emphasis on voting rights and an essentially nineteenth-century liberalism to a doctrine of broader social and economic equality. In 1911 Gaffre told a Brazilian Church conference that "if Democracy and the Church are created to be in agreement, because they have the same origin, the same aspirations and the same Ideal, we are going to see that Democracy, when it turns into socialism, no longer has anything in common with the Church and becomes its enemy."[74] As Catholic democrats have come to look more favorably on aspects of socialism, the growth of Catholic nationalism and collaboration with national policies has often reinforced traditional distrust of the radical left. Venezuelan bishops follow a line similar to that of the Venezuelan government and declare communism's clear and present danger. They point out that it wins support in Venezuela's schools and universities by appealing to the natural idealism of youth, claim that it has brought only tragedy to their sister republic of Cuba, and quote Pope Pius XI's prohibition on all collaboration with Communists.[75]

For their own purposes, diverse Catholic groups use the concept

74. L.-A. Gaffre, *Le Christ et l'Église dans la Question sociale. Conférences données au Brésil. Lettres-Préface de plusieurs Évêques et Notabilités de l'Église brésilienne* (Paris: Librairie Bloud & Cie., 1912), p. 58.

75. *Carta pastoral colectiva del episcopado venezolano: Estadísticas de educación gratuita* (n.p.: Publicaciones del Secretariado Permanente del Episcopado Venezolano, n.d.), pp. 9–10.

123

of anticommunism to discredit their opposition. Conservatives are most apt to depend upon anticommunism. Instead of seeing the Guatemalan Church battling against dedicated Communists as the rightist revolutionaries of 1954 were to allege, Mary P. Holleran concludes that the religious struggle after the overthrow of Jorge Ubico in 1944 was only the traditional contest between clergymen and anticlerical politicians. Her field research in Guatemala in 1944 and 1946 indicates that only the nomenclature of the struggle had changed, as clerics, who had come to be called Falangists, tried to discredit the anticlerical group by calling them Communists.[76] The term "Communist" is now regularly used to discredit the Catholic left, as when Chilean conservatives give the name of "black Communists" to the members of the Catholic labor movement. Even United States conservatives denounce progressive Catholicism as being tainted by Marxism. After declaring that the Christian Democratic party in Chile is becoming "a mass-party of opportunists," Thomas Molnar finds that "it is exasperating to hear faded Communist slogans from Jesuits and Dominicans as well as Catholic university professors and students. Their misguided romanticism and inadequate knowledge of the real situation are actually blocking the work of improvement they so desperately want."[77] What such criticism of the Christian Democrats fails to appreciate is that the traditional, "real situation" of exploitation in Latin America has made superficial Marxist slogans actually seem to apply. The criticism neglects the very different, antiauthoritarian way in which progressive Church leaders wish to solve the problems which both they and the Marxists perceive and decry.

Rejecting the newer programs, the Brazilian right has put forward an especially virulent opposition to communism and the Catholic left. In a special catechism designed to tell Brazilian

76. Mary P. Holleran, *Church and State in Guatemala* (New York: Columbia University Press, 1949), pp. 242–43. Although Holleran is correct in showing that the shift in epithet by the anticlericals was partly one of terminology, it was also more than that. The leaders of the 1944 revolution in Guatemala genuinely opposed the ties between the Franco regime and that of Jorge Ubico in Guatemala, and they resented the support for Franco which was uniformly voiced by the Church hierarchy and by *Verbum*, the Guatemalan Church periodical.
77. Thomas Molnar, "Christian Socialism's Day," *National Review* 19, no. 13 (April 4, 1967): 348–49.

Catholics what they can and cannot believe about communism and social change, Archbishop Geraldo de Proença Sigaud answers catechistic questions such as "What is Communism?" "Can a Catholic be a socialist?" and "What do the popes say about modern socialism?" The answers invariably show why Christianity opposes the advance of world communism.[78] In distinguishing in another message between "Communists" and "Communists," Bishop Castro Mayer does not suggest that some leaders in Communist countries are not as reprehensible as others. Instead, he adheres to the stereotyped distinction between evil Communist leaders and the nominally Communist masses who, he alleges, detest the cruel domination under which they live.[79] Brazilian rightists also perceive world politics in Cold War terms, as when bishops condemn the Soviet Union for the very type of "economic imperialism" of which the Catholic left often accuses the United States.[80]

Catholic reformers use the concept of anticommunism in the very different sense of backing reform and their own acquisition of power in order to implement reform. In anticipation of Chilean elections, Church spokesmen have written lengthy treatises on why Catholics could not support the Communist party or a Communist coalition.[81] In the 1964 campaign one of the most effective devices for Eduardo Frei was an allegedly authentic picture showing a poor Cuban in worker's clothes kneeling with a priest at his last confession, while the members of a *fidelista* firing squad that was about to execute him laughed heartily in the background. Christian Democrats utilize anti-Communist propaganda for their own ends, but those ends are sharply opposed to those of Catholic traditionalists.

If Christian Democrats and Catholic conservatives sometimes

78. Geraldo de Proença Sigaud, S.V.D., *Catecismo anticomunista,* 3d ed. (São Paulo: Editôra Vera Cruz, 1963).

79. Antonio de Castro Mayer (Bispo Diocesano de Campos), *Carta pastoral prevenindo os diocesanos contra os ardis da seita comunista,* May 13, 1961, 2d ed. (São Paulo: Editôra Vera Cruz, 1961), pp. 22–23.

80. "Declaração dos cardeais, arcebispos e bispos do Brasil," *Revista da Arquidiocese* (Goiânia, Goiás) 2, no. 7 (julho, 1958): 68–69.

81. See José Aldunate L., S.I., "Los pactos electorales, un problema de conciencia," in Julián Rentería Uralde, ed., *La Iglesia y la política* (Santiago de Chile: Ediciones Paulinas, 1963), esp. pp. 47, 68–71.

reject communism for conflicting reasons, they also reject it because of a joint, realistic appraisal of its likely effects on religion. Policies advocated in Havana and Peking threaten Catholicism. The Cuban approach to religion appears in *Trabajo y lucha,* an introductory textbook for secondary schools that Fidel Castro's Ministry of Education issued in 1961. Although the text finds that Christianity "arose as a protest movement among the oppressed and exploited majority," it goes on to emphasize that "by the Third Century, Christianity . . . had become a magnificent instrument in the hands of the governing minority."[82] Catholics recognize that Chinese Communist propaganda in Latin America has stressed the historical issues that seem to make the Church oppose freedom and social development,[83] while the announced goals of Chinese communism clearly give the churchmen reason to oppose it. As frankly proclaimed in a seven-page pamphlet published in Peking soon after the Castro victory in Cuba, the official Chinese position advised Communists to "bring an end to the influences and activities of the Catholic Church," a Church that the Chinese claim is only a "source of counter-revolutionary activities in the popular democracies." Although the Chinese pamphlet advocates destruction of the Church by devious means rather than by a frontal attack,[84] the intent of Chinese Communism is unmistakable.

Catholic reformers set out lucid explanations of the genuine threat that Communism poses for their programs. Their apprehension was most obvious in a defense of social reform that twenty-four Chilean bishops issued in September, 1962. After an urgent plea for reform and for economic development, the bishops enumerate the reasons they believe that "Communism diametrically opposes Christianity." Communism would destroy both the idea of

82. Quoted in Dudley Seers, ed., *Cuba: The Economic and Social Revolution* (Chapel Hill, N. C.: University of North Carolina Press, 1964), p. 360.

83. Héctor Samperio G., "Communists and Other Marxists," in Considine, ed., *Social Revolution in the New Latin America,* p. 79.

84. Li Wei Han, "The Catholic Church and Cuba: Program of Action." A translation and condensation of this pamphlet appears in *CIF Reports* 1, no. 10 (March, 1963): 470–75.

God and the workers' right to free trade unionism. Also, allegedly, it would try to destroy national loyalties and the ties which bind families together. Although it has spread because of its promises to alleviate real abuses and provide a just distribution of wealth, it would simply give supreme power to the Communist party once it took over. In short, the bishops reject communism because they find that it does "not offer the remedy for the evils which we wish to exterminate." In almost direct confrontation to the position that Father Camilo Torres and others have taken, the bishops declare that "the desire to take advantage of Communism to attain power with the intention of ignoring its doctrines and opposing its action, once power has been obtained, constitutes immorality which cannot be justified and which pre-supposes a lack of talent and intelligence on the part of Communists, which they certainly do not lack." In special defense of their own authority to prevent collaboration with Communists, the bishops conclude that "of course, it is clear in this delicate matter, more than in any other, that proper prudence and filial obedience to the directives of the Church are advisable."[85]

Church-supported propaganda booklets spread this Catholic message, as they denounce communism and praise religious freedom as one of the prime benefits of democracy. A recent Brazilian pamphlet, for example, contains multicolor illustrations of a happy democratic family voting, building their own home, and enjoying freedom in education, in labor union organization, and in free access to uncensored information. By contrast, pictures in unrelieved red and black depict a Communist society where children inform on their parents, the state dominates education, and common citizens futilely try to escape or overturn their Communist oppressors at the Berlin Wall, in the Hungarian revolution, and in Communist Cuba. On the two special pages devoted to the Church, the pamphlet contrasts the happy members of a Catholic procession in a democracy with the broken windows, the rubble, and the

85. "Social and Political Duties in the Present Time," in *Recent Church Documents from Latin America*, CIF Monographs, no. 2 (Cuernavaca, Mor.: CIDOC, 1963), pp. 28–29.

headless saints' statues of a church building desecrated by Communists.[86] This combination of a comparatively subtle Catholic emphasis on family happiness and solidarity with an extraordinarily blunt form of anti-Communist propaganda is fairly typical of the Church's general response to the competition of communism.

But ideological differences and the Communist threat to the institutional Church are not the only motivation for Catholic opposition; members of the Catholic hierarchy also work against communism out of concern for their own positions. They naturally fear limitations on their authority under Communist regimes. Declaring that the real fight "is not of Communism against Capitalism, but of Communism against Religion," Bishop Samuel Ruiz of Chiapas, Mexico, points out that victorious Communists would expel the Catholic hierarchy and attempt to sever the connections between Rome and the hierarchy and between pastors and the faithful.[87] Prelates also use the advance of communism to show why hierarchy and discipline are necessary in the Church. Just as communism gains strength from its tight organization and the unquestioning obedience that subordinates give to superiors, so Catholics must "blindly obey" the Church hierarchy in order to combat communism.[88]

A final reason for anticommunism has been the influx into Latin America of missionary priests who fought communism in Spain and China. In 1960, when Spaniards made up 54 per cent of the foreign clergy serving in Latin America,[89] many of the Spanish priests had come with the attitudes of the anti-Communist crusade of the Spanish Civil War. Another group of missionary priests who had been driven out of China after the Communist victory of 1949 has interpreted the Latin American situation in light of their experiences with Chinese communism. Some opponents of Catholicism have exaggerated the secret intentions of these priests, as

86. *Duas vidas* (Belém: Publicações Liguori, Padres Redentoristas, n.d.), pp. 21–22.
87. Samuel Ruiz García (Obispo de Chiapas), *Exhortación pastoral*, Oct. 2, 1961, p. 6.
88. Bernardino Echeverría R., O.F.M. (Obispo de Ambato), *Carta pastoral a propósito de los ejemplos de Cuba*, June 24, 1961 (Ambato: Editorial "Pío XII," 1961), p. 12.
89. Pike, "Catholicism in Latin America Since 1848," p. 72.

when Manhattan claims that the Vatican has been in conscious conspiracy with Franco's Spain to bring authoritarian government to Latin America.[90] Although Franco's Hispanidad movement has tried to win support in Latin America and although Spanish priests serving in Latin America have often manifested the authoritarian attitudes of Spanish fascism, the notion of Vatican conspiracy is clearly mistaken. Instead of genuinely favoring either authoritarian or democratic regimes, the Vatican tries to work with whatever government is in power. Although the motives of the Spanish missionary priests should not be exaggerated, therefore, their influence has at least worked to strengthen opposition to communism in the Latin American Church.

The analogy to the Spanish Civil War, which Catholic rightists have used to oppose communism, may be even more applicable than they believe. They have long held that laws passed by Communists do not have to be followed. A 1938 article in *La Religión,* the Venezuelan newspaper, claimed that there was no obligation to follow laws that violated a Catholic's conscience or contravened human dignity. Just as the Spanish Church at the time had the right and duty to oppose a legally established government in order to fight communism, so, if communism should take power in Venezuela, the Church must similarly oppose it.[91] When the Church officially opposes a leftist reform government, however, it forces that government to accept more and more aid from Communist countries, as in the case of the Spanish Republicans. Furthermore, if the attempt to unseat the reform government is successful as it was in Spain, Catholics may well see only a traditionalist, antidemocratic, and antireform government arise in its place. As younger Spanish priests have recently concluded, trying to reform this type of government from within can prove to be a frustrating enterprise. The Spanish missionary priests who have come to Latin

---

90. Avro Manhattan, *Spain and the Vatican* (London: Watts & Co., 1946), pp. 34–35. See also Avro Manhattan, *Vatican Imperialism in the Twentieth Century* (Grand Rapids, Mich.: Zondervan Publishing House, 1965).

91. "La Iglesia en Venezuela," *La Religión,* Dec. 22, 1938, as reprinted in Juan de la Cruz Palacio, *La Iglesia y el Estado: Un problema en pie* (n.p.: Tipografía Standard, 1939), pp. 23–25.

America in the last decade have been more and more critical of authoritarianism and insistent upon social reform.

Despite the various reasons for anticommunism in the Church, opposition to communism on religious grounds is probably not as potent a factor in Latin American politics as some observers have initially proposed. Martin Needler, in his detailed study of the military coup that deposed Ecuadorean President Carlos Julio Arosemena Monroy in July, 1963, found religious opposition to communism to be much less significant than he had originally expected. Before studying the coup in detail, Needler hypothesized that the military acted to oppose communism because of its atheism, as well as to maintain order and to prevent economic reforms that might hurt the class position of the military elite. After discussing the coup with Ecuadoreans of different political persuasions and with such pivotal personnel as the staunchly anti-Communist minister of defense, however, Needler concluded that the military acted not from any religious or ideological opposition to communism but from the simple, selfish fear that the Communists would disband the regular military establishment and replace it with a militia.[92]

Latin American humorists underscore this conclusion on the superficiality of Catholic influence by lampooning the connection that conservatives make between Catholicism and anticommunism. One of the most piercing recent satires, *Manual del gorila* by Carlos del Peral, ridicules the anti-Communist "gorilla" who co-operates with a domestic oligarchy, the United States government, and the International Monetary Fund. "It is generally convenient," Peral says, "for the gorilla to profess Christianity, especially when it relates to the Christian Western World or helps to keep his wife faithful to him." The gorilla believes, however, that Christ was a young Roman patrician rather than a poor carpenter, that the advice about the camel and the eye of a needle was sheer demagoguery, and that the Star of the East should be renamed the "Star of the West." Especially, he believes that "Christ did not throw the

92. Martin C. Needler, *Anatomy of a Coup d'État: Ecuador, 1963* (Washington, D. C.: Institute for the Comparative Study of Political Systems, 1964), p. 41.

money changers out of the temple. Knowing that they were among the strongest defenders of the free world, he joined them in order to suppress Communism."[93] Such humor reflects as much on the values of the humorist as on those of his subjects. To some Latin Americans, conservative Catholicism appears to negate the essential Christian opposition to individual and group selfishness.

Actually, for many churchmen who appear to be the most outspoken anti-Communists, their stance is not so much a negation of these values as it is a special interpretation of them. Churchmen whose view of communism as an international conspiracy makes them appear to be spokesmen for the conservative right are sometimes also sincere advocates of a particular brand of social reform. One such Church leader was Mariano Rossell Arellano, the archbishop of Guatemala from 1939 to 1964, whose dedication to reform was nearly as great as his more famous opposition to communism.

As he has been pictured in most accounts, Archbishop Rossell Arellano was certainly a dedicated anti-Communist. As early as 1945 he and other Guatemalan bishops attacked communism on the grounds that, in seeing man as a productive machine rather than as an individual, it denied human liberty and dignity.[94] He warned Guatemalans to side with God and Western culture against "the barbarity of Moscow and the culture of Genghis Khan,"[95] and he later saw Communists behind a burlesque of

93. For a translation and condensation of Peral's booklet, see "The Handbook of the Gorilla," *CIF Reports* 4, no. 24 (Dec. 16, 1965): 183–87.

94. Mariano Rossell Arellano (Arzobispo de Guatemala), Jorge García y Caballeros (Obispo de los Altos), and Raymundo M. Martín, O.P. (Administrador Apostólico de Verapaz y Petén), *Carta pastoral colectiva sobre la amenaza comunista en nuestra patria,* Oct. 1, 1945 (Guatemala: Tipografía Sánchez & de Guise, 1945), p. 6. On the development of Guatemalan Catholicism, see Richard Newbold Adams, *Crucifixion by Power: Essays on Guatemalan National Social Structure, 1944–1966* (Austin, Tex.: University of Texas Press, 1970), chap. 5, "The Renaissance of the Guatemalan Church"; Anita Frankel, "Political Development in Guatemala, 1944–1954: The Impact of Foreign, Military, and Religious Elites" (Ph.D. diss., University of Connecticut, 1969); and Francis X. Gannon, "Catholicism, Revolution and Violence in Latin America: Lessons of the 1968 Guatemala Maryknoll Episode," *Orbis* 12, no. 4 (Winter, 1969).

95. Mariano Rossell Arellano (Arzobispo de Guatemala), *Instrucción pastoral al pueblo católico de Guatemala sobre el deber y condiciones del sufragio,* July 8, 1948 (Guatemala: Imprenta Sansur, 1948), p. 8.

Church ritual put on by Guatemalan university students.[96] He issued pastoral statements telling Guatemalan Catholics not to vote for candidates suspected of Communist affiliations.[97] When members of the government of President Juan José Arévalo claimed that the Church was intervening in party politics, Rossell Arellano defended the Church's right to counsel Catholics against communism.[98]

The archbishop's view of communism in Guatemala depended partly on the activity of European and Asian Communists. He interpreted the persecution of the Church in Eastern Europe as one of the most atrocious that the Church had ever suffered, but not one different in kind from those imposed by Liberals and Freemasons in Latin America.[99] He strongly attacked Soviet suppression of the Hungarian revolution in 1956,[100] and indeed much of his opposition to international communism seems to have been based on its antagonism to religion in Eastern Europe, the Soviet Union, and China. Seeing communism as an international conspiracy, he sharply denounced such "pseudo-Communist" organizations as the Alianza Femenina Guatemalteca that grew up in Guatemala during the early 1950's. He reminded Catholics of Pope Pius XII's excommunication of supporters of such Communist organizations and explained that they represented the new Communist policy of infiltration rather than outright attack on the Church.[101]

96. *Amonestación pastoral del Excelentísimo y Reverendísimo Monseñor Mariano Rossell Arellano, Arzobispo de Guatemala, al pueblo católico, con ocasión de la huelga estudiantil, llamada "De Dolores,"* March 20, 1956 (Guatemala: Centro Editorial, 1956).

97. Rossell Arellano, *Instrucción pastoral al pueblo católico de Guatemala sobre el deber y condiciones del sufragio*, p. 7.

98. Mariano Rossell Arellano (Arzobispo de Guatemala), *Aclaraciones sobre la recta y firme postura de la Iglesia de Guatemala con relación al presente momento político, y protesta por las insidiosas calumnias de partidos políticos contra el clero de nuestra patria*, May 25, 1950 (Guatemala: Tip. "Sánchez & de Guise," 1950), pp. 2, 5–6.

99. Mariano Rossell Arellano (Arzobispo de Guatemala), *Exhortación pastoral para pedir oraciones por la "Iglesia del silencio,"* Nov. 1, 1953 (Guatemala: Unión Tip., 1953), p. 1.

100. Mariano Rossell Arellano (Arzobispo de Guatemala), *Mensaje pastoral en que pide oraciones por la salvación del pueblo húngaro y de los demás países que gimen bajo la esclavitud del Soviet*, Nov. 3, 1956 (Guatemala: Editorial "San Antonio," 1956).

101. *Declaraciones del Arzobispo de Guatemala, Excmo. y Revmo. Monseñor*

Detailed studies of Guatemalan politics conclude that the Church and especially Archbishop Rossell Arellano played a major role in the revolution of 1954,[102] and this view is substantiated by the statements of the archbishop himself. In the aftermath of the Castillo Armas coup which the CIA engineered to overthrow the regime of Jacobo Arbenz Guzmán, the archbishop said that "every Guatemalan knows the work of the Church in the Liberation of the fatherland has been great."[103] He praised those who "rejected the mercenary sale of Guatemala to International Communism." Overstating his case, he announced Communist "jailings, torturings and assassination of hundreds of workers and campesinos" and the alleged fact that "Guatemalan Communism had taken root in the Soviet Style: blood, prison, death, desolation."[104] In a statement at funeral services held for those who died opposing the Arbenz regime, he decried "the air-rending cries of those victims. . . . Such evil! The inconceivable, the diabolical cruelty in cutting down the lives of those national heroes for having revealed themselves as opposed to anti-Guatemalan and anti-Christian Communism!"[105] Although the bodies of some Guatemalans killed by Communists were found in hidden graves, a wry sense of the excesses of his anti-Communist rhetoric lies in his description of the

---

Mariano Rossel Arellano, al pueblo católico (Guatemala: Imprenta M. Ortiz H. & Cía., 23 mayo, 1952).

102. See Mario Monteforte Toledo, *Guatemala: Monografía sociológica* (México: Instituto de Investigaciones Sociales, Universidad Nacional Autónoma de México, 1959), pp. 176, 322.

103. *Alocución del Excelentísimo y Reverendísimo Mons. Don Mariano Rossell Arellano, Arzobispo de Guatemala, el domingo 10 de octubre en la Catedral Metropolitana en la misa de las 19 horas* (Guatemala: Unión Tip., 1954). For a similar assertion that, without Church aid, Guatemala would have become a "lackey satellite of the Soviet," see *Amonestación pastoral del Excelentísimo y Reverendísimo Monseñor Mariano Rossell Arellano, Arzobispo de Guatemala, al pueblo católico, con ocasión de la huelga estudiantil, llamada "De Dolores"* (Guatemala: Centro Editorial, 1956).

104. Mariano Rossell Arellano (Arzobispo de Guatemala), *Carta pastoral sobre la paz, fruto de la justicia y del amor*, July 2, 1954 (Guatemala: Tip. Sánchez & de Guise, 1954), p. 1.

105. Mariano Rossell Arellano (Arzobispo de Guatemala), *Oración funebre pronunciada en los funerales celebrados en la Catedral Metropolitana por el eterno descanso de las almas de todas las víctimas asesinadas en Guatemala durante el terror comunista y de los muertos en los campos de batalla*, July 7, 1954 (Guatemala: Tip. Sánchez & de Guise, 1954), p. 2.

Communist "cruelty reaching such an extreme that even the bodies of its victims can not be found."[106]

For a prelate whose picture was often taken with Guatemalan Fascists in the years shortly after he became archbishop in 1939, Rossell Arellano combined a surprising support for liberty with his opposition to Communism. Like other Guatemalans who overthrew the dictatorship of Jorge Ubico in 1944, he praised the Atlantic Charter as a basis for authentic democracy.[107] He distinguished sharply between liberty and libertinism, between actions taken freely after consideration of the consequences and actions resulting from blind passion. Christian charity would help, he thought, to create a union of wills, prevent liberty from degenerating into license, and so build a "great and beautiful Fatherland" in Guatemala.[108]

As he backed the sort of liberty that the Church would keep from becoming libertinage, Rossell Arellano denounced the anticlericalism of the liberal governments of Guatemala. But he did not advocate a return to the most extreme clerical conservatism. Instead, he advocated the principle of Christian social justice rather than secular power for the Church. Although his stand might at first appear to be an ordinary, right-wing denunciation of communism and liberalism, it was really far more than that. He used his anti-Communist pastorals to promote the ideas of social justice that he advanced during the 1940's and the 1950's. His pastorals set up no programs of reform, and they sometimes seemed naive in their belief that Christian love could heal social conflict, but they certainly did not fall into the error of preaching a sterile anti-communism. Long before the era of Pope John XXIII, the Guatemalan archbishop used the social teachings of earlier popes to justify what he called "social and distributive justice." In fact, one is tempted to conclude that he made his verbal opposition to com-

106. Rossell Arellano, *Carta pastoral sobre la paz, fruto de la justicia y del amor,* p. 6.

107. See Mariano Rossell Arellano (Arzobispo de Guatemala), "Declaraciones del Arzobispo de Guatemala sobre la posición de la Iglesia," *Verbum* 4, alcance al no. 119 (21 enero, 1945).

108. Mariano Rossell Arellano (Arzobispo de Guatemala), *Exhortación pastoral con ocasión de los últimos acontecimientos,* July 14, 1944 (Guatemala: Tipografía Sánchez & de Guise, 1944), pp. 3–4.

munism so extreme partly in order to curry favor with its right-wing opponents and so encourage them to back the social reforms that he favored.

Rossell Arellano also showed great concern for the position of the Church. Six weeks before Arévalo was elected to the presidency on March 13, 1945, the archbishop issued a circular intended to influence political leaders more than the "faithful" to whom it was addressed. It proclaimed that there was no better "soldier of the Fatherland" than the militant in the ranks of Christ and optimistically promised that the new government could count on the 98 per cent of the population that was Catholic, those civic-minded Catholics who were allegedly "chaste in their habits, removed from vice, respectful of the goods and reputation of their neighbors, obedient to authority, [and] models in the home."[109] The Arévalo and Arbenz governments chose not to depend primarily upon Catholic support, however, and the archbishop came to lament the decline of the Church's authority both in Guatemala and in the world. He saw the worldwide danger of new "machines of war" such as nuclear weapons arising from man's rejection of the moral principles of Christianity.[110] In sincerely denouncing the violence and brutal murders committed in Guatemala, he clearly wanted the moral authority of the Guatemalan Church to increase. He hinted at the possibility of violence even in Christmas messages, where he said that peace and Christian social justice were inseparable and that one could not be realized without the other.[111]

The Arévalo and Arbenz regimes were not in fact hard on the Church, so that Rossell Arellano's bitter opposition to communism cannot be explained as a reaction to any attempt to weaken the Guatemalan Church. As measured by the number of priests allowed to practice in the country, the leftward movement of Guatemalan politics between 1944 and 1954 did not interfere with religious activity. The total number of diocesan and regular

109. *Circular del Arzobispo de Guatemala a sus fieles,* Feb. 1, 1945.
110. Mariano Rossell Arellano (Arzobispo de Guatemala), *Carta pastoral en que exhorta a los fieles a mayor santidad de vida, en las dolorosas circunstancias actuales* (Guatemala: Tipografía Sánchez & de Guise, 1944), p. 4.
111. Mariano Rossell Arellano (Arzobispo de Guatemala), *Mensaje al pueblo católico en la navidad de 1948* (Guatemala: Unión Tip., 1948), pp. 6–7.

priests in Guatemala rose from 114 in 1944 to 195 in 1954, even though it rose more rapidly to 242 in 1955 after the rightist revolution of Castillo Armas.[112] The archbishop was genuinely discouraged, however, by the failure of Arévalo and Arbenz to effect the sorts of social reforms that were backed by the Church. Rossell Arellano decided that a new regime was required and that he himself might encourage the regime to accept the Catholic approach to social justice. When the new government took over in 1954, he hoped that the Church would work more effectively with it. In an official statement to the National Constituent Assembly that met in the spring of 1955, he and other Guatemalan Church leaders asked for recognition of the Church's rights and social role. They linked social reform to anticommunism in the Church's position, telling the Assembly that "to fight communism there is only one efficient and lasting way, Social Justice, and the Church with its specific doctrine is the most effective force to 'pacifically' conquer the hearts and wills of those who have fallen to communism." Therefore, the Assembly ought to give all support to the social work of the Church "in the destruction of communism."[113]

The archbishop's commitment to reform was not put forward merely as a substitute for more radical programs. In a pastoral message in 1946, before the leftward drift of Guatemalan politics had gotten well underway, he told workers that their just claims conflicted with prevailing notions of property and capital. Since the Church was the "mother of the poor," it would enter no alliances with oppressive capitalism.[114] After tracing the history of the Church's concern for the poor, he concluded that the Church sought workers' welfare not by the destruction of capitalism but

112. Alonso and Garrido, *La Iglesia en América Central y el Caribe,* pp. 190–91, 271. Compare Table 3 on p. 184. The 1954 figure of 195 priests was taken from Table 3, rather than from the Alonso and Garrido volume, which gives a 1954 figure of 192.

113. Mariano Rossell Arellano (Arzobispo de Guatemala), Raymundo M. Martín, O.P. (Obispo de Verapaz y Administrador Apostólico de El Petén), Miguel Ángel García Arauz (Obispo de Jalapa y Administrador Apostólico de Zacapa), and J. Rafael González Estrada (Obispo Titular de Matrega y Administrador Apostólico de las Diócesis de Quetzaltenango, Sololá y San Marcos), untitled statement to the National Constituent Assembly, April 18, 1955 (mimeographed), p. 2.

114. Mariano Rossell Arellano (Arzobispo de Guatemala), *A las clases laborante y patronal,* Sept. 1, 1946 (Guatemala: Imprenta Hispania, 1946), p. 1.

by the distribution of wealth.[115] This viewpoint was not truly progressive, for it focused on distribution rather than on the generation of new wealth through economic development, but it at least manifested a sincere concern for social justice. Furthermore, Rossell Arellano's thinking later developed with the times. In 1954 he upbraided "exploiters" and said that "the Church recognizes the just right of association of the economically weak, of proletarians, against their exploiters."[116] Before the elections of 1957, he told Guatemalans that their most pressing national needs were improving the welfare of workers and peasants, creating consumer cooperatives, and stopping the exploitation of agricultural laborers.[117]

An intriguing question is the motivation for Archbishop Rossell Arellano's dedication to social reform. Does the Guatemalan case show the first instance of Catholic reformism really spurred by the threat of Latin American communism, or did the archbishop himself derive some of his own reform orientation from the reformist tendencies of the Arévalo and Arbenz policies which he criticized? Probably neither answer is fully correct. Anticommunism encouraged his reformist pronouncements, but he was not moved so much either by or against the Guatemalan leftists as he was by the Catholic social tradition in which he believed. His calls for "distributive" reforms, his tying of reform to papal encyclicals, and his adamant opposition to Communist brutality are all quite consistent with his concept of Catholic social justice. Far from being classified simply as "rightists" or "reactionaries," such leaders as Rossell Arellano should be appreciated for their genuine commitment to reform as well as for their apparently dogmatic rejection of international communism. Rossell Arellano was a traditionalist rather than a reactionary. The thinking of contemporary traditionalists as well as contemporary reactionaries needs to be studied,

115. *Ibid.*, p. 7.
116. Mariano Rossell Arellano (Arzobispo de Guatemala), *Carta pastoral sobre los avances del comunismo en Guatemala*, April 4, 1954 (Guatemala: Tip. Sánchez & de Guise, 1954), p. 7.
117. Mariano Rossell Arellano (Arzobispo de Guatemala), *Mensaje al pueblo de Guatemala en vísperas de elecciones presidenciales y de diputados al Congreso de la República*, Oct. 15, 1957 (Guatemala: Imprenta San Antonio, 1957), pp. 5–7.

not only for its own sake, but also because it has held back other Catholics from more openly accepting the new reformist position, and because a fresh reaction against its uncompromising nature has pushed one wing of the Catholic progressives into even more radical positions than they would otherwise have taken.

IV ~

Catholic Revolutionaries:
Radicals or Avant-garde?

Although Catholic traditionalists remain in control of many positions of authority within the Church, many individuals and organizations of the Catholic left have come openly to defy that authority. Multifarious left-wing Catholic movements operate in very different national contexts, from ONIS in Peru, to Golconda in Colombia and Tercer Mundo in Argentina.[1] The new militants of the Catholic left go far beyond the *freista* progressives in that they advocate violent revolution, tactical cooperation with the Communists, and radical reform of the hierarchical organization and attitudes of the Church itself. They have voiced sharp criticism of both United States foreign policy and the missionary endeavors of North American Catholics. As sincere social critics, most members of the Catholic left have come to believe that only their prescriptions can save Catholicism. This apocalyptic attitude

1. For descriptions of the positions and activities of these groups, see Gonzalo Arroyo, "Católicos de izquierda en América Latina," *Mensaje,* no. 191 (agosto, 1970). A particularly thoughtful discussion of the role of ONIS in Peruvian politics may be found in "The Catholic Church in Politics: The Peruvian Case," a paper presented by Carlos A. Astiz at the Eighth World Congress of the International Political Science Association, Munich, Germany, Sept., 1970.

in itself suggests a need to analyze the validity of the left's assumptions, as do the implications of those assumptions for both United States foreign policy and the processes of Latin American political development.

With the rise of the Catholic left in the 1960's, the "radical" reformers of the Latin American Church have grown in number, in self-consciousness, and in militancy. Regimes of the left have long tried to legitimize their programs by tying them to Catholic calls for reform. Responding to criticism of domestic programs by Guatemalan bishops in the early 1950's, for example, the government of Jacobo Arbenz Guzmán supported the publication of Tulio Benites' *Meditaciones de un católico ante la reforma agraria,*[2] a closely reasoned book showing that the agrarian reform law of the Arbenz regime followed Catholic doctrine. Benites' position directly opposed that of the Guatemalan hierarchy, which fiercely denounced the policies of the Arbenz government as Communistic. More recent statements against the hierarchy have gone even further, at times calling into question the allegiance of Catholics to the Church itself. In a short study entitled *A Igreja esta com o povo?,* Father Aloísio Guerra suggested before the Brazilian revolution of 1964 that the Church hierarchy in Brazil was reactionary and divorced from the people. He saw no incompatibility between socialism and Catholicism and praised a priest from Pernambuco who had told him in 1962 that "we ought to be on the side of the people even against the Church."[3] Such priests as Father Guerra, as representatives of the Catholic left, have often assumed that being "on the side of the people" means advocating violent revolution and opposing the United States.

THE ACCEPTANCE OF VIOLENT REVOLUTION

Father Camilo Torres Restrepo, the former Colombian priest who was killed while fighting as a guerrilla in the sierra in 1966, has

2. Guatemala: Editorial del Ministerio de Educación Pública, 1952.
3. For a discussion of Father Guerra's pamphlet, see Manoel Cardozo, "The Brazilian Church and the New Left," *Journal of Inter-American Studies* 6, no. 3 (July, 1964): 318–19.

become the most widely respected Catholic advocate of revolution. His thinking deserves careful analysis, not only because it was clearly formulated or because it has gained wide respect, but also because it is often alleged to reflect the views of other priest-revolutionaries such as Father Jean-Baptiste Georges in Haiti[4] and Father Juan Carlos Zaffaroni in Uruguay.[5] Concern for human welfare prompted Father Torres to advocate violent revolution. To justify revolution, both in his own mind and to others, he worked out an explanation whose logic is unassailable so long as one accepts the central premise of insurmountable barriers to pacific change. In a special study of revolution as a Christian imperative, he presented fraternal charity as the major test of human achievement. He emphasizes that God's judgment of men is "based fundamentally in the efficacy of our charity" and that decisions on eternal salvation will depend on the amount of food, drink, hospitality, clothing, and shelter that a man has been able to provide for others. In the developing countries, a Christian can best fulfill his ultimate duty of charity by finding and furthering the most effective strategy for economic growth.[6] Unfortunately, as

4. For a discussion of Father Georges' revolt against François Duvalier in 1963 as that of "the first Christian Socialist guerrillas in Latin America," see "Guerrilla Priest," *CIF Reports* 6, no. 4 (Feb. 16, 1967): 28–29. When conducting interviews in Haiti itself, I received a very different impression of Father Georges from the Catholic stereotype of a revolutionary priest fighting for liberty and justice. Charges of self-interest are repeatedly leveled at this former member of Duvalier's government. Partly because of President Duvalier's positive campaign of black nationalism and partly because of his personal importance in the vodun folk religion, the president has more support in Haiti than is commonly believed.

5. The fact that Torres' ideas and motives were close to those advocated by Zaffaroni appears clearly in the latter's writing. See especially Juan Carlos Zaffaroni, *Camilo Torres, el sacerdote guerrillero* (Montevideo: Ediciones Provincias Unidas, 1967); and Juan Carlos Zaffaroni, "La juventud uruguaya frente al ideario político de Camilo Torres," in Zaffaroni, *Tres conferencias* (Montevideo: Ediciones Provincias Unidas, 1968).

6. Camilo Torres Restrepo, "La revolución: Imperativo cristiano," in *Por el Padre Camilo Torres Restrepo (1956–1966)* (Cuernavaca, Mor.: CIDOC, 1967): 203, 236. Popularizers of Torres' ideas have also issued this study as a separate, inexpensive book: Camilo Torres, *La revolución: Imperativo cristiano* (n.p.: Editorial Sandino, 1968). An English edition of his work is Camilo Torres, *Revolutionary Writings* (New York: Herder and Herder, 1969). For a succinct, critical view of the relationship between Torres' life and his ideas, see John Womack, "Priest of Revolution," *CIDOC Informa*, Document 69/180. A far more sympathetic interpretation of his role, with numerous photographs and reprints of letters and newspaper statements concerning him, appears in Germán Guzmán Campos, *Camilo: Presencia y destino* (Bogotá: Ediciones Publicidad, Servicios Especiales de Prensa, 1967), and, without the photographs, in the trans-

Torres interpreted the development process, the barriers to progress are simply too numerous and too substantial to be overcome without violence.

Torres compiled a staggering list of barriers to peaceful change. He pointed out that developing countries like those of Latin America lack true national markets, nationally integrated systems of production, and adequate numbers of technically trained personnel. Domestic capital is scarce, while the industrialized Western states provide only meager funds because of their Cold War preoccupations, their general preference for private enterprise, and their desire to invest only where political stability is assured. When developing countries try to keep most of their economies under private control, they face the problem of fitting private investment into an overall plan. Heavy investment in military equipment and inefficient bureaucratic personnel rather than in technical training perpetuates the crucial deficiency in technicians, while the "brain drain" to higher-paying countries further aggravates the deficiency.

These economic barriers reinforce barriers of class structure and attitude. Monopoly control of production and concentration of economic and political power is held by the narrow group Father Torres calls the "directing class," which allegedly lacks the foresight to see that major change is necessary. With a prestige system that prevents the rise of Schumpeterian entrepreneurs by making prestige derive from the possession of goods rather than from the effective direction of industry and mass production, the directing class chooses to make profits through high prices and low production levels. Altruistic attitudes motivate some members of the class, but their number and influence are simply too limited to keep the class from being oppressive. Inadequate channels of com-

lation of this book by John D. Ring, as *Camilo Torres* (New York: Sheed and Ward, 1969). Other sources on the topic include Norberto Habegger, *Camilo Torres, el cura guerrillero* (Buenos Aires: A. Peña Lillo, 1967); Alejandro del Corro, ed., *Colombia: Camilo Torres, un símbolo controvertido, 1962–67* (Cuernavaca, Mor.: CIDOC, 1967); Camilo Torres Restrepo, *Obras escogidas* (Montevideo: Ediciones Provincias Unidas, 1968); and John Álvarez García and Christian Restrepo Calle, eds., *Camilo Torres, His Life and His Message,* trans. Virginia M. O'Grady (Springfield, Ill.: Templegate, 1968).

munication and information between the directing class and the "popular class" prevent the upper group from recognizing the imperative need for change. Simultaneously, because of a minifundia individualism among the members of the popular class, they lack self-confidence and awareness of how they can work together for their common needs.[7] Change in the social structure is necessary to break these barriers of class structure and attitude and to give the mass of citizens the technological orientation required for economic growth.

As a professor of sociology in Bogotá, Camilo Torres found that both stagnation and degrading inequalities characterized the Colombian social system. On the basis of a broad range of statistics on salaries, caloric intake, and the cost of living, he tried to prove the real poverty and the progressive proletarianization of the working class of Bogotá.[8] He sharply attacked the amounts of money that the Colombian armed forces spent on planes, ships, and tanks, and appealed directly to Colombian soldiers to come over to the side of the fatherland and the workers.[9] He said that the Conservative and Liberal parties in Colombia had lost their ideological and religious differences, that they gave party members a sense of personal security, and that they led members of the lower class to work with the middle and upper classes. In doing so, he complained, these "poly-class" parties frustrated the rise of class-based parties and the working-class movement.[10]

Optimistically, Father Torres believed that changes in political decision-making could solve many of these problems. He found that the only way to break the "vicious circles" preventing development was by "a decision on the part of those who control the factors of power."[11] Given the inadequate foresight of the directing class, however, only violent revolution could put properly oriented

---

7. Torres, "La revolución: Imperativo cristiano," pp. 213–27.

8. See Camilo Torres Restrepo, *La proletarización de Bogotá: Ensayo de metodología estadística,* Monografías Sociológicas, no. 9 (Bogotá: Universidad Nacional de Colombia, Facultad de Sociología, 1961), esp. p. 10.

9. See "Ataque a políticos hizo Camilo Torres en Palmira," *El Tiempo,* Aug. 1, 1965.

10. Camilo Torres, "Posibilidades de la izquierda," *Tercer Mundo,* no. 13 (mayo, 1965): 4.

11. Torres, "La revolución: Imperativo cristiano," p. 215.

decision-makers into positions of power. Violence had become part of the institutionalized, "legalized" system in Colombia for maintaining social inequalities, justifying its use in attempts to overcome those inequalities.[12] Father Torres felt that groups which he called "Marxist" would probably lead the revolution, and that Christians should therefore collaborate with the Marxists as much as their principles would permit. In this way, Christians could prevent the worst evils of revolution and work constructively for the common good. Torres here lent support to Marxists but not necessarily to Communists, since he distinguished sharply between Marxists and disciplined Communist party members.[13] He recognized that many Latin American intellectuals and reformers think of themselves as Marxists and yet maintain no ties with Russian, Chinese, or Latin American Communist parties.

When Camilo Torres joined the guerrilla band in which he died, part of the Colombian press wrote him off as a doctrinaire Marxist. *El Espectador* said that "events have shown that he was a priest neither in the vanguard, nor of a modern type, nor of special sensibility. He was simply a convinced Marxist, in the habit of a priest, neither more nor less."[14] Torres' position did indeed resemble that of other leaders who had come to call themselves Marxists, and the United Front that he supported against the Colombian oligarchy brought together the same Marxist-Catholic coalition that Fidel Castro had called for to oppose United States "imperialism."[15] As Castro had said in a speech on March 13, 1962, "All progressive elements, all patriotic elements, should be united and . . . in that front there should be not only the sincere Catho-

12. See "Violencia: Sólo con una patria sin miseria será posible la paz," *Frente Unido,* Aug. 26, 1965. For a forceful, religious and pragmatic attack on this sort of advocacy of violence, see Enrique Colombres, "El mito de la violencia," *Criterio* 43, no. 1603 (10 septiembre, 1970).

13. Torres, "La revolución: Imperativo cristiano," pp. 230–31, 236.

14. "Se desconoce el lugar donde esté operando Camilo Torres," *El Espectador,* Jan. 9, 1966. The *New York Times* similarly called Camilo "a defrocked Roman Catholic priest who had turned Communist." See "Guerrilla Cleric Slain in Colombia," *New York Times,* Feb. 19, 1966.

15. For a statement of the aims of the United Front and its relationship to other political movements in Colombia, see Julio César Cortes, "¿Qué es el Frente Unido? Ni comunista, ni demócrata cristiano. Es la organización de los no alineados para realizar la revolución colombiana," *Frente Unido,* Sept. 16, 1965.

lic, who has nothing to do with imperialism or with latifundismo, but also the old Marxist fighter."[16] Moreover, Torres' example sanctioned collaboration between Communists and the Catholic left. Diego Montaña Cuéllar, a leading Communist with whom Camilo had worked in the United Front, underlined this collaboration shortly after Camilo's death, saying, "I was told that Father Camilo was crazy . . . but crazy to save Colombia, because he saw that all the nonviolent means of struggle were already at an end."[17] A cartoon in the Communist press showed Camilo lying dead at the end of a long, smoking rifle. A large figure of Uncle Sam held up the butt of the rifle, while carrying it and directing it toward Camilo were the tiny, malevolent figures of a Colombian businessman, government official, general, and bishop.[18] Although the Communists have tried to claim him as a martyr of their own, he was much more genuinely a martyr of the Catholic left. In his own acceptance of revolution he is best seen, not as a doctrinaire Marxist, but as a man whose study of his country led him to believe that the development process could not be altered without recourse to violence.

A vocal group of Latin American Catholics has joined Father Torres in this viewpoint, although few have followed his example of revolutionary participation. Widely respected Catholic leaders have come to the point of declaring that "solutions along the lines of 'ferment among the masses' is desirable. When this is not possible, the use of the word 'Christian' in organization names should be used with extreme caution."[19] Paulo de Tarso, a leading Chris-

---

16. Quoted in Dorothy Day, "Pilgrimage to Cuba," *CIF Reports* 1, no. 10 (March, 1963) : 472. This article is made up of excerpts from material that appeared first in *The Catholic Worker* in the fall of 1962.

17. Quoted in " 'El Padre Camilo no consultó a nadie su camino': Diego Montaña," *El Espectador,* Feb. 19, 1966. The Colombian Communist party later claimed that *El Espectador,* the leading Liberal newspaper, was trying to malign Camilo by implying that he was mentally ill. See "Diego Montaña habla sobre Camilo Torres: Rectificación a 'El Espectador,' " *Voz Proletaria,* March 3, 1966.

18. *Voz Proletaria,* Feb. 24, 1966. The lead article accompanying this cartoon is entitled, "La oligarquía mató a Camilo."

19. "The Church's Responsibility in Latin America: Theological and Sociological Aspects," *CIF Reports* 6, no. 6 (March 15, 1967) : 48. This article summarizes a larger study made in collaboration with Father Comblin in Chile, Father Houtart in Belgium, Professor de Almeida in Brazil, and others.

tian Democrat who was twice elected to be a federal deputy in Brazil, once cited numerous statements of Latin American Catholics to indicate why Catholic doctrine does not absolutely condemn violent revolution. Speaking for himself, he then found that violent revolution is justified when pacific means of change are exhausted, when injustice is unbearable, when the postrevolutionary "structure" will be clearly superior to the existing structure, when the revolution has a good chance of success, and when it will create better conditions for the common people rather than simply changing the groups that control the government.[20] Because of the nonrevolutionary line now taken by the Soviet-oriented Communist parties of Latin America, such arguments of the Catholic left go further in their advocacy of violence than do those of many Communists.

In the aftermath of the 1964 revolution in Brazil, however, Paulo de Tarso and many other Brazilians have come to feel that violence is not the way to bring constructive change. Pragmatically, de Tarso argues, the violent strategy is impractical and counterproductive because it alienates the United States and so "can never win," because it might tear Brazil apart in an ultimate North-South struggle, because the Brazilian people are not receptive to violence, and because its threat merely leads to military takeovers which attempt to "stabilize" the situation. Personally, on religious and moral grounds, de Tarso also rejects violence. He would rather die than kill. His ideas on the feasibility of an alliance between Communists and the Catholic left have also changed since 1964, as he now advocates independence and a Christian Democratic stance for the Catholic left, feeling that a group cannot join a Communist alliance and realistically expect to come out ahead.[21]

The older form of militancy has nevertheless associated the Catholic left with secular reformers who present the image of Christ as a revolutionary. One leader who did this effectively was Francisco Julião, the organizer of the Peasant Leagues in northeastern Brazil who came to live in Cuernavaca, Mexico, after his

20. Paulo de Tarso, *Os cristãos e a revolução social* (Rio de Janeiro: Zahar Editores, 1963), pp. 110–12.
21. Interview with Paulo de Tarso, in Santiago, Chile, Aug. 1, 1968.

exile in the military revolution of 1964. As Julião told the peasants:

> You give the soldier to defend the fatherland. And the fatherland forgets you. You give the hired killer to the *latifundio*. And the hired killer tyrannizes you. You give to the Church. And the Church asks you for resignation in the name of Christ. But Christ was a rebel. And for that reason he ascended the cross. And like Christ and the good St. Francis of Italy, I also stand by your side. And two who are still alive, Mao Tse-tung of China and Fidel Castro of Cuba.[22]

The debate between conservatives and the Catholic left is accurately summed up in the different images of Christ which they present, in images which alternatively stress patience and long-suffering or an adamant demand for new human relationships for which life itself must be sacrificed.

The advocacy of violence is by no means confined to the Catholic left and its ideological allies. Carlos Lacerda, the former governor of Guanabara who supported the military takeover in Brazil in 1964, tried to justify its violence by claiming that "to be a Catholic is to be a fighter. It is to fight with enthusiasm and valor, even using violence if necessary, in order to preserve all that is sacred and all that flows from sacred doctrine, the true Christian Doctrine."[23] Even though some clergymen spoke out against the excesses of Conservative party violence in Colombia under the government of Laureano Gómez from 1950 to 1953, ultraconservatives oppressed Liberals and Protestants in the name of the Catholic religion as well as in the name of the Conservative party.[24] The most inexorable opponents of the Catholic left, therefore, including Carlos Lacerda and the Colombian Conservatives, have at times found violence just as necessary as have the Catholic revolutionaries whom they oppose.

22. Quoted in Frank Bonilla, *Rural Reform in Brazil,* American Universities Field Staff Reports Service, East Coast South America Series 8, no. 4 (Oct., 1961): 10.
23. *O Dia,* April 19–20, 1964, as translated and reprinted in *CIF Reports* 3, no. 1 (April 16–30, 1964): 7.
24. See Vernon Lee Fluharty, *Dance of the Millions: Military Rule and the Social Revolution in Colombia, 1930–1956* (Pittsburgh, Pa.: University of Pittsburgh Press, 1966), pp. 118–23.

Violence is also a prime concern for progressives like Father Manuel Aguirre in Venezuela, whose personal views on the subject have reached outside his own country to influence both other progressives like Bishop Mark McGrath in Panama and self-styled revolutionaries like the Melville brothers in Guatemala. Father Aguirre has studied extensively the French Revolution of 1789 and sees many parallels to it in contemporary Latin America, including the advocacy of revolution by some priests who—like French priests in the 1780's—do not really understand the excesses to which mass violence leads. Aguirre himself believes that massive violence is coming to Latin America, even though he denounces it as an ineffective and brutal way to settle conflicts and bring constructive change.[25] What may be tragic in the orientation of such progressives is that, if violent revolution is not in fact inevitable, their assumption that it is may work as a self-fulfilling prophecy to help bring on the very situation that they decry.

Other observers concentrate on the role of Catholicism after violence and revolution. Segundo has suggested that, although Christians may serve in massive revolutions, the real function of Christianity will come after such revolutions. In their aftermath, in a period of self-questioning and reflection, Christianity will allegedly bring a sense of solidarity and harmony to overcome the factionalism of revolution.[26] Although this seems a most laudable role for Catholicism to play, and although a sense of Catholic solidarity would certainly affect the actions of some Latin Americans, the force of contemporary Christianity is simply not strong enough to bring abiding unity to opposing political factions. If unity does come in postrevolutionary situations, it will probably come through common weariness and rejection of open conflict, through an ethic of cohesive nationalism, or through an authoritarianism that silences dissent. Catholics may link their pleas for solidarity to postrevolutionary regimes which promote nationalist

25. Interview with Manuel Aguirre Elorriaga, S.J., in Caracas, Venezuela, June 14, 1968.
26. Juan Luis Segundo, *Función de la Iglesia en la realidad rioplatense* (Montevideo: Barreiro y Ramos, S.A., 1962), pp. 79–80.

cohesion or forbid dissent, but the ethics of those regimes will be neither originally nor preponderantly Catholic.

In contrast to both the clearcut advocacy of violence and the postrevolutionary concerns of Juan Luis Segundo are the somewhat more ambiguous positions of two leaders often associated with the Catholic left: Ivan Illich of the Centro Intercultural de Documentación (CIDOC) in Cuernavaca, Mexico, and Dom Hélder Câmara, the archbishop of Recife, Brazil. Concluding that only the Latin American masses can develop programs that adequately meet their own needs, Illich has rejected the approaches of traditional Catholicism, most contemporary political leaders in Latin America, and the United States government.[27] Church leaders, politicians, and Yankees now voice concern that more must be done for common citizens in Latin America, but Illich differs in believing that truly constructive change can be effected only by them. As a result of his opposition to formalistic solutions provided by others, he has not provided a precise recipe for Latin American development other than the clear statement that change must come from the mass of Latin Americans themselves.

In its implication of mass violence and its evident renunciation of direction by the clerical, political, and foreign groups that are now most directly concerned with the Latin American status quo, the Illich position startles many of his contemporaries. If the mass of Latin Americans should rise to the call that he and others have sounded, the Church would benefit greatly from having priests and former priests associated with the very beginnings of innovation. As Mexicans have looked fondly back on Father Hidalgo and Father Morelos, Catholics in the future could champion Illich and his followers as forerunners of policies that their ideas encompass in whole or in part.[28] If development should come to Latin America

27. For a sympathetic evaluation of Illich's concern with the masses, see Thomas G. Sanders to Richard H. Nolte, June 1, 1967 (TGS-1 in series of field reports distributed by the Institute of Current World Affairs), pp. 6–12.

28. For evaluations of the actual programs of Hidalgo and Morelos and their subsequent lionization as prototype reformers, see Hugh M. Hamill, Jr., *The Hidalgo Revolt: Prelude to Mexican Independence* (Gainesville, Fla.: University of Florida Press, 1966); and Frederick C. Turner, *The Dynamic of Mexican Nationalism* (Chapel Hill, N. C.: University of North Carolina Press, 1968), pp. 30–32.

through mass involvement, then Illich's impact on Latin American Catholicism could be great. If Latin American development should progress or merely proceed through politicians' efforts, redirections of Church initiative, or the cooperation of enlightened foreign aid, however, Illich may remain cut off from the official mainstream of Catholic thought. In this case, his thinking will appeal mainly to other Catholics and reformers who feel similarly alienated from many of the contemporary policies of the Church.

Although the reforms advocated by Dom Hélder have antagonized fewer churchmen than have the stinging criticisms of Illich, the positions of these two men have much in common. The 5-foot 4-inch, 120-pound archbishop, whose penchant for activity has given him the nickname of the "electric mosquito," was born in the dry northeastern state of Ceará in 1909. His mother taught school; his father was a bookkeeper and a Freemason.[29] Some observers have based conclusions about his programs upon such simple biographic data, assuming that his deep concern for the poverty of northeastern Brazil arises in part from his early background. Whether or not this is true, the archbishop has now become strongly identified with the concept of development from the masses. Although rejecting violence himself, he has said that "our best young people are now convinced that violence is the only solution."[30] His direct reliance on the masses has caused Carlos Lacerda to carp that Dom Hélder "cultivates misery" as one cultivates lettuce in his garden.[31]

Dom Hélder has been one of the most audible critics of the Brazilian military since the revolution of 1964 but, with a surprisingly characteristic ambivalence, he has not always been an-

29. For popular discussions of Dom Hélder's background and activities, see David St. Clair, "The Battling Bishop of Brazil," *The Sign* 44, no. 4 (Nov., 1964); Thomas B. Morgan, *Among the Anti-Americans* (New York: Holt, Rinehart and Winston, 1967), pp. 13–33; and José De Broucker, *Dom Helder Camara: The Violence of a Peacemaker,* trans. Herma Briffault (Maryknoll, N. Y.: Orbis Books, 1970).

30. Quoted in Frances M. Foland to Richard H. Nolte, Nov. 4, 1967 (FMF-9 in series of field reports distributed by the Institute of Current World Affairs), p. 21. The best source on Dom Hélder's more recent and better-known thinking is his book entitled *Revolução dentro da paz* (Rio de Janeiro: Editôra Sabiá, 1968).

31. See Frances M. Foland to Richard H. Nolte, Oct. 4, 1967 (FMF-8 in series of field reports distributed by the Institute of Current World Affairs), p. 2.

tagonistic to the military. When the military finally allowed João Goulart to take over as president after the resignation of President Jânio Quadros in August, 1961, Dom Hélder told a North American audience that "it scandalized the American press that it was the military which provided the check to disorder and chaos. Are not federal troops in Little Rock a bit of the same scandal? For us, as for you, the military is a means of weathering crisis within the constitutional framework and without the shedding of blood. . . ."[32] When the military deposed Goulart in 1964, Dom Hélder claimed that it was performing a very different role.

Besides the inconsistency evident in his stand on the political involvement of the Brazilian military, there are other issues on which Dom Hélder's position can be questioned. In the 1930's he backed the fascistic *integralistas* whom Getúlio Vargas suppressed, and in the early 1960's he championed the left-wing reforms that proved so ineffective under Goulart and led to the revolution of 1964. Both the *integralistas* and the followers of Goulart supported labor and created enthusiasm among students and activists, but neither they nor Dom Hélder enunciated genuinely effective programs of reform. With a messianic rather than a programmatic approach to reform, Dom Hélder's practical policies have relied on charitable handouts to the poor as well as on the program of basic education that he helped to establish.[33]

Dom Hélder accepts Raúl Prebisch's explanation that the economic problems of Latin America stem largely from a decline in its terms of trade, so that he concludes that development should be financed by requiring the developed countries to pay considerably more for Latin America's exports and not by promoting such programs of foreign aid as the Alliance for Progress. Although he frequently quotes President John F. Kennedy, the archbishop

32. "Who Has Real Democracy," *CIF Reports* 1, no. 3 (June, 1962): 115. This article is taken from a speech that Dom Hélder made at Georgetown University in the fall of 1961.

33. For reasoned criticism of Dom Hélder on these grounds, see Foland to Nolte, Oct. 4, 1967. On the 1970 campaign in the Brazilian press against Dom Hélder and his approach to development, see "Brasil: Campaña contra Dom Hélder," *Mensaje* 19, no. 194 (noviembre, 1970). This article was written by one of the most perceptive critics of Brazilian politics under the pseudonym of João Brasileiro.

interprets Brazilian cooperation with the United States as suppressing reform. In doing so, he neglects the genuine supporters of reform who still remain in the United States. If programs are needed which do more than support labor and excite students, if the Brazilian army remains a decisive base of power whose own reformist inclinations must be encouraged rather than opposed, if the real need of the poor is for vocational training rather than charity, if the polemics of Raúl Prebisch's old argument outweigh its validity, and if groups in the United States can help to further Brazilian goals through the Alliance or private enterprise, then some of the assumptions of Dom Hélder need to be questioned. If so, then the ultimate importance of his thought may lie in the issues that he raises and the consciences that he pricks rather than in the partial answers that he has provided.

COMMUNISM AND THE CATHOLIC LEFT

Anticommunism goes easily with religious faith. It is no coincidence that John Foster Dulles was both one of the most determined anticommunists of the twentieth century and the only American religious leader ever to become Secretary of State.[34] Among Catholics, many of the spokesmen who have gained the greatest respect also reject the antireligious tendencies of Marxist thought. In the words of Lebret, whose various works have been translated into Portuguese and found an appreciative audience in Brazil, Marxist materialism is "radical, absolute." It "negates the spirit" and the transcendency of the spirit and so can lead only to a "mutilated humanism."[35] Like Dulles or Lebret, most moderate Catholics as well as the conservatives have seen communism as a worldwide danger to political freedom and especially to the freedom of religion. This tendency not only isolates the Catholic left

34. See Louis L. Gerson, *John Foster Dulles* (New York: Cooper Square Publishers, 1967), esp. pp. xi–xii, 17–29.

35. L. J. Lebret, *O drama do século XX: Miséria, subdesenvolvimento, inconsciência, esperança,* trans. Benevenuto de Santa Cruz and Fátima de Souza, 3d ed. (São Paulo: Livraria Duas Cidades, 1966), pp. 177–78. For a collection of Marx's own statements on religion, see K. Marx and F. Engels, *On Religion* (Moscow: Foreign Languages Publishing House, n.d.).

in Latin America, but also makes the reasons for its rapprochement with the Communists especially significant.

Part of the apparent connection between Communists and the Catholic left arises of course from the tendency of conservatives to group them together indiscriminately. Brazilian anti-Communists openly accuse Catholic progressives of being seduced by Communists despite their good intentions. The rightists find "crypto-Communist" journalists writing for Frei Josaphat's *Brasil-Urgente,* and they denounce Communist infiltration into organizations supported by the Catholic left such as the União Nacional de Estudantes (UNE), the Juventude Universitária Católica (JUC), and the Movimento de Educação de Base (MEB).[36] Many conservative apprehensions are exaggerated. Communists advocate united actions between Catholics and themselves but, so that they can shape the direction that those actions take, they specifically tell progressive churchmen such as Father Roger Vekemans that their religious duties prevent *them* from intervening in politics in any way.[37]

One reason collaboration has been possible between Communists and the Catholic left is that the groups view crucial issues of Latin American development from similar ideological perspectives. The Catholic left often thinks in Marxist categories. As Thomas Sanders defines the Brazilian Catholic concept of *conscientização* ("consciousness" or "awareness"), for example, it holds that "the failure of the masses in underdeveloped societies to promote structures consistent with their interests stems from a lack of consciousness conditioned by illiteracy, social tradition, political manipulation, economic desperation, and lack of organization." To promote *conscientização,* Catholics should further the masses' "self-awareness so that they can shape their destinies, in conformity with their own interests rather than those of a dominating minority."[38] The analogy between *conscientização* and Marxist, proletarian class-consciousness is clear.

36. *Infiltração comunista no Brasil,* Cadernos Nacionalistas 1 (Rio de Janeiro: Instituto de Pesquisas e Estudos Sociais, 1963), pp. 36–38.

37. Orlando Millas, *Los comunistas, los católicos y la libertad* (Santiago de Chile: Editorial Austral, 1964), p. 93.

38. Thomas G. Sanders to Richard H. Nolte, Sept. 7, 1967 (TGS-4 in series of field reports distributed by the Institute of Current World Affairs), p. 8.

Efforts to increase *conscientização* have so far met general disappointment. The real force of Ação Popular (AP), the militantly socialistic group of Catholic intellectuals in Brazil, was to engage Catholics actively in the reformulation of the national life. Like the activity of Catholic youth groups and MEB, AP worked to educate Brazilians to an increased consciousness of their situation and the need for change.[39] Ironically, with the firm opposition of the military to these movements of the Catholic left after the revolution of 1964, their form of education for "consciousness" has become less immediately relevant to official programs of reform. Since the military government has defined their efforts as counterproductive, the positive effects of those efforts will be felt only in the long run if at all. The frustration that gave rise to the concept of *conscientização* is thus maintained, and so is the ideological rationale for collaboration between Communists and the Catholic left.

Such frustration naturally leads Catholics to denounce aspects of the capitalist system, and those denunciations again resemble those that the Communists are voicing. Frustration with human misery and the absence of change lies at the base of Catholic plans for radical action. In Colombia, Camilo Torres' belief that only revolution would allow social reform prompted critics to accuse him of being a Communist dupe, but Camilo actually declared instead that "Communism with all its dexterity and its errors has arisen from the absence of an active love translated to secular structures in a scientific manner." To the Colombian clergy he suggested only that its main preoccupation be the "welfare of humanity rather than the protection of it from Communism."[40] Although he unequivocally declared that he was not a Communist and that Communists work sometimes for just and sometimes for unjust causes, Camilo became willing to fight with them against

39. See Cândido Mendes, *Memento dos vivos: A esquerda católica no Brasil* (Rio de Janeiro: Tempo Brasileiro, 1966).

40. From an article entitled "¿Comunismo en la Iglesia?" that Camilo Torres wrote in response to the charge of Colombian President Guillermo Valencia that Communists had infiltrated the Church. The article appeared originally in *La Hora* in May, 1965, and is reprinted in *Por el Padre Camilo Torres Restrepo (1956–1966)*, pp. 267–71.

what he called "the oligarchy and the domination of the United States." Perhaps because he felt that the experience of Poland has shown that Communists can govern without destroying Catholicism,[41] he fought in a struggle that might conceivably have led to a Communist takeover. Although his death and the failure of the Colombian movement for which he worked make speculation rather fruitless, his criticisms of communism indicate the distinct possibility that he might have turned openly against the Communists if they had won power and failed to implement the reforms for which he fought.

Before such a victory brings the actual day of reckoning with the Communists, however, it is easy for both Catholics and Communists to blame failures in Latin American society on exploitative capitalism or Anglo-Saxon imperialism. The differences between religionists and atheists can be subsumed or temporarily forgotten while placing the blame for underdevelopment on someone else. As Pike points out, the Church could be stronger in its anti-Communist stand if it more openly embraced capitalism, and a better-supported capitalist system might go far to build the general economic growth upon which the social justice programs of the Church must depend.[42] Pragmatic leaders in the Latin American Church have worked to modify capitalism in the very respects that they believe will make it more productive and responsive to social needs, but against them stands an undercurrent of militant Catholicism which believes that capitalism cannot be saved.

In addition to ideological similarities and a tendency to blame the same causes for underdevelopment, the necessity for Catholics to live under the Communist regime of Fidel Castro has also occasioned collaboration. The antireligious tendencies of the Castro revolution have hurt its chances elsewhere in Latin America, and numerous advocates of far-reaching reform became oriented during the mid-1960's to the Catholic rather than the atheist left. But within Cuba the need for collaboration is incontestable. As priests have

41. Camilo Torres Restrepo, "Mensaje a los comunistas," in *Por el Padre Camilo Torres Restrepo* (*1956–1966*), pp. 329–31.
42. Fredrick B. Pike, "The Catholic Church in Central America," *Review of Politics* 21, no. 1 (Jan., 1959) : 112.

worked with the reform policies of the Castro government, some of them have found real justification for such action. Speaking for many of the priests who remained in Cuba in 1963, a priest who had worked there since 1959 declared that out of Cuba's "misfortune will come a Church closely identified with social and economic reform and progressive intellectual conceptions of modern-day political philosophy, a Church purged of reactionary and outdated members of the clergy."[43] After years of work in Castro's Cuba, Yvan Labelle generalized this growing spirit of accommodation among the religious personnel on the island. Labelle upbraids the religious who oppose the Cuban revolution, saying that either they are discouraged and secretly wish to leave Cuba or they fall uselessly into "sacramentalism" in an effort not to imply approval of Castro in any public statements. Increasingly, however, the priests who have remained in Cuba accept the revolution as a social reality and try to work as best they can with it rather than trying to subvert it.[44]

This accommodation points up the benefits of mutual toleration. In early 1968, 210 churches, 31 religious communities, and numerous religious bookstores and Catholic hospitals operated on a regular basis in Cuba, while the Castro government put up no opposition to the three new bishops named to Cuban sees late in 1967 and even allowed the duty-free import of forty Volkswagens for the use of the clergy. Monsignor Cesare Zacchi, who had served since 1960 as the apostolic nuncio in Havana, formally enunciated the rapprochement between Castro and the Church as necessary so that the Church could carry out its spiritual functions. Monsignor Zacchi indicated that the Cuban clergy had gotten to know a new class of Catholics after the old middle class and the priests who supported it had left Cuba. In justifying the need for Catholics to work constructively in the "irreversible" context of the Castro revolution, he even suggested that Catholic youth might join the youth of the Communist party and that in his opinion Fidel Castro was, ethically, a Christian.[45] Castro has certainly not been loath to

43. Quoted in "Statements and Views on Cuba's Revolution," *CIF Reports* 2, no. 7 (Dec., 1963) : 323.
44. Yvan Labelle, "The Church in Socialist Cuba," *CIF Reports* 4, no. 7 (April 1, 1965) : 49. This article is a condensation of lectures that Labelle gave at CIDOC in Cuernavaca, Mexico.
45. *Latin America* 2, no. 8 (Feb. 23, 1968) : 57–58.

use religious symbolism for his own purposes, as when during the 1960 Christmas season *fidelistas* produced a special nativity scene showing the baby Jesus lying in a Cuban peasant home and portraying the three wise men as Castro, Ernesto Guevara, and a leading Negro officer in Castro's army.[46] Some Catholic groups outside Cuba have also remained open to the possibility of cooperation with Communist regimes in Latin America.

A need for cooperation with communists operates especially in contexts of domestic politics where socialists and communists have come to exercise increasing power. In Chile, the lack of a Christian Democratic majority in the Senate encouraged President Frei to remain open to the Russian-oriented wing of the Chilean Communist movement, and such an opening proved crucial for Christian Democratic influence on the Chilean government after the presidential victory of Salvador Allende in 1970. Partly as a result of the strength of the Marxist left, numerous Chilean Catholics have long tried to state their reformist aims in terms acceptable to the less militant of the doctrinaire Marxists. Alberto Moreau, writing in the theoretical journal of the United States Communist party, has interpreted the trend toward mutual toleration between Catholics and Marxists as resulting from Catholic recognition that "anti-Communism was isolating the Church from the people."[47] Although Moreau exaggerates the strength of communism in his implicit assumption that "the people" accept it, Chilean as well as Cuban Catholics have been genuinely concerned to demonstrate that the thoroughgoing reforms they seek can be reconciled with the ends if not all the means that Marxists advocate.

Such concern should not uniformly lead progressives to join the Catholic left in united action with Communists, because a tie with Communists could rob the progressives of their appeal to many Latin Americans. Dealing with the frustration of Catholic programs for paternalistic "reform from the top" that began in the

---

46. Edwin Tetlow, *Eye on Cuba* (New York: Harcourt, Brace & World, 1966), p. 96.

47. "Catholics and Marxists in Latin America," *Political Affairs* 45, no. 7 (July, 1966): 68. For a general description of relations between Communists and Chilean nationalists, see Ernst Halperin, *Nationalism and Communism in Chile* (Cambridge, Mass.: M.I.T. Press, 1965); and Malcolm W. Browne, "Chilean Marxists' Split Is Deepening," *New York Times*, April 2, 1968.

1920's, Fredrick Pike has found that they failed because they became associated with fascism and the failure of fascism in both Europe and Latin America by 1945.[48] In a parallel manner, the efforts of the Catholic left in the 1960's and 1970's for what might be called "reform from the bottom" may similarly be brought to naught by too close an association with Communist or *fidelista* movements. If the Communist example continues to be discredited in Latin America, then it can bring only discredit to Catholic groups aligned too closely with it.

Instead of allying with Communists, the Catholic left could in most contexts work more effectively with Catholic progressives of the *freista* variety. Because of the progressives' urgent programs in the areas of land reform, education, fiscal affairs, and nationalization, they generally provide the most feasible alternative for implementing the goals of the Catholic left. When a Marxist leader takes power, as Salvador Allende did in Chile in 1970, prudence dictates that Christian Democrats join the president in a tactical alliance in order to realize specific reforms; in such situations the *freista* emphasis on the maintenance of civil liberties takes on particular importance. Although conservatives both inside and outside the Church are then likely to claim once again that the progressives as well as the Catholic left are more "communist" than the Communist party, their Christian humanism provides a counterweight to Communist despotism of the Stalinist variety.

ANTI-AMERICANISM AND THE EXOGENOUS CHURCH

A large segment of foreign opinion assumes that Catholics welcome the foreign missionaries who come to Latin America from outside the area. In commenting on the social service activities of North American religious personnel, a standard textbook in the field of Latin American politics states that "here at the grass roots, priests

48. Fredrick B. Pike, *Church and State in Mid-Century Latin America: A Catholic's View* (New York: National Council of the Churches of Christ in the U. S. A., 1965), p. 9. This pamphlet is the text of an address that Professor Pike delivered at the Symposium on the Churches and the Changing Order in Latin America, at the Church Center for the United Nations, in New York, May, 1965.

158

and ministers are devoting their lives to helping the many under-privileged in society. It is obvious that here there are no Ugly Americans."[49] There are "Ugly Americans" here, however, and Latin American Catholics as well as Communists have denounced them. The reactions against proselytizing by fundamentalist Protestant sects are well known, but less widely known is the severe criticism that Latin Americans have leveled against foreign Catholic missionaries from outside Latin America. The xenophobic responses are perplexing, because they issue for different reasons from each segment of the Latin American Church. Traditionalists, progressives, and the avant-garde have all decried foreign intervention, and they have sometimes done so for diametrically opposed reasons. A spirit of nationalism underlies all such opposition but, whereas traditionalist opposition to United States influence has attacked it as liberal, democratic, and Protestant, the criticism of avant-garde militants now upbraids it as a colonialist attempt to maintain the status quo. In simultaneously assailing the United States for allegedly trying to prevent change and for trying to push change too rapidly, Catholic radicals and conservatives point up the difficulty of the United States position as well as the diversities within Latin American Catholicism.

The extent of the influence of foreign priests is one of the fundamental reasons for attacks upon them. Of the 12,000 priests in Brazil in 1966, at least a third were non-Brazilians.[50] Foreigners make up more than three-quarters of the clergy of Bolivia. In 1950 Bolivia had only 204 native diocesan priests for a population of about 3 million, and by 1964 the number of native diocesan priests had fallen to 172 in a total population of 4.5 million.[51] In Haiti the proportion of French priests has been as high as the proportion of Spanish and North American priests in South America. A study carried out between 1958 and 1961 indicated that 67.3 per cent of the diocesan priests in Haiti were French, while only 30.2 per

49. Alexander T. Edelmann, *Latin American Government and Politics: The Dynamics of a Revolutionary Society* (Homewood, Ill.: Dorsey Press, 1965), p. 178.

50. *Friends of Latin America* 3, no. 4 (Sept., 1967): 27. This newsletter is a translation of a report of the College for Latin America founded at Louvain, Belgium, in 1953, under the patronage of the Catholic University.

51. Vicente O. Vetrano, "Algunas reflexiones sobre la Iglesia en Bolivia," *Criterio* 39, no. 1517 (9 febrero, 1967): 80.

cent were Haitian nationals. Out of a total of 278 diocesan priests in Haiti, 187 were French and 84 were Haitian along with 3 North American, 2 Belgian, and 2 Canadian priests. Out of an additional 185 regular priests, only 4 were native Haitians.[52]

Foreign influence in the Latin American Church extends well beyond the presence of such high proportions of foreign priests. The heavy financing that Chilean Catholics have received from Germany is well known, as are the large sums that North American prelates have sent to the Andean republics in aid of missionary endeavors. Foreigners, like the North Americans who serve as bishops in Brazil, Bolivia, and Panama, have also risen to commanding positions in the Latin American Church hierarchy. Even where bishops were born in Latin American countries, they are often the first-generation sons of foreign immigrants. Instead of coming from the old Catholic aristocracy of Buenos Aires, for example, the most easily distinguishable group of Argentine bishops has been the sons of families that immigrated to Argentina after 1880. A recent study of the origins of Argentine bishops has found 39, out of a total of 49 bishops, to be the sons of immigrants. In terms of the origins of their parents, 19 of these bishops were Italian, 12 Spanish, 5 German, 2 Irish, and 1 Arab.[53]

It would be quite wrong to assume that Latin Americans oppose all of these foreign religious personnel. In fact, opposition to foreigners often arises from the assumption that they are unconcerned rather than that they have become too much concerned with developments in Latin America. As Richard Shaull points out, basing his contention on his extensive missionary work in Latin America, many Latin Americans criticize Yankees for busying themselves with beautiful church buildings and spiritual revival in the United States while remaining thoroughly disinterested in the connection between religion and socioeconomic change in Latin America.[54] Although some Catholics are certainly perturbed by an absence of

52. Isidoro Alonso and Gines Garrido, *La Iglesia en América Central y el Caribe: Estructuras eclesiásticas* (Bogotá: FERES, 1962), pp. 25–27.

53. José Luis de Imaz, *Los que mandan* (Buenos Aires: Editorial Universitaria de Buenos Aires, 1964), pp. 174, 176.

54. M. Richard Shaull, *Encounter with Revolution* (New York: Association Press, 1955), pp. vii–viii.

North American awareness, others are disconcerted to see the extent of foreign influence that foreign concern has so far brought.

Nationalist pride is a regular cause for opposition to this foreign influence. Cultural conflict and the superior airs of some Yankee churchmen appear in the comment of a Colombian Jesuit who, after studying in the United States, asked Father John Considine, "What is there in the U. S. Catholic that makes him, despite his lamentable ignorance of South American ways and religious traditions, assume the role of the Eternal Father himself in tendering us unsolicited advice as to what we must do to lift ourselves out of our shame? Heaven knows we need help but why not offer it to us not as our masters but as our brothers."[55] The force of nationalist pride is by no means limited to Colombia or Latin America. It operates in Asia and Africa as well, and it is one of the strongest forces working to make both the personnel and the objectives of the Church more attuned to the particular needs of the developing countries. Showing the vitality of nationalist opposition to foreign clergy in a very different context, President Sékou Touré of Guinea declared that any foreign clergy remaining in his country after June 1, 1967, would be expelled. With an evident dislike of foreign direction of Church activities in Guinea, President Touré said, "We demand total Africanization because in 20 centuries, in the history of Christianity, no African or colored person has been raised to the dignity of archbishop or even bishop in any European country."[56]

Nationalism plays a special part in Haitian opposition to Catholic missionaries, as Haitian nationalists associate Catholicism with foreigners and exploitation and see vodun as the religious medium through which to mobilize mass support. In one of the best analyses of the political effects of religion in Haiti, Rémy Bastien concludes that the nineteenth-century French missionaries who came to Haiti had "a secret mission: to create a climate of opinion favorable to a voluntary association of Haiti with France."[57] The missionaries con-

55. Quoted in John J. Considine, *New Horizons in Latin America* (New York: Dodd, Mead & Company, 1958), p. xi.
56. Quoted in *Christian Science Monitor,* May 17, 1967.
57. "Vodoun and Politics in Haiti," in Harold Courlander and Rémy Bastien, *Religion and Politics in Haiti* (Washington, D. C.: Institute for Cross-Cultural Research, 1966), p. 45.

centrated on the education of the upper-class elite and tried to show this elite the inherent superiority of French culture. Although this cultural indoctrination failed to recreate political association between Haiti and France, it did alienate the upper classes from native Haitian culture. When François Duvalier expelled the foreign clergy in the early 1960's, therefore, he did so in the name of opposition to the combination of the foreign clerics and domestic bourgeoisie which rejected native Haitian values and culture.

Foreign priests may, of course, adapt to the nationalistic viewpoints of the countries that receive them. As Vladimiro Boric, the Salesian bishop of Punto Arenas, Chile, pointed out with obvious pride, Salesian teachers stress Chilean patriotism in all of their schools, whether in the far north or three thousand miles to the south in Punto Arenas itself. The fact that foreign priests teach in Chilean schools does not reduce the nationalist content of education, because, he says, Italian and other foreign Salesians enthusiastically teach Chilean folklore and national songs to the Chilean children.[58] The situation of Chile, where foreign priests come from many countries and already share similar racial and cultural backgrounds with most Chilean priests and parishioners, stands in sharp contrast to the Haitian case, where the folk customs of this black republic differ greatly from those of the white priests, who traditionally came to Haiti from France and French Canada.

Charges of exploitation and cultural imperialism have been leveled more widely at the United States. As a sociologist and a "man of the left," Father Camilo Torres claimed that the mass of Colombian citizens held antigringo sentiments. In a short but most interesting mimeographed statement written in 1964, Torres presented a Marxist interpretation of Colombian class structure and attitudes.[59] He found that the most significant breakdown was into only two classes, which respectively represented 15 per cent and 85 per cent of the population and which were continually becoming more dissimilar, independent, and antagonistic. In differentiating be-

58. Interview with Bishop Vladimiro Boric in Punto Arenas, Chile, July 27, 1968.
59. Camilo Torres Restrepo, "La desintegración social en Colombia: Se están gestando dos subculturas," in *Por el Padre Camilo Torres Restrepo (1956–1966)*, pp. 195–99.

tween these groups, Torres gave what he believed to be their responses to key phrases and concepts. The upper class would allegedly interpret the term "oligarchy" as an "insult," while the lower class would interpret it as "privilege." The upper class would see the Colombian National Front as a "policy of coexistence," while the lower class would see it as a "union of the oligarchies." The upper class would see agrarian reform as "illegal expropriation" and the Church as an "institution working for order," while the lower class would see agrarian reform as "acquisition of land by the poor" and the Church as a "reactionary force."

Camilo Torres' assumption of mass anti-Americanism comes out clearly in the responses which he postulated to key phrases concerning the United States. He claimed that the upper class would interpret the Alliance for Progress as "North American aid," while the lower class would see it as "imperialism." The upper class would find "imperialism" to be a "Marxist slogan" and Peace Corpsmen to be "altruistic volunteers," while the lower class would find "imperialism" to be "gringo influence" and Peace Corpsmen to be "tourists or spies." Father Torres' assumptions would have much more meaning for social scientists if, as a trained sociologist, he had actually surveyed upper- and lower-class reactions to these key words to see if real responses agreed with his subjective impressions. In the absence of sound empirical research to substantiate his interpretation of class breakdown and attitude, the interpretation really tells more about Torres' viewpoint than it does about the depth and location of anti-Americanism in Colombia. The interpretation is both accurate and significant in another sense, however, in that it reflects the anti-Americanism which a sizable group of Catholic leftists both feels and attributes to the Latin American masses.

One of the greatest critics of United States influence is Ivan Illich, himself a former North American churchman. Illich upbraids what he and other members of the Catholic left describe as the "colonial" nature of the Latin American Church, writing that:

. . . Foreign generosity has enticed the Latin American Church into becoming a satellite to North Atlantic cultural phenomena and policy. Increased apostolic resources intensified the need for their continued flow and created islands of apostolic well-being, each day farther beyond the capacity of local support. The Latin American Church flowers anew by returning to what the Conquest stamped her: a colonial plant that blooms because of foreign cultivation.[60]

At CIDOC in Cuernavaca, Illich has become particularly concerned with the inadequacies of North American Catholics who go to work in Latin America. Noting that North American lay volunteers come from both "the best and worst types of people for this work," he commented shortly after the formation of CIDOC that "they're either very mature and will pay the price of sacrifice because they love the Lord, or they're escapists and self-appointed prophets."[61]

Some of Illich's severest criticism appeared in the January 21, 1967, issue of *America,* the Jesuit weekly, and produced a strong counterstatement from Richard Cardinal Cushing at the annual meeting of the Catholic Inter-American Cooperation Program held in Boston at the end of January. After specifically mentioning Cardinal Cushing's support for the South American Church, the article declares that "it is easy to come by big sums to build a new church in a jungle or a high school in a suburb, and then to staff the plants with new missioners. A patently irrelevant pastoral system is artificially and expensively sustained, while basic research for a new and vital one is considered an extravagant luxury." Illich alleges that the Latin American Church is "over-staffed" and that North American priests work diligently to stifle "revolutionary awakening" in Latin America. He claims that "the 'padre' stands on the side of W. R. Grace and Co., Esso, the Alliance for Progress, democratic government, the AFL-CIO and whatever is holy in the Western pantheon." Illich sees the influx of North American and European priests as postponing the necessary crisis that would make Latin American prelates think more seriously of such reforms as a married diaconate and the widespread use of laymen for evangelical tasks. He even questions whether bishops ought to "close up shop" and suggests that "a healthy sense of values empties the seminaries and the ranks of

60. Ivan Illich, "The Seamy Side of Charity," *America* 116, no. 3 (Jan. 21, 1967): 88–89.
61. Quoted in "Training to Help the Latins: A Picture Story," *The Sign* 41, no. 4 (Nov., 1961): 19.

the clergy much more effectively than a lack of discipline and generosity."[62]

Latin American moderates have turned Illich's criticism of North American missionaries into a traditional call for more native vocations. In a typical response to the Illich article, Father Hermann González comments that "to accuse the North American Catholic Church of being an unconscious agency of ESSO, the Grace Line, and Yankee imperialism must offend United States Catholics." Writing from a Venezuelan perspective, Father González goes on to say that in Venezuela the North American priests and religious form only an insignificant minority compared to numerous groups of Spanish, Italian, Belgian, French, and German clergy. He admits that the predominance of foreigners among the Venezuelan clergy has sometimes created "open tensions," but he concludes that the foreign clergy remains necessary and that the only lasting problem would be a failure to recognize that the native Venezuelan clergy must come to replace the foreigners through new vocations.[63] Although this kind of approach admits the existence of some of the tensions to which Illich points, its major effect is to blunt and minimize the severity of his criticisms by converting the criticisms into a standard call for vocations.

Other Latin American churchmen, instead of minimizing the Illich criticism, have tied it to a more general criticism of United States foreign policy. Dom Hélder Câmara upbraids the United States and the Soviet Union in the same terms, seeing them both as having failed to bring sufficient aid to the developing countries. In a speech on August 25, 1967, he condemned the "total incomprehension of the super-powers—the U. S. A. and the U. S. S. R.—to create effective means for the development of the underdeveloped coun-

62. Illich, "The Seamy Side of Charity," pp. 88–91. For a good discussion of Illich's ideas and basic orientation, see Joseph P. Fitzpatrick, S.J., "What Is He Getting At?," *America* 116, no. 12 (March 25, 1967). For praise of Cardinal Cushing's activities and those of the Society of St. James the Apostle that he supported, see Gary MacEoin, "U. S. Priests Among the Latins," *The Sign* 41, no. 3 (Oct., 1961); and Juan Cardinal Landázuri Ricketts, "The Bright Light of Progress," in John J. Considine, M.M., ed., *Social Revolution in the New Latin America: A Catholic Appraisal* (Notre Dame, Ind.: Fides Publishers, 1965), pp. 174–75.
63. Hermann González, S.J., "Sacerdotes y religiosos importados," *Sic* 30, no. 294 (abril, 1967): 169–70.

tries."[64] The United States comes in for special attack from Dom Hélder and the Catholic left, however, because of American backing for the Brazilian military. In his assumption that the United States is working to preserve the status quo through its support for the military, Dom Hélder speaks for some United States observers as well as for a significant group of Latin American Catholics.[65]

Further cause for attacks on the United States appears in the fact that North American Catholics have denounced the Catholic left and tried to create firmer bonds between the Latin American Church and the United States government. Professor Manoel Cardozo, the head of the history department at the Catholic University of America, presents a typical North American attack on the Catholic left in his criticism of *Brasil Urgente,* the radical publication of the left that ceased publication in 1964. Professor Cardozo complains that "Father Carlos Josaphat and those who worked with him were not so much interested in truth as in fixed ideas, and in the process of explaining what they thought, were guilty of the most outrageous departure from truth."[66] Such criticisms naturally displease the Catholic left, but even more galling is the defense of intervention. Some North American priests defend United States intervention in Latin America in the same way that the late Cardinal Spellman defended intervention in Vietnam. Alleging North American altruism in the Dominican Republic intervention of 1965, for instance, Father James A. Clark writes that "for the first time in history, American soldiers had to come to help the common people, not to support bond holders or dictators but to preserve peace for the ordinary citizen." Father Clark echoes the thought of Latin American progressives in his view that the United States and the Church should place themselves "solidly on the side of the masses of people," but he angers the nationalists in his stress on the coincidence of interest between the United States government and the Latin American

64. Quoted in Foland to Nolte, Nov. 4, 1967.
65. For a North American statement of this same criticism, see Joseph Page, "Facade in Brazil," *New Republic* 157, no. 111 (Sept. 9, 1967): 8. Opposition to the wealth and self-satisfaction of the developed countries also comes out strongly in Hélder Câmara, "The *First* World Is the Problem" *Cross Currents* 20, no. 3 (Summer, 1970).
66. Cardozo, "The Brazilian Church and the New Left," p. 316.

Church. Seeing the community of interest between the United States and the Church in wishful but exaggerated terms, Father Clark even proposes that North American aid to such countries as the Dominican Republic be channeled through Catholic and Protestant organizations in order to prevent graft and make the aid effective.[67]

As Catholic critics alternatively support or decry United States policies in Latin America, it is revealing to see how directly some North American and papal statements have corresponded with one another. In the *Populorum Progressio* encyclical of March, 1967, and the Declaration of the Presidents of the Americas of April, 1967, the Vatican and the United States government each called for measures such as expanded international trade, Latin American economic integration, and arms control.[68] This coincidence of program indicates neither collaboration nor, as critics of both Rome and Washington have implied, Vatican or North American policies designed to cover their desires to subvert Latin America. Neither the Vatican nor the United States government can solve Latin American problems, but each has been motivated to suggest what appear to it to be genuinely beneficial programs.

Protestant activity in Latin America, on which both the Vatican and the United States government remain diplomatically silent, continues to spur further xenophobia. An underlying cause for anti-Americanism in Catholic circles continues to be fear of the alien Protestantism and the democratic tendencies that Catholic conservatives have traditionally opposed. Expediency has sometimes forced Protestants and Catholics to work together, as in the 1964 Christian Democratic fight against Salvador Allende in Chile in which Protestants staunchly supported Eduardo Frei, choosing a Catholic alternative over the apparent atheism of Allende and the Frente de Acción Popular (FRAP). The ecumenical movement now encourages further cooperation with Protestantism, and the continuing threat of this alien faith encourages Catholics to make their own faith

67. James A. Clark, *The Church and the Crisis in the Dominican Republic* (Westminster, Md.: Newman Press, 1967), pp. 103, 192, 199.
68. For a detailed comparison of the two documents, see Eduardo Fernández, "Encíclica y Declaración: Una valoración por contraste," *Sic* 30, no. 295 (mayo, 1967): 226–29.

more directly relevant to secular problems. But, in the main, denunciations and attacks against Protestants take considerable time and energy for many Catholics, and their anti-Protestantism detracts from their efforts for social welfare.

Cultural differences have long provoked friction between North American missionaries and the Latin Americans whom they wish to convert. In a rabid condemnation of Protestant missionaries accusing them of seriously undermining Franklin Roosevelt's Good Neighbor policy, John W. White complained in 1943 that "average South Americans are far better educated and much more cultured than many of the United States missionaries and bitterly resent being treated as heathen and in need of 'saving' by Protestant agents from the United States, many of whom do not command the respect of their own fellow citizens."[69] Protestant missionaries have frequently applied an ethic of Yankee puritanism which is offensive to Latin Americans. In an evangelical denunciation of drinking that typically ignores the general acceptance of wine in the South European and Latin American countries, George P. Howard offends Chileans by writing that alcoholism is Chile's "greatest social problem," that annual wine consumption is 79.5 liters, and that the number of imprisoned Chilean drunkards rose by 200,000 from 1943 to 1944.[70] Although all missionaries have not presented such unsympathetic criticisms, their foreign values and ethnocentric attitudes have nevertheless set them apart.

Past practices of the government and missionaries of the United States, which have now largely been given up, have also provided Latin Americans with major causes for resentment. Besides being strongly disliked in Latin America for gunboat diplomacy and the encouragement of Panamanian separatism, President Theodore Roosevelt alienated Latin Americans by pushing the revocation of anti-Protestant domestic laws in Peru, Ecuador, and Bolivia.[71] More

69. *Our Good Neighbor Hurdle* (Milwaukee, Wis.: Bruce Publishing Company, 1943), p. 133.
70. *We Americans: North and South* (New York: Friendship Press, 1951), pp. 108-9.
71. See John Lee, *Religious Liberty in South America, With Special Reference to Recent Legislation in Peru, Ecuador, and Bolivia* (Cincinnati, Ohio: Jennings and Graham, 1907), pp. 197-98, 204-5.

recently, in dealing with primitive Indian groups in Amazonian areas, missionaries have cajoled the Indians into giving up their old styles of life and taken them out of their surroundings only to see many of them die off. The Sirionó, for example, were taken out of their jungle environment in eastern Bolivia after they were converted. By 1967 about 90 per cent of the Indians had contracted tuberculosis. The number of Indians in the tribe had decreased in only a few years from 1,000 to 600, and the remaining Indians were not expected to survive long.[72] Although comparatively few Latin Americans have concerned themselves with Roosevelt's assistance to Protestantism or with experiences like that of the Sirionó tribe, those who have naturally resent the foreign intervention.

A more immediate cause for Catholic xenophobia is the danger that Protestant missionaries appear to pose. In an overall sense, Protestantism threatens the values that Latin Americans admire. Since much of the Protestant missionary work is done by fundamentalists, it appeals to individuals concerned initially with forgiveness for their sins. In concentrating upon personal conversions, it often deprives religion of the pageantry and elegance that Catholics have come to revere. Jehovah's Witnesses have been particularly offensive to Latin American Catholics by their practice of standing at the doors of Catholic churches and giving anti-Catholic literature to communicants coming from mass.[73] As Robert H. Dix emphasizes in the case of Colombia, parish priests have also felt threatened by Protestant missionaries who portray priests as well as the Church in general as being reactionary and corrupt.[74] Protestants have posed a particular challenge in such programs as their use of the creole folk language in Haiti, where their appeals are especially well adapted to local conditions. They have won especially large numbers of converts in Brazil, where the appeals of fundamentalist sects and spiritualists fit the requisites of socioeconomic change and the

72. *New York Times,* July 22, 1967.
73. Peter Masten Dunne, S.J., "The Church in Latin America," in Waldemar Gurian and M. A. Fitzsimons, eds., *The Catholic Church in World Affairs* (Notre Dame, Ind.: University of Notre Dame Press, 1954), p. 412.
74. *Colombia: The Political Dimensions of Change* (New Haven, Conn.: Yale University Press, 1967), pp. 309–10.

169

psychological needs of individuals caught up in the process of change.[75]

The foreign financing available for Protestant missionaries has seemed to make them a particular threat. Latin American Catholics resent missionary invasions that, with what Father Eduardo Ospina calls their "dollars in abundance," try to convert Catholics into Protestants. Protestant colleges that offer large scholarships and tantalizing opportunities to learn the English language, Protestant radio propaganda such as the "Voice of the Andes," and Protestant books and fliers such as those distributed widely by Jehovah's Witnesses and the Seventh-Day Adventists provoke numerous outcries from Catholic leaders.[76] In Colombia and other Latin American countries Catholic activists have also occasioned attacks on the Protestant proselytizers, ranging from tire slashing to the breaking up of meetings.

Friction with foreign missionaries is particularly inopportune, because it reinforces the pattern of intellectual separateness and religious difference that has traditionally made it so difficult for North Americans to gain a genuine sympathy and understanding for Latin American affairs. As Richard M. Morse suggests in explaining the deficiencies of Latin American studies in the United States, "Our present *doctrinal* diversity and toleration obscure for us the fact that we are integrally a Protestant nation, insensitive and vaguely hostile to the *sociological* and *psychological* foundations of a Catholic society."[77] The doctrines and the action-oriented imperatives of Latin American Catholicism are now becoming more and more diverse, and as they do so attempts at achieving greater understanding of them become even more necessary and more difficult. Militant reformers in the Latin American Church are alienated not only from Protestant missionaries but also from North American Catholics

75. See Emilio Willems, "Religious Mass Movements and Social Change in Brazil," in Eric N. Baklanoff, ed., *New Perspectives of Brazil* (Nashville, Tenn.: Vanderbilt University Press, 1966).

76. For a typical example of this position, see Eduardo Ospina, S.J., "La penetración del protestantismo en la América Latina," *Ecclesiástica Xaveriana* 5 (1955). For a contrasting Protestant interpretation, see Emmanuel Chastand, *Drame d'une Minorité Religieuse: Le Martyre de l'Eglise Protestante en Colombie* (Anduze, France: Imprimerie du Languedoc, 1961).

77. "The Strange Career of 'Latin-American Studies,' " *The Annals of the American Academy of Political and Social Science* 356 (Nov., 1964) : 111. Morse's italics.

whose verbal support for "social reform" is outstripped by their deeper fear of upsetting social relationships or North American interests. If this situation should become more general, then the development of genuine inter-American sympathy and cooperation will be further postponed.

So far, a tendency to change the traditional orientation of foreign missionaries has mitigated the militancy of Catholic xenophobia. In an interview promoting the Papal Volunteers for Latin America, Father John Considine claims that "sensible North Americans have gotten rid of the idea that we're torch bearers going down into the valley of ignorance."[78] Such American periodicals as *U. S. News & World Report* credit much of the innovation in Latin American Catholicism to the influence of the United States, German, Belgian, and French priests who came to Latin America after World War II.[79] Upholding the view of Father Considine and American periodicals has been the example of the new breed of missionaries: Protestants like Richard Shaull and Catholics like Ivan Illich. Besides being among the most outspoken advocates of change, these men have been the greatest critics of Yankee complacency and ethnocentrism. Shaull, who is now a professor at the Princeton Theological Seminary, has won the sympathy of Catholic reformers by declaring that liberal democracy and traditional Christian activities in social service are "completely irrelevant" in the context of Latin American efforts for reform.[80] Illich has trained a series of missioners and reformers at his Cuernavaca center, as has Father François Houtart at Louvain. In quantitative terms it even appears that American priests are among the greatest advocates of social change. In Joseph Fichter's study of Catholic attitudes in Santiago, 74.2 per

78. "Two Ways to Aid the Latins: An Interview with Father John J. Considine, M.M.," *The Sign* 42, no. 10 (May, 1963): 13. For a good case study of the new missionary attitudes, see Frank Bonilla, *A Franciscan Bishopric in the Amazon: Some Contemporary Problems of Brazilian Catholicism,* American Universities Field Staff Reports Service, East Coast South America Series 8, no. 5 (Nov., 1961). This report details the wide-ranging educational and social service activities of Dom Tiago Ryan, the titular bishop of Margo and prelate nullius of Santarém, and the priests and brothers who came with him from Chicago and St. Louis to work in Brazil.

79. "Changing Role of the Church in Latin America," *U. S. News & World Report,* Oct. 16, 1967, p. 94.

80. Richard Shaull, "Recientes estudios sobre el desarrollo político en Asia, Africa y América Latina," *Cristianismo y Sociedad* 1, no. 2 (1963): 50.

cent of the North American priests answered that the pace of Chilean social change was not rapid enough. Only 54.3 per cent of the priests born in Chile and only 55.8 per cent of the European priests gave this answer, however.[81]

Xenophobia has not prevented rapport between reformers in North and South America. The influence of North American Catholicism has often, both advertently and inadvertently, supported reform and progress. On the grounds of preserving separation of Church and State, North American Catholics indirectly aided the reforms of Puerto Rican Governor Muñoz Marín by criticizing the Puerto Rican bishops who ordered Catholics not to vote for him.[82] Some Catholic leaders have seen the United States not as an exact model that can be copied but at least as a positive exemplar whose political characteristics can be admired. Eduardo Frei in 1948 contrasted "the marvellous example of the United States, whose union and political judgment have allowed them to construct the most powerful democracy" with those Latin American "operetta republics in which riots and military coups follow one another between intervals of anarchy."[83] Furthermore, North American critics have come to see progressive Church leaders as their natural allies. In an edition of *I. F. Stone's Weekly* needling the Americans for Democratic Action for not condemning the Vietnam war thoroughly enough, Stone thus praises Pope Paul's encyclical *On the Development of Peoples*. He interprets the encyclical as a slap at United States support for military dictatorships and contrasts the Catholic left with the leaders in Latin America and elsewhere who oppose reform or support the Vietnam war. Six months before the death of Che Guevara, Stone asked, "Could it be that Che Guevara, instead of being in Bolivia, is hiding in Rome? Maybe we'd better put a Green Beret on Cardinal Spellman and drop him by parachute in Vatican

81. Joseph H. Fichter, *Cambio social en Chile: Un estudio de actitudes* (Santiago de Chile: Editorial Universidad Católica, 1962), pp. 65, 70.
82. See "Puerto Rican Pastoral," in Thurston N. Davis, S.J., Donald R. Campion, S.J., and L. C. McHugh, S.J., eds., *Between Two Cities: God and Man in America* (Chicago: Loyola University Press, 1962), pp. 429–33.
83. From an editorial in *Política y Espíritu* that is reprinted in Eduardo Frei Montalva, *Sentido y forma de una política* (Santiago de Chile: Editorial del Pacífico, 1951), pp. 119–21.

City, fully equipped for counter-insurgency, including if necessary our favorite form of baptism—by napalm."[84] If commitments at home and in other parts of the world did not limit United States resources, it could much more adequately support progressive regimes like that of Eduardo Frei and so counteract the xenophobic tendencies of the Catholic left.

REORGANIZATION IN THE CHURCH

Under the dual impact of changes in Latin American society and Catholic attitudes toward that society, churchmen are questioning the relevance of the traditional Church organization. They ask whether the old organization of the Church is best suited to effect new desires for political and economic development, as well as to draw more of Latin America's burgeoning population into a personal acceptance of the faith. One aspect of the new thinking deals with the crucial area of priestly recruitment, raising such issues as whether priests should marry or be recruited from the lower classes, whether the education that the priests receive should be radically altered, and whether more laymen should be used. Another aspect of the debate deals with the relationships between priests and parishioners and raises the whole issue of the efficacy of hierarchical organization. Although there is as yet little consensus on the lines of administrative change, the ideas put forward so far indicate that attitudes toward reorganization and eventually reorganization itself will be among the most potent forces shaping the evolution of the Catholic Church.

The fundamental desire behind discussions of Church restructuring is to make the Church better able to deal with popular wants and needs. Since more effective recruitment and utilization of religious personnel will be required to accomplish this, numerous plans have been suggested for better recruitment and utilization. Monsignor Elías Andraos of Buenos Aires advocates allowing marriage among one section of the priesthood, not to prevent some

84. "Pope's New Encyclical Read in Latin America As Attack on U. S. Policy," *I. F. Stone's Weekly* 15, no. 14 (April 10, 1967) : 3.

priests from renouncing their vocation in order to marry but rather to draw a new group of men into the priesthood in order to help overcome the shortage of priests.[85] A large assembly of Ecuadorean priests and bishops, meeting in Quito during 1970, similarly advocated that priestly celibacy be made voluntary, and that further study be devoted to the possibilities of ordaining married men and allowing men who are now priests to marry and continue their vocations.[86] Although such plans hold out a promise of potential relief, the present reluctance of the Vatican to accept the idea of a married clergy means that reformers must look elsewhere for solutions.

Another suggestion has been that the Church try much more actively to recruit priests from the lower class. Father Poblete's survey research in Chile has shown that the upper class is still overrepresented in vocations, with just over 20 per cent of the vocations coming from this class, which comprises no more than 10 per cent of the total population. Chilean worker and peasant backgrounds accounted for only 12.8 per cent of the seminarians in the survey, while the middle class spawned over 66 per cent of the seminarians.[87] A partially untapped source of vocations would thus seem to exist in the lower sector of Latin American societies, and interview data suggest that members of this sector might be willing to consider entering the priesthood if they could obtain an education by doing so. Many priests interviewed during 1968 frankly admitted that they themselves first went to seminaries because of the opportunity there for free education and upward mobility, and they attributed such motivation to the majority of priests from lower- and lower-middle-class backgrounds.[88] In the seminaries the opportunities for pastoral service became more evident, so that the seminarians who decided to continue their vocations rather than using their education for other purposes have tended to do so for more deeply religious and altruistic rather than simply personal reasons.

85. Elías Andraos, "La escasez de clero: Un problema asuciante y una propuesta de solución," *Criterio* 40, no. 1519 (9 marzo, 1967) : 150–52.

86. "Conclusiones de la Primera Convención Nacional de Presbíteros del Ecuador," *Nadoc,* no. 141 (22 abril, 1970) : 4–6.

87. Renato Poblete Barth, S.J., *Crisis sacerdotal* (Santiago de Chile: Editorial del Pacífico, 1965), p. 65.

88. Based on personal interviews during 1968 with about thirty Latin American priests, particularly in Venezuela, Paraguay, Argentina, Chile, and Colombia.

A further reason for lower-class recruitment has been the view that men from the lower class would more readily understand its needs. Whether or not David Mutchler is correct in assuming that "an overwhelming majority of Brazil's priests are from upper class families," it is certainly true that Dom Hélder and other prelates have tried to increase the reform orientation of Brazilian clergymen by increasing vocations most among the lower classes.[89] The underlying assumption that priests recruited from lower socioeconomic backgrounds will more easily side with the progressives may be inaccurate, and it needs to be tested by empirical research. Even in its unverified form, however, the assumption is one on which leaders of the progressives and the Catholic left have come to act.

Illich's calls for reform go much further than calls for a married clergy or lower-class recruitment. He demands basic changes in the bureaucratic structure of the Church and suggests that within this generation a majority of the personnel of the Church may abandon their positions unless such changes occur. He does not advocate ordaining married priests as a way to remedy lagging vocations and clerical dropouts because, as he says, "we have more than enough unmarried ones." Instead, he proposes what he calls "the necessary and inevitable secularization of the ministry." Laymen would take over the leadership functions of priests, and "diaconia" would replace parishes as the basic ecclesiastical unit. Instead of going to weekly mass, Christian friends would meet periodically to read the Bible and discuss messages from their bishop. They would all be self-supporting, so that there would be no need to support the large and expensive clerical establishment that Illich believes to be increasingly concerned with bureaucratic red tape.[90] Even if such forms of lay organization should become more common, however, their existence might well work to maintain rather than destroy the

89. David E. Mutchler, S.J., *Roman Catholicism in Brazil: A Study of Church Behavior Under Stress,* Studies in Comparative International Development 1, no. 8 (St. Louis, Mo.: Social Science Institute, Washington University, 1965), p. 110.

90. Ivan Illich, "The Vanishing Clergyman," *CIDOC Informa* 5, no. 2 (June 18, 1967): 5–9, 13. As in the case of ecclesiastical structures, Illich has similarly called for the dissolution and fundamental restructuring of educational institutions. See Ivan Illich, "Education without School: How It Can Be Done," *New York Review of Books* 15, no. 12 (Jan. 7, 1971).

Church hierarchy. As Gianfranco Poggi suggests in his study of Catholic Action in Italy, the mobilization of laymen has so far tended to preserve and strengthen—rather than dilute—the authoritative, hierarchical system in which popes and bishops exercise command.[91]

Illich notwithstanding, priests should remain essential in the organization of the Latin American Church for some time to come. In this situation, ways must be found to make priestly activity more directly relevant to popular needs and to reorient the education that the priests receive. Brazilian bishops, who have become acutely aware of past failures to actually reach the poor, dealt directly with the issue of priestly activity in their "Emergency Plan" of 1962. The plan criticized the "passivity" of the majority of Catholics attending mass, censured the subjects of the sermons delivered to them for being far from their real interests, and found the language of the sermons to be alien to their colloquial ways of speech.[92] The clear implication is that priests should not concentrate exclusively on spiritual or intellectual activities, or use language with which their listeners do not feel comfortable. Instead, they should provide grass roots leadership on matters that are of real concern to their parishioners. Similarly, Brazilian churchmen have begun to alter seminary training to allow priests to take on new roles. Under the influence of Dom Hélder and student activists, the study of poverty and social development has entirely replaced traditional Thomistic philosophy at the Regional Seminary of the Northeast, where future priests learn to deal as much with the secular as with the religious problems facing the people of the region.[93]

Numerous churchmen share the Brazilians' desire to make the relationship between the priesthood and laity one of intimacy

91. *Catholic Action in Italy: The Sociology of a Sponsored Organization* (Stanford, Calif.: Stanford University Press, 1967), pp. 11–12.

92. " 'Emergency Plan' of the Bishops of Brazil," in *Recent Church Documents from Latin America,* CIF Monographs, no. 2 (Cuernavaca, Mor.: CIDOC, 1963), pp. 14–15.

93. For a description of the new program of study, see Thomas G. Sanders to Richard H. Nolte, Aug. 5, 1967 (TGS-3 in series of field reports distributed by the Institute of Current World Affairs), pp. 5–6.

rather than distance and awe. In a striking example of this tendency in the Church, Alberto Devoto, the bishop of Goya, Argentina, issues his regular pastoral letters in a one-page mimeographed form that has every appearance of being a personal letter between a bishop and his people. His practice contrasts those of other bishops who rarely send pastorals, who read pastoral messages over the radio, or who have lengthy pastorals printed up as small books or pamphlets. A careful reading of the pastorals of Bishop Devoto and other bishops like him indicates the depth of their concern with their people. When a flood drove many citizens from their homes in the spring of 1966, Bishop Devoto made personal visits to the refugees. He tried to counteract indifference by saying that, since the flood most deeply affected poor families who were already suffering most, it could not be simply a punishment from God. Departing from the usual form of address in order to stress his feelings, Bishop Devoto appropriately concluded his pastoral on the flood: "YO SIEMPRE ESTARÉ CONTIGO."[94]

Many churchmen have decided that to become more effective they must modify their styles of life. A congregation of bishops, priests, religious, and laymen meeting in La Paz, Bolivia, early in 1968 affirmed that, instead of wanting to be served by men, the Church is the servant of men and the "animator of profound transformations." In order to encourage change and incidentally to alter its own image, the Bolivian clergy declared that all clergymen would have to adopt a pattern of life much closer to the style of the people among whom they were living.[95] Such declarations parallel statements from Latin American bishops saying that they must give up the use of large black automobiles, or palatial residences, or even episcopal coats of arms, in order to reduce their symbolic separation from the common people.

Rejection of churchly symbols confirms the open, nonhierarchical view that progressive churchmen take toward the distinctions among men. Although conservatives contend that it is the pride

94. Alberto Devoto (Obispo de Goya), untitled pastoral letter, March 8, 1966. The capitalization is Bishop Devoto's.
95. "La Iglesia da trascendentales orientaciones con relación a la realidad que vive el país," *Presencia* (La Paz, Bolivia), Feb. 6, 1968.

of mediocre men that encourages doctrines of egalitarianism,[96] the force of human pride works with at least equal strength to support hierarchical interpretations of human achievement. It is only natural that, out of a sense of psychological self-justification and esteem, the comparatively secure and powerful members of Latin American societies see fundamental distinctions among men as partly responsible for their high status. They generally have intelligence and initiative, and they see these qualities, rather than luck or family background, as largely responsible for their success. Their experience as well as their vanity tells them that most other men lack the same degrees of intelligence and initiative and that the marks of homage accorded bishops or presidents are therefore justified. It is a mark of genuinely Christian humility, in the approach to questions of hierarchy and leadership as well as pomp, which encourages churchmen like Dom Hélder or Bishop Devoto to erase some of the symbols separating bishops from other citizens.

As calls for reorientations of both the personnel and the symbols of the Church have increased, prelates have come to worry that the reforms will go too far and make a mockery of priestly activity and the most sacred rites. The bishop of Tacna, Peru, complains that newspaper headlines have come to refer to the mass as "Misa a Gó Gó, Misa a la Boliviana, a la Gaucho, a la Chilena, a la Guaraní," and he warns that tailoring ritual too closely to fit nationalist and modernist predilections will seriously detract from the majesty and respect that Catholicism demands.[97] Father Renato Poblete, a Jesuit sociologist at the Bellarmino Center in Santiago, is universally recognized as one of the leading Catholic progressives, but he nevertheless believes in the continuing importance of religious symbolism. He feels, quite justifiedly, that respect for the Church is threatened under such allegedly advanced practices as the holding of the mass by a priest—who comes in off the street dressed in ordinary clothes rather than his vestments—at the ordi-

96. Antonio de Castro Mayer (Bispo de Campos), *Castidade, humildade, penitência: Características do cristão alicerces da ordem social,* Aug. 15, 1963 (São Paulo: Editôra Vera Cruz, 1963), pp. 25–29.

97. Alfonso Zaplana Bellizza (Obispo de Tacna), *Exhortación pastoral con motivo de las nuevas normas conciliares de la Iglesia,* Nov. 20, 1967.

nary supper meal of a Catholic family.[98] Since a great many other bishops and priests share such fears, they will at least serve to retard the pace of symbolic innovation in the Church.

One built-in check to rapid reorganization of the Church is its hierarchical organization and the advanced ages of the prelates who lead it. Despite the Vatican's recent urging that bishops offer to resign at age seventy-five, the pope's refusal to accept key resignations even at this advanced age means that many bishops still remain in their leadership positions for very considerable periods of time. In 1961, for example, 40 per cent of the bishops of the Argentine Church had been bishops since at least 1946. As José Luis de Imaz points out, this gave Church leaders a far longer continuance in office than was enjoyed by Argentine military or business leaders. At the time of the Church attack on Perón in 1954, seven Argentine bishops were over 65, ten were between 55 and 65, and only three were under 55.[99] The practice of tenure appointments similarly makes the average age of religious leaders significantly higher than that of their secular counterparts in the other Latin American countries, and modern medicine is now keeping the ruling prelates at the helm at even more advanced ages than in the past.

Hierarchy and episcopal longevity have occasioned numerous attacks on the administrative patterns of the Church, as priests resent the strict obedience that they must give to older bishops with whose ideas they disagree. Father Badanelli comments bitterly on the need to propagate bishops' ideas to the largely female congregations of Latin America, quipping that *"to obey,* canonically speaking, means to renounce all intellectual dignity in order to turn oneself into a lamb leading a flock of ewes. . . ."[100] Catholics have also become more sharply critical of the conservative members of the Latin American hierarchy. After describing a 1966 rebellion against the authority of the Argentine hierarchy, José Carlos Mújica

98. Interview with Renato Poblete Barth, S.J., in Santiago, Chile, July 28, 1968.
99. Imaz, *Los que mandan,* pp. 171–72.
100. Pedro Badanelli, *Perón, la Iglesia y un cura,* 4th ed. (Buenos Aires: Editorial Tartessos, 1960), p. 13. Badanelli's italics.

concludes that the Church in Argentina is suffering a structural crisis. The members of its structure suffer from "motivational asynchronism"; they respond to current problems with motivational patterns derived from the Catholic attitudes of such different times in the past that it is extraordinarily difficult for them to deal coherently with specific crises facing them here and now.[101] The same opinion appears in a 1966 editorial in *Inquietudes,* a liberal Colombian journal. As *Inquietudes* proclaims, "On one hand, we have a world becoming constantly more pluralistic, a Latin America in revolution through social change; on the other, a 'triumphalist' hierarchical structure, linked to an inadequate and unjust establishment."[102]

Despite such criticism and the statistical evidence on the conservatism and advanced ages of the hierarchy that can be marshaled to support it, a comparison of the ages and orientations of the religious hierarchies of the different Latin American countries indicates that no automatic correlation exists between advanced age and conservatism. At first, one might be tempted to explain the reputation for progressivism of the Chilean hierarchy in terms of its apparent youth. Instead of being men past the normal retirement age, twenty-two out of the twenty-seven Chilean bishops in 1959 were sixty years of age or younger, and eight of the bishops were under fifty. The average age of the Chilean hierarchy was 53.3 years.[103] When compared with neighboring republics, however, the Chilean hierarchy does not seem strikingly young. During the same year the average age of the Peruvian hierarchy was 51.1 years, while that in Bolivia was 55.8 years.[104] The Peruvian and Bolivian hierarchies were neither significantly older nor significantly

101. "A Church Revolt: Argentina," *CIF Reports* 5, no. 14 (July 16, 1966) : 107.

102. *Inquietudes* 2, no. 12 (Dec., 1966), as translated and reprinted in *CIF Reports* 6, no. 2 (Jan. 16, 1967) : 3.

103. For a careful survey of the ages of the Chilean hierarchy, showing their dates of birth and consecration and the percentage of bishops in different age groups, see Isidoro Alonso, Renato Poblete, and Gines Garrido, *La Iglesia en Chile: Estructuras eclesiásticas* (Bogotá: FERES, 1962), pp. 74, 201. To compare these Chilean data with those of other Latin American countries, the best statistical source is the *Annuario Pontificio* for the year in question.

104. Isidoro Alonso, Gines Garrido, Dammert Bellido, and Julio Tumiri, *La Iglesia en Perú y Bolivia: Estructuras eclesiásticas* (Bogotá: FERES, 1962), p. 184.

more conservative than that of Chile. Although age and degrees of progressiveness may correlate positively in individual cases, therefore, the comparison of age structures between the Chilean, Peruvian, and Bolivian hierarchies shows that such correlations cannot be generalized in aggregate terms. Tradition, environment, and individual background as well as age need to be analyzed and compared in explanations of the progressive viewpoint.

Hierarchical organization and lifetime tenure have not prevented an institutional liberalization in Latin American Catholicism that has become apparent in the evolving role of CELAM, the Latin American Bishops' Council which was founded in 1955. As Thomas Sanders emphasizes, the council was at first strongly conservative in its orientation.[105] Instead of locating the CELAM secretariat in a center of liberal Catholicism such as Santiago de Chile, the Vatican located it in the conservative stronghold of Bogotá, Colombia. Dom Jaime de Barros Câmara, the late cardinal archbishop of Rio de Janeiro, served as first president of CELAM from 1955 to 1959. Dom Jaime's interpretation of communism as Latin America's major problem has consistently aligned him with conservative forces. The orientation of CELAM shifted in 1959 when Archbishop Miguel Darío Miranda of Mexico City became president and when the two vice-presidential posts were filled by two of the leading progressives in the Latin American Church, Dom Hélder of Brazil and the late Bishop Manuel Larraín of Talca, Chile. The council has continued to be led by moderates and progressives, and they strengthened its new tendencies in 1963 with a complete reorganization and the creation of new departments including one on social action. Rather than reinforcing the conservatism of Latin American bishops as it originally did, therefore, CELAM has come to challenge and refashion that conservatism.

While the role of the Bishops' Council has thus changed significantly, a more fundamental issue in the debate over Church re-

105. For discussions of the changes of CELAM, see Thomas G. Sanders to Richard H. Nolte, July 17, 1967 (TGS-2 in series of field reports distributed by the Institute of Current World Affairs); and Cecilio de Lora Soria, S.M., "History, Structure, and Present Activities of CELAM," in Henry A. Landsberger, ed., *The Church and Social Change in Latin America* (Notre Dame, Ind.: University of Notre Dame Press, 1970).

structuring has been the assumption that enough priests will not be forthcoming to serve adequately the religious needs of Latin America's burgeoning population. Churchmen regularly use the supposition of inadequate native vocations to call either for large vocational campaigns or for the importation of foreign priests, so agilely sidestepping the fact that it is the explosion of population *in relation* to the number of priests that causes the most pressing inadequacies. On the other hand, critics from the left like Ivan Illich assume that the situation of the "vanishing clergyman" will require, not new vocations or more foreign priests, but fundamental reorientations in Church organization and practices. Although hard data on the growth of the Latin American priesthood cannot resolve this fundamental debate between the conservatives and the leftists, statistics can seriously question the immediacy of the crisis in clerical recruitment that both groups assume to be true.

Data on the inhabitants-per-priest ratio between 1949 and 1969 do in fact challenge this basic assumption. Tables 3 and 4 indicate, at five-year intervals between 1949 and 1969, the increasing numbers of priests and changes in the inhabitants-per-priest ratio for each of the twenty major Latin American countries.[106] Since the

106. These data were compiled from the editions of the *Annuario Pontificio* published by the Tipografia Poliglotta Vaticana in Vatican City in 1950, 1955, 1960, 1965, and 1970. The *Annuario* publishes, on a yearly basis, statistics for every diocese in the world on the number of diocesan priests, religious order priests resident in the diocese, nuns, brothers, seminarians, new priests ordained during the year, parishes, population, number of Catholics, and other related items. The *Annuario*, which is published during the middle of each calendar year, regularly provides statistics for the beginning of the preceding year, e.g., the 1970 *Annuario* prints data supplied by the diocesan Curias for the diocesan situation on Dec. 31, 1968. In cases where the Vatican does not receive up-to-date information from a particular diocese, it publishes the previous year's figures, and this situation leads to inadequacies in the data that it is virtually impossible to rectify after the fact.

Since the *Annuario* does not regularly provide data on the basis of countries or regions, I have calculated the national and aggregate inhabitants-per-priest ratios by determining the total number of priests and population in each country. The total population figures compiled in this way differ slightly—but not extensively—from other estimates of the yearly populations of the different Latin American republics. The *Annuario* population figures seem preferable for present purposes, because they reflect the estimates by personnel in each diocese of its current population and because they allow the calculation of the inhabitants-per-priest ratio for each diocese and the later comparison of figures for different types of dioceses. In the few cases where religious statistics for a particular diocese were not included in the *Annuario* for a given year, I have included an estimate of the relevant statistic which equals the mean

total number of priests in these republics rose from 26,825 to 44,818 during this period, the greater increase in their populations only made the inhabitants-per-priest ratio rise from 5,543 in 1949 to 6,063 in 1969. Furthermore, as Figure 2 graphically illustrates, the ratio actually went down in 1954 and again in 1959, rising again in 1964 and surpassing the 1949 level in 1969.

The assumption of a current recruitment crisis appears to be even more dubious when the countries are considered individually rather than in the aggregate. From 1949 to 1969, the inhabitants-per-priest ratio for twelve of the twenty republics went down, indicating that the growth in the priesthoods was faster than the growth in their general populations. This held true for all six of the Central American countries, and for such countries of inter-

---

between the figures given in the *Annuarios* for five years before and five years after the year in question.

It is difficult to compile religious statistics for whole countries from the *Annuario* much before 1950, because they were not reported on a regular basis in the earlier years. In 1945, for instance, all of the data for Brazil and Mexico are not listed, and neither are those for the subdiocesan units. Information on the number of priests or the inhabitants-per-priest ratio for earlier years must be drawn from other sources, as that on the Chilean ratio in 1750 and 1845 was drawn for Fig. 5 from Poblete, *Crisis sacerdotal,* p. 19. Data on individual dioceses are available well before 1950, however, and worthwhile research remains to be done in compiling and comparing the inhabitants-per-priest ratio and other information for dioceses in different countries and in urban and rural areas before and after 1950.

The religious statistics given above should be an improvement over those previously published in such compilations as Yvan Labelle and Adriana Estrada, *Latin America in Maps, Charts, Tables. No. 2: Socio-Religious Data* (*Catholicism*) (México: CIDOC, 1964). The Labelle and Estrada volume drew its data secondhand from FERES (the International Federation of Catholic Institutions of Social and Socio-Religious Research) and other sources. The data are completely inconsistent within the volume, as four different sets of figures are given for the number of priests and the inhabitants-per-priest ratio for the year 1960 (pp. 86, 90, 93, 96). Sometimes these errors are easy to trace, as when they arise from projecting 1960 figures from the 1957 edition of the *Annuario Pontificio* (p. 90), and in other cases they arise from widely differing estimates of the number of priests and from different sources of population estimates.

The contradictions of the Labelle and Estrada compilation contrast the consistency of the 1945–1965 statistics given in Isidoro Alonso, "Les statistiques religieuses en Amérique latine," *Social Compass* 14, nos. 5, 6 (1967). Although the Alonso data differ in the years considered from those provided above, both sets of data lead to the same practical and theoretical conclusions. Readers should, however, be aware of the problems involved in determining the religious statistics for Latin America and compare the methods of data-gathering as well as the resulting figures in different published sources.

Table 3: *Growth of the Latin American Priesthood, 1949–1969*

	1949	1954	1959	1964	1969
Argentina	3,900	4,434	4,731	5,232	5,530
Bolivia	504	612	689	788	855
Brazil	7,231	8,296	10,326	11,332	12,427
Chile	1,980	1,758	2,351	2,481	2,459
Colombia	2,874	3,586	3,807	5,191	4,858
Costa Rica	168	219	246	296	367
Cuba	620	670	723	225	215
Dominican Republic	162	190	310	382	446
Ecuador	892	1,093	1,201	1,403	1,585
El Salvador	214	241	277	355	395
Guatemala	132	195	298	464	517
Haiti	333	378	450	466	410
Honduras	130	125	156	206	260
Mexico	4,327	5,454	6,301	7,204	8,649
Nicaragua	167	198	222	281	300
Panama	120	142	171	198	257
Paraguay	292	265	312	411	446
Peru	1,346	1,542	1,770	2,225	2,311
Uruguay	649	740	688	797	627
Venezuela	784	1,097	1,292	1,871	1,904
Total:	26,825	31,235	36,321	41,808	44,818

mediate size as Venezuela and Peru, as well as for small countries like Bolivia, Ecuador, Paraguay, and the Dominican Republic. It was only in the largest republics—Brazil, Mexico, and Argentina—as well as in Chile, Colombia, Haiti, Cuba, and Uruguay, that the growth of the priesthood failed to surpass the growth in population.

The sheer weight of the Brazilian experience helps to account for the overall trend. Containing almost one-third of Latin Ameri-

Table 4: *Changes in the Inhabitant-per-Priest Ratio, 1949–1969*

	1949	1954	1959	1964	1969
Argentina	4,584	4,298	4,552	4,443	4,722
Bolivia	6,331	5,139	5,314	4,863	5,419
Brazil	6,802	6,627	6,166	6,940	7,764
Chile	2,794	3,454	3,064	3,064	3,443
Colombia	3,783	3,385	3,684	3,469	4,263
Costa Rica	7,937	4,175	4,400	4,300	4,347
Cuba	7,832	8,837	8,770	29,389	38,003
Dominican Republic	13,470	11,365	9,346	8,887	8,945
Ecuador	3,915	3,549	3,261	3,322	3,845
El Salvador	9,269	8,320	7,785	7,382	8,222
Guatemala	25,667	14,611	10,612	9,577	7,951
Haiti	8,874	8,579	7,644	7,960	11,005
Honduras	9,471	12,103	10,236	10,990	8,942
Mexico	5,183	4,765	4,985	5,249	5,947
Nicaragua	7,844	5,412	4,968	5,086	5,992
Panama	5,417	5,650	4,768	6,030	5,128
Paraguay	6,318	6,329	5,555	4,966	4,594
Peru	5,956	5,599	5,783	5,160	5,500
Uruguay	3,606	3,223	4,086	3,271	4,354
Venezuela	5,145	5,505	5,014	4,321	4,852
Total:	5,543	5,265	5,211	5,381	6,063

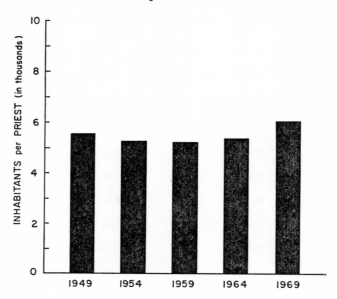

Figure 2: Average Number of Inhabitants per Priest in the Twenty Latin American Countries, 1949–1969

ca's population and nearly 28 per cent of its priests in 1969, Brazil's high inhabitants-per-priest ratio of 7,764 has significantly raised the twenty-republic average. As a comparison of Figures 2 and 3 makes clear, there was a close correspondence between changes in the Brazilian and the aggregate ratios during the twenty-year period.

Although the ratios for several other republics shifted even more radically during the two decades, most countries did not change to any great degree. The sharpest, contrasting alterations in the inhabitants-per-priest ratios appear in the cases of Cuba and Guatemala, shown in Figure 4. The Guatemalan ratio fell consistently from 25,667 in 1949 to 7,951 in 1969, in considerable part because of an influx of missionary priests from outside Guatemala. It naturally proved much easier to make the growth in the number of priests outdistance the rise in the population for a small country like Guatemala than it would have for a huge country like Brazil. In an opposing development, the Cuban ratio rose from 7,832 in 1949 to 38,003 in 1969, primarily because of

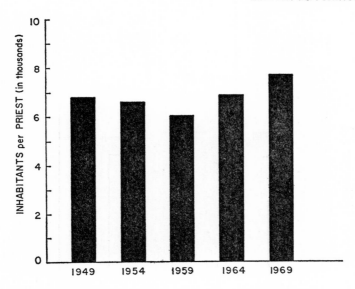

Figure 3: Inhabitants per Priest in Brazil, 1949–1969

Fidel Castro's expulsion of priests after 1960. The Cuban case shows the potential threat to the clergy from a socialist revolution, and it also neatly illustrates what the situation would be in Latin America if the number of priests were merely to stand still while the population of the region continued to grow at its present rate. The number of priests in Cuba fell only from 225 to 215 between 1964 and 1969, but—as Table 4 and Figure 4 illustrate—population growth during the same five years made the inhabitants-per-priest ratio rise significantly from 29,389 to 38,003.

In none of the other Latin American republics was change in the proportional size of the priesthood so great during the twenty years before 1969. Paraguay and the Dominican Republic experienced fairly steady reductions in their inhabitants-per-priest ratios, and the ratio in Costa Rica fell sharply after 1949. When the ratios are as high as Guatemala's 25,000 and 14,000 in 1949 and 1954, or Cuba's 29,000 or 38,000 in 1964 and 1969, there are already so many persons for every priest that regular pastoral care of any kind becomes virtually impossible. When the ratio falls from 6,318 to 4,594, however, as it did in Paraguay from 1949 to

187

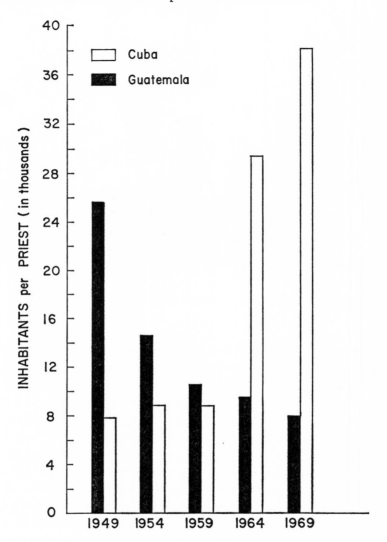

Figure 4: Inhabitants per Priest in Cuba and Guatemala, 1949–1969

1969, a real possibility exists for improved pastoral care. But few other republics experienced a decrease in the ratio as consistent or as significant as that of Paraguay, and, in such prominent countries as Chile or Brazil, the ratio rose considerably. In most coun-

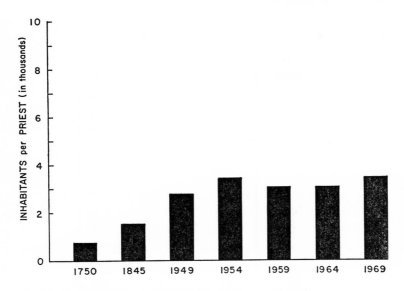

Figure 5: Inhabitants per Priest in Chile, 1750–1969

tries, such as Argentina, Peru, Ecuador, Panama, or Venezuela, the slight increase or decrease in the ratio simply did not show any major change at all.

In the short run, therefore, the experience of most Latin American countries does not support the contention that Church structures must change because growth in the priesthood cannot keep pace with the growth of the population. But the experience of the two decades after 1949 does not, of course, show what will happen during the last decades of the twentieth century, and much of the experience of this period may relate to temporary phenomena. The significant reduction in the aggregate inhabitants-per-priest ratio during the 1950's, for example, arose in no small part because of an influx of foreign priests. This influx was more feasible at the time, because of the forced exodus of missionary priests from China after the Communist victory in 1949.

Furthermore, when seen in the longer perspective of the last two centuries rather than recent decades, the relative size of the priesthood does in fact appear to be in dramatic decline. In the case of Chile, as Figure 5 illustrates, the inhabitants-per-priest ratio rose from some 779 in 1750, to 1,548 in 1845, to 2,794 in 1949, and to 3,443 in 1969. Over this longer period, such factors as the difficulties of a celibate priesthood in the sexually oriented context of Latin America, or the steady growth of appealing careers of service and personal advancement in secular society, would seem to have more significance than the short-term ability to send priests from other parts of the world to fill gaps in Latin America's native vocations.

In judging the future size of the Latin American clergy, evaluations must adequately account for the divergent and potentially misleading tendencies of related indicators. Research at the Rand Corporation has shown a strong and statistically significant relationship between per capita GNP and the size of the Catholic clergy in different Latin American countries; in population-related indices, wealthier countries also have more religious personnel. The correlation coefficient between the variables was 0.487, and its significance at the 5 per cent level provides considerable confidence in the relationship. A high correlation was also found between the proportion of religious personnel in different Latin American countries and the countries' levels of urbanization and the percentages of their working forces engaged in agriculture. Countries with greater urbanization, and lower proportions of their working force in agriculture, also have more religious personnel per 100,-000 population.[107]

These data do not indicate, however, that as per capita income in Latin America rises, the number of priests, brothers, and nuns will also rise. The past experience of this region suggests that per capita economic growth may be very slow and, even where it does move consistently ahead, this growth will not necessarily increase the proportion of clergymen. An analogy to earlier hypotheses in the theory of political development may be in order at this point. Among the most questionable aspects of the general literature on development have been the assumptions (1) that, after a certain

107. Luigi Einaudi, Richard Maullin, Alfred Stepan, and Michael Fleet, *Latin American Institutional Development: The Changing Catholic Church* (Santa Monica, Calif.: Rand Corporation, 1969), pp. 21–24. Since this study drew its data from the 1968 edition of the *Annuario Pontificio,* its Church statistics actually refer to the situation in 1967 rather than, as it claims, to the situation in 1968.

stage of growth has been reached, regular increases in per capita GNP will occur, (2) that this regular economic growth will provide the motor which drives society to become more politically participant and to evolve "democratic" institutions of government, and (3) that this general "development syndrome" can be effectively measured by such apparently objective and unambiguous indicators as the growth of urbanization. Latin American experience has not measured up to the canons of this "development syndrome," however. Despite modest increases in per capita income and urbanization, Latin America may continue to have strongly authoritarian tendencies in government and remain in what Alfred Stepan has called a situation of developmental "stagnation" and a "crisis of immobility."[108] By analogy, to generalize from the static picture of a correlation between per capita income and the proportion of religious personnel at one point in time may well be as misleading as these earlier generalizations about the assumed connection among Latin American economic growth, urbanization, and democracy.[109]

The fact that those Latin American countries with higher per capita incomes also tend to have more clergymen indicates most clearly, perhaps, that they can now afford to support the religious personnel, but it says nothing about vocational recruitment in the future. That recruitment depends in considerable part on the desire of young men to enter the priesthood, which in turn depends upon the perceived hardships and attractions of the priesthood as opposed to other occupations, upon the environmental encourage-

108. "Political Development Theory: The Latin American Experience," *Journal of International Affairs* 20, no. 2 (1966): 225, 234.

109. Another interesting parallel appears here between the situation of Catholicism and development in Latin America and the situation of the dominant Partido Revolucionario Institucional (PRI) in Mexico. In a manner similar to the above interpretation of Catholicism and development, Ames has found that, although the PRI has a lower percentage of electoral support in areas which are comparatively developed in terms of urbanization and related indices, this fact does not mean that the PRI will become weaker or lose its dominance in Mexican politics as development continues. As Ames rightly points out, such an interpretation of a weakening PRI, which one might draw from a static view of the present situation, is questionable in part because the PRI made its strongest electoral gains from 1952 to 1967 precisely in the most developed areas of Mexico. See Barry Ames, "Bases of Support for Mexico's Dominant Party," *American Political Science Review* 64, no. 1 (March, 1970).

ment or discouragement that the young man finds toward the priestly vocation, and particularly upon the availability or non-availability of a sympathetic priest with whom a boy can personally identify.[110] As the data on changes in the inhabitants-per-priest ratio indicate, priests are becoming scarcer in Latin America, even though the highest proportions of religious personnel are in the wealthier countries and even though Latin American countries are gradually increasing in per capita wealth. This trend does not show any sign of immediate reversal, so that more of the reasons for it need to be explored. In order to gauge more effectively the extent to which the recruitment patterns, attitudes, and institutions of Latin American Catholicism can permanently change in nature, it becomes necessary to evaluate the real causes and possible consequences of recent developments in the Church.

110. On the basis of survey research on the attitudes and backgrounds of seminarians and students who showed no interest in a religious vocation, Father Renato Poblete found that friendship and respect for an individual priest were of special importance in the vocational decision of young Chileans. Poblete, *Crisis sacerdotal*, pp. 170–71.

V ~

The Origins and Future of Activist Catholicism

       In order to gauge the likely future paths of activist Catholicism in Latin America, it is necessary to trace the genuine causes for the changes in Catholic approach that have become apparent so far. In a more limited sense, to estimate the future directions and rapidity of change in Catholic thought, one needs to consider the motive forces that have shaped its past evolution. Has the rise of Catholic progressivism come mainly in response to new economic and social currents, or has it responded to papal encyclicals, Vatican II, and the new trends in European Catholicism? Has it come in part from a fearful recognition of declining Church influence and, if so, what are its chances of overcoming such a decline? Differences of opinion both within and outside the Church have enshrouded such questions in controversy and have not provided clear answers on which churchmen could act. To the extent that clear answers do exist, however, they need to be carefully stated and evaluated as a basis for future action.

       With a justification that is more functional than it is rational, one cause for progressivism proposed by Catholic activists is predestination. Because they believe they are aiding a predetermined process, many Christian Democrats conceive of their role in social change in terms surprisingly similar to those of their Marxist opponents. Implicit assumptions about God's actions in history lead them to a belief in the inevitability of beneficial social development that, without the concepts of class conflict and revolution, strikingly resembles the vision of orthodox Marxism. As Rafael Caldera puts it, all the social structures of Latin America are going to change because "they have to change" and because "destiny and the needs of Latin America" require it. The role of Christian Democrats is therefore to "accelerate" this development.[1] More explicitly, Father Hoffman writes, "It seems that God is presently setting us free from undue preoccupations with the life and program of a religious institution—even with its reform and renewal—so that we may concern ourselves first with the suffering and hopes of man on the road to the future. . . ."[2] As in the case of Marxists who help along an historical program that they believe to be inevitable, Christian Democrats and churchmen frequently see themselves as playing a more effective role in the process of historical development because they understand the direction that the process is destined to take. It would be impossible to convince such leaders that alterations in human affairs do not ultimately depend on the decisions of the God in which they believe, and from the standpoint of sanctioning social change it would be counterproductive to question their assumption that God now wants such alterations. Although it seems helpful and reassuring to Christian Democrats and Church leaders to believe that their new attitudes and roles are foreordained, the secular causes of those attitudes and roles run far deeper and are far more complex.

The experience of Latin American Catholicism questions not only a theological interpretation through predestination but also a sociological interpretation through moral continuity. In one of the most challenging views of causation presented so far, Pareto

1. *El bloque latinoamericano* (Santiago de Chile: Editorial del Pacífico, 1961), p. 109.
2. Ronan Hoffman, O.F.M., "Social Change in Latin America: The Mission of the Church," *CIF Reports* 6, no. 8 (April 16, 1967): 67.

saw what he called "Catholic Modernism" in terms of static moral precepts. As "the Divinity of Christ is now disappearing to make room for the Divinity of Humanity," Pareto believed that "neo-Christianity keeps the morality of traditional Christianity, changes the theology, and justifies the change by the common morality."[3] Pareto may have been premature in this early analysis of Catholic modernism, however. Since he published *A Treatise on General Sociology* in 1916, Catholic questioning of older moral precepts on birth control, the acceptance of human inequalities and subordination, and the value of meek acceptance of poverty indicates considerable rethinking in the area of morals.

If this is so, then how does the chain of social causality differ from that suggested by Pareto? It may do so in that changes in the needs of society allow changes in morality, which in turn produce changes in theological justifications. Many social needs such as the general prohibitions against murder or incest do not change, so that much of traditional morality appears to remain the same. Despite this appearance of moral continuity, however, morality may be the key transitional entity, affected by shifts in social requisites and through shifts in theology. Although theology at times changes more sharply and more perceptibly than morality in order to justify the new moral climate, it may do so in reality only to maintain the morality necessary in an altered social situation.

SOCIAL AND ECONOMIC ADAPTATION

In Latin America as elsewhere, religion adapts to the environment in which it exists. As a result, social and economic developments within Latin America have generally influenced the progressive thrust of contemporary Catholicism far more than have directives from Rome or the thinking of foreign intellectuals. Latin Americans have become dissatisfied with the slow rates of change in their

3. Vilfredo Pareto, *The Mind and Society: A Treatise on General Sociology,* trans. Andrew Bongiorno and Arthur Livingston, 4 vols. (New York: Dover Publications, 1963), 3: 1070–73.

societies, especially as they have become more generally aware of the possibility of twentieth-century technology and the example of the developed nations of Europe and North America. Spurred on by leaders like Lázaro Cárdenas, Luis Muñoz Marín, or Juan Perón, Latin Americans increasingly demand at least verbal protestations of the need for secular progress even from the leaders of such traditional institutions as the army or the Church. The thought and statements of Latin American clergyman have shifted as they have come to recognize both the possibility of social development and the general demand for it.

In a fundamental sense, alterations in religious thought and doctrine depend either upon new functions that the religion performs or upon new techniques through which it performs more traditional functions. Following Freud, Ostow and Scharfstein find that religion has "three functions: to exorcise the terrors of nature, to reconcile man to the cruelty of fate, and to make amends for the painful restraints that communal life imposes."[4] If these continue to be the primary functions of Latin American Catholicism, however, the changing nature of technology and social relationships is altering the ways in which the functions are performed, and the different life situations and expectations of Latin American classes and social groups are establishing variant patterns in which the functions are performed. Technology has given men greater control over nature and reduced their fear of it, while such groups as Haitian peasants or Yucatecan and Andean Indians, who still feel subject to the terrors of nature, calm their fears through vodun or traditional Indian beliefs with only a veneer of Catholicism. Even for the lower groups whom urbanization is bringing into close proximity to the wealth of others, the realization of material gains by upper and middle groups has made the "cruelty of fate" seem less certain and the "restraints of communal life" less unavoidably painful.

Poverty for most Latin Americans has seemed distressingly constant, despite new beliefs that it can be overcome on a more massive scale. Although the Church has amassed considerable ma-

4. Mortimer Ostow and Ben-Ami Scharfstein, *The Need To Believe: The Psychology of Religion* (New York: International Universities Press, 1954), p. 147.

terial wealth in comparison to other sectors of society, it has operated in a context of poverty that remains remote from the experience of middle-class North Americans. Viteri elucidates the difference in context, writing that:

Church buildings in the States are simple, bright, functional. Church buildings in Latin America are old if not ancient, of complicated architecture; many of them bear fortunes in gold and gold leaf and in the labor of artisans who were unhampered by any conflict between the perfection of their work and the time in which it had to be achieved. These pieces of history are crowded with an invisible army of fleas, coming and going with the occupants of the pews. When money is to be contributed, you see in the United States the almost military movements of collectors parading baskets before the people, who drop in envelopes with bills of all denominations. In Latin-American churches, a little girl or an old woman dressed in mourning black goes around with a small platter receiving the sporadic fraction of a peso, sol, bolivar, or sucre that might have bought a few more drops of watery milk for the baby at home.[5]

It is in part to change this atmosphere of degrading poverty that surrounds their parishioners and themselves that Catholic leaders have taken the progressive stands. Behind their decision to do so lie the technological innovations that have made social progress possible.

When confronted with the situation of poverty, Catholic activists have alternately responded with intensive study of the issues involved and with the proposal that the Church should turn away from concern with religious ritual in order to concentrate on aiding the common people. Latin American Jesuits have made particular contributions in the areas of research and teaching. In addition to the widely known and circulated studies that have come from such Jesuit research centers as the Centro Bellarmino in Santiago, Chile, other Jesuit groups—in countries as disparate as Paraguay and Venezuela—have produced long, important studies of national development whose distribution in mimeographed form has been

5. Miguel H. Viteri, *For a Federated Latin America: The One Answer to Twenty Problems* (New York: Exposition Press, 1965), pp. 10–11.

largely limited to the countries involved.[6] On the other hand, stressing commitment rather than analysis, Father Clark is typical of many other activists in averring that the Church "must serve the poor at great cost to itself. It ought to abandon the rich, who can always provide for their religious needs, and become the servant of the people."[7] By neglecting the rich, the Church would seem to be in danger of losing a prime source of its support. To Father Clark and others, however, a full-fledged championing of the interests of the Latin American masses appears to be the only way to maintain the long-run influence of the Church. Therefore, such calls for abandonment of the rich in fact demand reorientation in order to maintain rather than to dismiss the authority of the Church.

If poverty is a conscience-provoking phenomenon that encourages Catholic progressivism, it is also a theoretical justification that progressives invoke for their movement. Most churchmen argue that deficiency in "moral capacity" results from inadequate living conditions, and that the Church must consequently work to improve those conditions in order to help parishioners to follow its moral teachings. Superficially, this reasoning seems to be both in keeping with the higher proportion of practicing Catholics found among high-income groups in Latin America, and analogous to arguments frequently made to the effect that atheistic communism flourishes best among the poor. In fact, however, this interpretation is substantially mistaken on both counts.

The widely discussed, contemporary breakdown in morality in economically prosperous parts of "advanced" countries such as Sweden, Italy, or the United States indicates that increased prosperity is no automatic safeguard of traditional Christian morality, in either Catholic or non-Catholic countries. The Church is certainly right from its own standpoint to try to win the allegiance of new members of the middle class away from secular orientations,

6. See, for instance, "Paraguay: Survey, S.J.; Datos generales," mimeographed (Asunción, 1968); José Martínez Terrero, S.J., "Las cooperativas de Venezuela," mimeographed (Caracas: Centro Gumilla, 1968); and Carlos Acedo Mendoza, "El problema de la vivienda en Venezuela," and Ramón H. Silva T., "Introducción al estudio del sindicalismo venezolano," mimeographed (Caracas: Centro Gumilla, 1968).

7. James A. Clark, *The Church and the Crisis in the Dominican Republic* (Westminster, Md.: Newman Press, 1967), p. 201.

but it is questionable whether acceptance of the old Christian morality is a necessary concomitant of their middle-class status. It may have been merely a general concomitant of that status during an earlier stage of Western civilization. Moreover, while increased leisure and literacy have made members of upper-class groups in Latin America better able to grasp the intellectual content of Catholicism, their wealth and power have not made them obey the moral edicts of the Church. Latin American men frequently keep a mistress as soon as they have enough capital to do so, using the mistress as a sign of success. The fidelity of their upper- and middle-class wives is certainly reinforced by Church teachings, but it is enforced in the first instance by the fact that, in masculine-dominated households, men have simply not allowed their wives to have affairs. On the related issue of communism flourishing among the poor, the past success of communism in prosperous countries such as France and Italy and the general rejection of it in far less prosperous countries such as India serve as a similar warning against common generalizations. Although the "moral capacity" argument thus rests on dubious intellectual foundations, its apparent logic has won wide acceptance. By serving as a ready justification for the present social teachings of the Church, the argument supports actions that seem worthwhile on other grounds even to observers who question its inherent validity.

Coinciding with new attitudes toward poverty, technology has spurred the new lines of Catholic thought in several ways. First, the technological possibility of materially raising the living standards of the broad mass of national populations has led to outcries that living standards actually be raised. As Eduardo Frei commented in 1967, "Our people know that they are living in poverty in a hemisphere full of riches. There is not only poverty in many sectors, but also consciousness of that poverty and of the real possibility of overcoming it."[8] Secondly, as technology has also given men new devices of self-destruction and repression, Church leaders have spoken out against warfare and repression. Thermonuclear weaponry allows a handful of men to make ultimate decisions

8. Quoted in *Christian Science Monitor,* May 5, 1967.

on the survival of most of mankind, and papal statements on the need for world peace repeatedly call upon both camps in the Cold War to prevent this possibility. In such Latin American countries as Perón's Argentina, cattle prods, machine guns, and tanks have helped to keep domestic groups subservient to a dictator. Here, partially under the influence of the new Catholic thought, many clergymen have condemned the use of the new technology for selfish and inhumane ends. Thermonuclear weapons have posed the more pressing danger, and Catholic statements have been more outspoken on it than they have on the dangerous issue of opposing regimes that appear dictatorial. When repressive uses of the new technology become more and more evident as they did in the case of Perón, however, the opposition of the Church has correspondingly increased. Limitations on the Church itself naturally call forth the bitterest clerical opposition, and the Church has championed the repression of its enemies by such leaders as Francisco Franco. Opposition to the dictatorial uses of the new technology results in part from the democratic tendencies of Catholic thought; it cannot be strong when democratic ideals are weak within the Catholic thought of a particular country.

In still another sense, scientific and technological changes have occasioned an examination of traditional Christian doctrines that carries over from the scientific to the social plane. When the theories of Copernicus gained ascendancy among astronomers, for example, Catholic thought gave up its insistence that Aristotelian theories of astronomy be accepted as part of the Christian faith. Rejection of the notion that the earth lay at the center of the spheres gave men a new perspective on themselves. Moreover, it showed that traditional doctrines of the Church were subject to major revision, opening the possibility of revision in such social doctrines as the advocacy of humility in ascriptive feudal societies. As churchmen and citizens have come to depend more and more upon rational modes of inquiry, the nature of Latin American Catholic thought has changed partly in response to the growing rationality of its audience. Pardo de Leygonier blames the lack of sophistication in Latin American Catholicism on the colonial situation in which missionaries became sorcerers and made up stories to cajole credulous natives into accepting Catholic beliefs. There was a need to control the Indians, so the missionaries played upon credulity rather than rationality and allowed the authoritarian tendencies of the autochthonous cultures to take precedence over the evolving democratic tendencies in Catholicism.[9] This view correctly finds that the level of general sophistication in Catholic thought adapts to the level of its mass audience; later developments in both Catholic thought and its audience bear out this interpretation. As the great majority of Latin Americans have become better educated and more concerned to improve their economic positions, Catholic thought has become less miraculous and more oriented to socioeconomic controversies.

Emphasis upon the rationalistic component of technological innovation led Sigmund Freud to predict the demise of religion. On the basis of Freud's analysis, one can interpret the trend from formalism to Christian humanism as resulting from the spread of general education and the "scientific spirit." Freud, who defines religion as an illusion that people are finding less and less credible, suggests that natural science now shows up the errors of religious dogma while anthropology illuminates the "fatal resemblance" between the religious notions that we revere and the religious beliefs of primitive tribes that we decry. The spread of education similarly makes religion incredible. Freud differentiates the stages of religious decline, finding that "the greater the number of men to whom the treasures of knowledge become accessible, the more widespread is the falling-away from religious belief—at first only from its obsolete and objectionable trappings, but later from its fundamental postulates as well."[10] If Freud's analysis is correct, then the shift toward Christian humanism in Catholic thought foreshadows a trend toward a kind of humanism devoid of its specifically Christian component. Interpreted in this way, the progressive tendencies of Latin American Catholic thought represent

---

9. G. F. Pardo de Leygonier, "Chrétienté Latino-Américaine," in Raymond Aron and others, *L'Église, l'Occident, le Monde* (Paris: Librairie Arthème Fayard, 1956), pp. 137–40.
10. Sigmund Freud, *The Future of an Illusion,* trans. W. D. Robson-Scott (Garden City, N. Y.: Doubleday & Company, 1964), pp. 62–63.

the stage in religious decline wherein sincere Catholics are rejecting the old "trappings" but still accepting the "fundamental postulates" of religion.

Technological innovation has also encouraged the reorganization and reorientation of religious communities. During the Middle Ages, the seclusion of monasteries and nunneries allowed them to fill important social needs. Through their isolation from the everyday mainstreams of the secular world, they provided sanctuaries and outlets for the humanitarian values and intellectual concerns that were largely absent from the rough world around them. The remoteness of the convent has become a social liability rather than an asset, however, with the rise of a new material technology, mass literacy and education, physical and occupational mobility, and the egalitarian ethic of welfare-state humanism. To individuals who desire a life of service to their fellow men, direct participation in the processes of social change seems more productive than a life of contemplation and purely religious devotion. Institutional attitudes and relationships within the Church can be expected to adapt to changing circumstances, therefore, and such a process of adaptation certainly seems to be well underway.

The practical issues that are evident in Latin America also appear in the radically different context of the United States, where restlessness and a desire to alleviate poverty and to utilize more fully the human talent of the Church have caught up many North American Catholics. A recent survey found that new vocations among United States nuns were down by nearly 50 per cent in a single year, and that out of approximately 180,000 sisters in the United States the dropout rate among professed sisters had reached 3,600 per year. These nuns rejected their vows not to give up their religion but to work more directly in civil rights and other fields. Lupe Anguiano, who left Our Lady of Victory Missionary Sisters after seventeen years in the order, typically went to work in Los Angeles in a federal antipoverty program. Decrying "the tremendous talent going to waste in the convents," she told an interviewer that "the Church is caught up with the status quo. Those in charge believe in the institution rather than in the people it should

try to serve."[11] Ironically, this deep commitment to activist humanism was propagated by Pope John XXIII in an attempt to alter the
very status quo that Lupe Anguiano rejects.

The worldwide influences of technological and social change do
not mean that ecclesiastical innovation in Latin America will
become a carbon copy of that in other parts of the world, because
the incentives for change outside Latin America frequently do
not operate within the particular contexts of the region itself. In
the United States, for example, pressures to secularize Catholic
universities have arisen through the growing strength of trade unionism and government subsidies. After stubborn resistance by both
clerical and lay faculty members at Saint John's University who
were dismissed partly over the issue of union affiliation, many
other Catholic universities in the United States have reconsidered
giving the faculty a major voice in administrative decisions. Since
courts in Maryland decided to withhold government funds from
institutions under purely religious control as a violation of the
separation of Church and State, many Catholic universities have
advocated increased secular participation on their governing boards
as a way to maintain the vital flow of public support. In the context
of Latin America, however, where professors do not form their own
pressure groups and where there is no tradition of a strict, North
American separation of Church and State, the twin forces of
unionism and government subsidies have had no similar effects.

Despite the inapplicability of the situations found in some foreign contexts, the supposition that Catholic humanism has arisen
from social factors in the Latin American environment is supported
by the fact that secular expressions of identical sentiments have
arisen simultaneously. The idea of creating greater social and
economic equality among the social classes of the area is neither
new nor exclusively Catholic in its Latin American application.
Manuel González Prada, who died in 1918, is only one of numerous intellectuals to set forth a social ethic strikingly similar to the
developing ideals of Catholic humanism. González Prada summed

11. Quoted in Robert Blair Kaiser, "The Nuns That Quit," *Ladies' Home Journal*
84, no. 4 (April, 1967) : 83, 140.

up his approach in two words, *Seamos justos,* "We must be just." Sensing the higher standards of living which could be realized in the twentieth century and calling for these standards to be extended to all classes, he wrote that:

Birth imposes on us the obligation to live, and this obligation gives us the right to grasp not only what is necessary but also what is comfortable and pleasant. . . . If the earth is a ship and we are passengers, let us do what we can to travel first class, with fresh air, a good berth and good food, instead of resigning ourselves to stay in the hold of the ship where pestilential air is breathed, rotting boards are slept on, and refuse from the fortunate is the only food.[12]

The difference between secular writers like González Prada and the Catholic humanists is not one of goals so much as it is one of the metaphysical rationale by which those human goals are justified.

Institutional self-interest works alongside the forces of conscience and technological innovation to change Latin American Catholicism. Progressive clergymen believe that ecclesiastical institutions can survive only if they adapt to changing environments. As devout but also deeply humanistic individuals, they want to preserve the Church for both religious and humanistic ends. Dom Hélder Câmara typically alleges that, in Brazil, "the Church must join the battle for development and social justice so that, later, people will not say the Church deserted them in their hour of need because it was compromised with big business. If that happens, the Church will suffer the consequences. The people will stay with the Church only in the measure that it is courageous in its defense of the people, and they will leave it in the measure that it is cowardly."[13] This interpretation sees Catholic participation in the struggle for social justice as vital to the preservation of the Church itself.

In this situation, given the proliferation of secular ideologies during the past hundred years, a need for accommodation has

12. Manuel González Prada, "El intelectual y el obrero," in Abelardo Villegas, ed., *Antología del pensamiento social y político de América Latina* (Washington, D. C.: Unión Panamericana, 1964), pp. 596–97.

13. Quoted in David St. Clair, "The Battling Bishop of Brazil," *The Sign* 44, no. 4 (Nov., 1964): 46.

supported increased diversity in Catholic attitudes toward competing, secular groups. If the Church in a particular country or region uniformly gives aid only to one type of movement in politics, the Church will be rewarded if that movement is successful in grasping and holding power. But a narrow political orientation aids the Church only so long as the orientation supports the dominant secular group. If, on the other hand, conservative, socialist, and populist movements all have some chance to come to power, then the Church is greatly aided by having a diversity of wings, at least one of which can make an effective rapprochement to whatever movement takes power at a particular time. In this sense it is partly a practical accommodation to the significantly enlarged ideological spectrum of competing power groups in twentieth-century Latin America that accounts for the increased diversity in the positions of Catholic spokesmen.

Similarly, some Catholics oppose dictators not so much from religious conviction as from individual self-interest. Complaining loudly about Castro's dictatorship and betrayal of the Church, a self-styled member of the Cuban middle class explained in 1962 that Castro would bring "extinction for the middle class."[14] Although dictators can hardly extinguish classes as such, they can displace many would-be members of those classes. Such individuals denounce the dictators and emphasize religious persecution as part of their denunciations. While opposition to the Church helps to alienate a dictator from parts of the populace, the dictator's threat to the economic and political interests of particular groups or individuals is a still surer way to alienate them from him.

With a secure foundation in a much broader form of mutual self-interest, support for progressive policies by Church and State may also result from common opposition to a third force or to common problems. This happened in the clerical conciliation in Mexico,[15] where the alliance between nationalist reformers and

14. David Finley, "One Cuban vs. Castro," *The Sign* 41, no. 9 (April, 1962) : 12. Instead of causing the "extinction" of the Cuban middle class, Castro's influence has been to replace the independent shopkeepers who once formed part of it with equally "middle-class" government workers.

15. See Frederick C. Turner, "The Compatibility of Church and State in Mexico," *Journal of Inter-American Studies* 9, no. 4 (Oct., 1967); and James W. Wilkie,

the Church dates back to the administration of Lázaro Cárdenas from 1934 to 1940. Cárdenas, in order to gain the support from Church leaders which proved useful in his expropriation of American oil companies, had to overcome his own reputation for anticlericalism. As a gesture of moderation to Mexican churchmen, he formally rejected Garrido Canabal, a vehement opponent of the Church from Tabasco. When in 1935 Garrido Canabal was ejected from the cabinet and forced into exile in South America, Catholic leaders became convinced of their propriety in supporting Cárdenas over Calles. Just as the Mexicans joined to uphold oil nationalization in the face of United States pressure, so Chilean churchmen and politicians have increased their attacks on poverty and inequalities as they have each become more urgently aware of the pressures of underdevelopment and Marxism. The kinds of pressures that may occasion the growth of Catholic progressivism, therefore, include the threats of foreign encroachment, domestic factionalism, and a kind of poverty that is defined as alienating citizens from both Church and State.

The timing of the progressive movement—both between countries and within Latin America as a whole—further indicates its direct relationship to a sense of dependence upon the mass of citizens. In Chile, the country longest noted for Catholic progressivism, a comparative lack of wealth has promoted the liberal policies of the Church. In a context where churchmen never amassed anything comparable to the wealth of the Mexican or the Peruvian Church, Chileans have long sanctified the ethic if not the practice of political egalitarianism. For Latin America as a whole, the inherited wealth of the Church has set it apart from real dependence on the common people, giving members of the clerical hierarchy far more conservative inclinations. In a 1942 study designed to increase the amount of money given to Protestant churches in Cuba, J. Merle Davis underscored this point by complaining that a major barrier to increasing financial revenues was the Catholic tradition of only irregular support in which the Protestant converts had grown up. The Catholic Church had so much inherited property

"Statistical Indicators of the Impact of National Revolution on the Catholic Church in Mexico, 1910–1967," *Journal of Church and State* 12, no. 1 (Winter, 1970).

and such ready access to men of wealth that, in contrast to the Protestants, it was not dependent on the free-will offerings of its members.[16] The Church no longer finds contributions from wealthy conservatives to be sufficient for its expanding needs, however, and both the growing potential of middle-class support and the alienation of some conservatives through the new Catholic progressivism require a broadening of the financial base from which the Church operates.

Both financial and political necessity have thus forced the Church to depend more and more upon a variety of groups now gaining positions of power. One of the most pervasive shifts in Catholic attitudes is the attempt to build support for the Church among the mass of citizens rather than relying in a political sense upon the backing of a narrow stratum of the old aristocracy or the self-made caudillos who once dominated the political process in most of Latin America. A sense of religious dedication has long prompted Catholic missioners to expand and deepen the religious commitment of the "nominal" Catholics in the area, but the new concern with the creation of social awareness has more earthly and immediate causes. As Father Camilo Torres observed in the Colombian case, mass rural violence opens new avenues of social mobility and can convert the peasantry into a "majoritarian pressure group."[17] Concern to broaden the real base of Catholic support is a pragmatic response to apparent developments in Latin American politics. As lower groups which were once marginal in terms of both economic and political power have come to demand and in some areas receive a fuller share of power, support from them has come to be more directly relevant to the institutional position of the Church. Churchmen have therefore acted to build that support.

The rise of the Latin American middle class, which stems in large part from economic innovation and the spread of advanced

16. *The Cuban Church in a Sugar Economy: A Study of the Economic and Social Basis of the Evangelical Church in Cuba* (New York: Department of Social and Economic Research & Counsel, International Missionary Council, 1942), pp. 80–82.

17. Camilo Torres Restrepo, "La violencia y los cambios socio-culturales en las áreas rurales colombianas," in *Por el Padre Camilo Torres Restrepo (1956–1966)* (Cuernavaca, Mor.: CIDOC, 1967), p. 165.

technology in industry and agriculture, has also worked to alter Catholic attitudes. In 1932 Ryan found that sharp class distinctions in Chile characteristically prevented joint action by Chilean Catholics and impeded the work of such groups as Catholic Action.[18] Although factionalism still characterizes Chilean politics, a disproportionate growth of the middle class has nevertheless eroded the strength of wealthy groups and created a middle-income group which has a vested interest in economic modernization. After seeing what Theodore Draper analyzes as Fidel Castro's "betrayal" of the middle-class revolution that he led in the late 1950's, many members of the middle class prefer to see modernization come with political stability rather than violence. In this context, they have tied their calls for reform to their religious beliefs and to the evolving pattern of Catholic humanism.

Since Latin American university students have the option of giving their allegiance to a wide range of secular ideologies, the Church must try to formulate its doctrines in a manner that will increase its appeal among them. As a leader of Juventud Cristiana Venezolana points out, Latin American youth has undergone an ideological, moral, and spiritual "disorientation" because of the clash of contemporary ideologies.[19] University students are particularly important in Latin American politics, since their small number assures most graduates of a leading role in society and since they regularly take a much more direct part in national politics than North American students have traditionally taken. Furthermore, like young people in other countries, Latin American students are far more impatient for change and more disdainful of past solutions than are their elders. In necessarily trying to capture and hold the allegiance of students and of youth, Catholic leaders have been encouraged to press harder for social reform.

Finally, the twentieth-century enfranchisement of Latin American women has further enlarged the sense of responsibility of Catholic political leaders. As William Clawson emphasizes in the

18. Edwin Ryan, *The Church in the South American Republics* (New York: Bruce Publishing Company, 1932), p. 56.

19. For the details of this position presented by José Hoffman, see *El Universal* (Caracas), Feb. 5, 1965.

case of Mexico, anticlericalism flourished until recently in a situation where the most faithful Catholics were women who had no direct political power.[20] During the 1940's and 1950's most Latin American women gained the franchise and the right to run for office, however, and their new power has increased the electoral chances of Catholic candidates who identify their programs in some way with the teachings of the Church. As in the Chilean presidential election of 1964, feminine support can provide a crucial margin of victory. Women have also become more active in interest groups and in industry, and by doing so they have made political leaders dependent upon a wider political base than was necessary for either the caudillo or the official elected with more limited suffrage. In order to win support from women as well as from students and from the middle and lower classes, therefore, both churchmen and secular politicians have drawn up programs that combine a sense of "Christian responsibility" with promises of reform.

PAPAL PRONOUNCEMENTS: AMBIGUITY AND REINFORCEMENT

In contrast to the social and economic forces that are working to alter the pattern of Catholic thought and action, many churchmen suggest that Catholic thought in Latin America has acquired more progressive dimensions because it has taken up the message of papal encyclicals. While encyclicals are far from the only cause of changing attitudes, they have picked up, expanded, and reinforced the themes of progressive Catholicism. In order to understand why they have not done so more consistently or more openly, one needs to appreciate the severe restraints that Church politics imposes upon papal innovation.

The effects of papal encyclicals should not be exaggerated, because strong forces of popular ignorance of their message, elitist reaction against their message, and a pattern of only partial alle-

20. William Marion Clawson, "The Influence of the Catholic Church on the Development of the Mexican Government and Its Relationship to Protestant Missions" (D.Th. diss., New Orleans Baptist Theological Seminary, 1960), p. 196.

giance to the authority that they represent all militate against them. The impact of a pope's proclamations depends on the degree of respect afforded them. As Edward Gibbon commented long ago, "The spiritual thunders of the Vatican depend on the force of opinion; and if that opinion be supplanted by reason or passion, the sound may idly waste itself in the air."[21] Advocacy of social reform by John XXIII and Paul VI has tried to win respect for papal authority from the mass of citizens who desire reform, but it has tried to do so without fully losing the respect of the powerful conservatives who oppose innovation. While the progressive encyclicals have won popular approval, their temperate tone and the conservative pronouncements of national churchmen have dampened their effect. The degree of respect for papal authority remains so narrow and so circumscribed by other forces in its attempt to influence the actual behavior of citizens, that the impact of the encyclicals is far more limited than their champions have proclaimed.

The traditional attitudes and power structure in Latin America have kept popes from speaking out more decisively. As Monsignor Cardijn, the founder of Jeunesse Ouvrière Chrétienne, commented after a trip through the region, if Pope Pius XII had come to most of the Latin American countries to speak on social problems, he would have been "jailed or expelled as a Communist."[22] In practice, Latin American churchmen have long acted as if papal jurisdiction were not uniformly binding on them. Despite strong papal opposition to Freemasonry, virtually all priests in Brazil were Freemasons by the middle of the nineteenth century. More than half of the Brazilian priesthood continued to be Masons as late as 1870, even after the Masonic movement in Brazil had developed open opposition to the papacy,[23] so that more stringent enforcement of papal directives would almost surely have caused disaffections.

In the present period as well, taking positive stands on pressing

21. *The Decline and Fall of the Roman Empire,* 3 vols. (New York: Random House, n.d.), 3: 855–56.
22. Quoted in Daniel E. Núñez (Bishop of David) to Frederick C. Turner, David, Nov. 13, 1967.
23. Ryan, *The Church in the South American Republics,* pp. 89–90.

issues in the secular world holds out real danger for the institutional position of the Church. As Xavier Rynne quipped during Vatican II, "It is said of one noted Jesuit theologian that he had his first doubt about infallibility the day he discovered that the reigning pontiff disagreed with one of his opinions."[24] It is far easier to maintain the facade of Catholic unity when episcopal statements are phrased in ambiguous language and, given the very real splits in Catholic attitudes, it is also much safer to do so. Vague statements on the need for "reform" or "social justice" bother no one, because every Catholic can interpret them according to his own viewpoint. To the extent that Catholic progressives institute activist programs of social change or ecclesiastical innovation, however, they naturally come into open conflict with the traditionalists in their own Church. The reforms that Pope John set moving through Vatican II have merely whetted the appetites of the avant-garde, although they have caused conservatives to question seriously where the Church is going. Catholics face the disquieting situation of innovations that bring underlying conflicts out in the open. Paradoxically, the innovations that were designed to produce unity have also produced growing self-awareness among the ideological factions within the Church.

The spectrum of Latin American Catholicism has made Vatican planning even more difficult. Latin Americans appreciate this fact, as sociologists have indicated the radically different religious orientations of groups in the area and shown that a particular papal policy will have very different effects among these groups. Luis Leñero O., for instance, differentiates the Mexican population into a 10 per cent Indian group with an "archaic" orientation, a 60 per cent majoritarian group with a "traditional rural" orientation, and a 30 per cent "modernist" group with an "urban-industrial" orientation. The Indian group interprets Catholicism in terms of the ancient Indian symbols and beliefs, while the rural traditionalists see it essentially in terms of the stereotyped conflict between Church and State in Mexican history. The urban modernists are

24. Xavier Rynne (pseudonym), *Letters from Vatican City. Vatican Council II* (*First Session*): *Background and Debates* (Garden City, N. Y.: Doubleday & Company, 1964), p. 237.

themselves split into numerous subgroups according to such criteria as their familiarity with changes in the Church outside Mexico, their desire for ecclesiastical reform, and the degree of their personal belief and practice of religious precepts.[25]

Differing social and religious ethics will naturally affect these groups in different ways. Paternalism brings the Indian group into progressive contact with the broader society, while it works to a certain extent as a useful social regulator in a traditional rural environment which lacks modern technology. In the modern urban environment, however, paternalism is a regressive ethic that produces social tension and underdevelopment. As Leñero emphasizes, Vatican planning is difficult because it must formulate policies which simultaneously consider the different levels of development, religious orientations, and changes going on among such groups in Latin America.[26] When differences between countries, ideological conflicts among Church leaders, and the worldwide endeavors of the Church are added to these problems of group separateness, the difficulty of overall Vatican planning becomes obvious.

These difficulties have led the Vatican to appeal for unity and to dress social pronouncements in ambiguous language. In one of the most characteristic types of pontifical statement, Pope Paul VI stresses the need for unity among individuals, among groups, and among republics in Latin America in order to realize the social goals of the region.[27] Papal pronouncements on Latin America go on to praise the recent efforts of Church personnel, invoke biblical statements to urge even greater efforts during the present period, and call attention to such issues as the need for vocations, activity among students and youth, and new religious uses of mass media. They demand social action to avoid violence and disorder, but they are careful not to prescribe specific reforms

25. Luis Leñero O., "Desarrollo y cambio socio-religioso," *Desarrollo,* no. 6 (enero-febrero, 1966): 26–27, 31–43.

26. *Ibid.,* pp. 15, 31, 42.

27. See the letter of Pope Paul to the Latin American bishops dated Sept. 29, 1966. The letter appeared in *L'Osservatore Romano* on Oct. 10, 1966, and is reprinted in *Notiziario della Pontificia Commissione per l'America Latina,* no. 10 (Nov., 1967): 6–9.

that would alienate particular groups, governments, and even seg-ments of the Latin American clergy.[28]

Resistance to innovation is built into the institutional process of episcopal selection and retirement. The fact that bishops can re-nounce their sees does not actually alter the older age structure and general conservatism of the hierarchy as much as it might appear to do. Canon law has long allowed the voluntary renuncia-tion of sees, and numerous bishops in the modern period have availed themselves of this privilege. There is no age at which retirement becomes mandatory, however, and popes have been most reluctant to use their power to force resignations. Further-more, when new bishops are selected, a pope regularly consults with existing bishops and with the papal nuncios concerning the best candidates. Since both bishops and nuncios tend to be con-servative, the candidates and the new bishops tend to be fairly conservative as well. The conservatism thus usually perpetuates itself even in the case of an individual bishop who decides to retire because of age.

Bishops as well as popes, therefore, have a tendency to define change in terms of the stability of tradition, so that changes in attitude may come from the laity rather than the hierarchy even in countries that are noted for the liberality of their prelates. Some Christian Democrats in Chile claim that it was they who liberalized the hierarchy, as they adopted the views of progressive Catholicism in the late 1930's and the Chilean hierarchy began to accept them only in the early 1950's.[29] In the evolution of Catholic attitudes in Cuba, Leslie Dewart similarly finds that the bishops' pronouncements have lagged far behind the common Catholic opin-ion.[30] Moreover, when the episcopacy does uphold new view-points, it states that the fundamental attitude of the Church has remained the same. Bishop Echeverría Ruiz, for example, in in-

28. See *La acción pastoral en América Latina trazada por el Papa Paulo VI* (Lima: Ediciones Paulinas, 1965).

29. Georgie Anne Geyer, "Latin America: The Rise of a New Non-Communist Left," *Saturday Review*, July 22, 1967, p. 23.

30. *Christianity and Revolution: The Lesson of Cuba* (New York: Herder and Herder, 1963), p. 293.

terpreting *Mater et Magistra,* simultaneously states that Pope John XXIII "categorically" supported the rights of private property and that from his encyclical a new concept of limitations on property rights will have to evolve.[31] This is in part an attempt, simply, to justify ideological innovation by appealing to continuity, a kind of justification that also appears in Marxism and other movements. It goes beyond this, however, in that it also allows a wide range of specific interpretations to be drawn from ecclesiastical documents and so serves to lessen overt factionalism within Church ranks.

Catholic leaders recognize the need for papal and episcopal ambiguity. Like members of the Catholic left in Latin America, the left in the United States does not take its stand from papal directives but rather sees the pope as curtailed in his efforts for reform by the need to reconcile the militantly antagonistic wings within the Church.[32] After a series of interviews in Cuernavaca, Thomas Sanders concluded that Ivan Illich and his CIDOC group have even come to act on "the assumption that papal social teaching is trivial and irrelevant."[33] Papal teachings do have the effect of making the radical criticisms of a man like Illich more acceptable to the mass of Catholics, but the left itself does not expect avantgarde leadership from the Vatican. As on the issue of family planning, even progressives openly admit that popes generally come to accept social innovations only after the majority of Catholics has accepted them.

Within the context of pontifical ambiguity, prelates and laymen use papal statements to champion the policies that they themselves advocate. When doing so, they presume that Vatican directives have both binding validity and a pervasive effect. Prelates sometimes use papal statements to conjure for reform. As the bishop of Avellaneda, Argentina, said in a public speech strongly endorsing *Populorum Progressio,* "The word of the pope is a truth for the world and, for

31. Bernardino Echeverría R., O.F.M. (Obispo de Ambato), *Carta pastoral sobre la encíclica de Juan XXIII Mater et Magistra,* Aug. 15, 1961 (Ambato: Editorial "Pío XII," 1961), pp. 20–23.
32. Warren Hinckle, "Left Wing Catholics," *Ramparts* 6, no. 4 (Nov., 1967) : 26.
33. Thomas G. Sanders to Richard H. Nolte, June 1, 1967 (TGS-1 in series of field reports distributed by the Institute of Current World Affairs), p. 10.

the faithful, the most authentic."[34] Latin Americans have also defended very different political ideologies by claiming that popes sanctioned or inspired them. In upholding private property against agrarian reform, rightist churchmen reprint selected papal statements to "prove" that disobeying civil laws is both unpatriotic and displeasing to God.[35] Father Pedro Badanelli defended Juan Perón and his ideology of *justicialismo* by claiming, as did Perón himself, that *justicialismo* was based on the papal encyclicals.[36]

Commentators on Latin American Catholicism regularly assume that the persons they favor have gained their insights from papal decrees. In praising such Catholic "revolutionaries" as those who have worked against the Somoza regime in Nicaragua, articles in the Catholic press emphasize that the revolutionaries developed their political attitudes from a personal reading of the papal social encyclicals.[37] Monsignor Germán Guzmán Campos, in his sympathetic study of Camilo Torres, similarly finds that Camilo began his dialogue with the Communists as the result of close study of *Mater et Magistra* and *Pacem in Terris*. Father Torres himself tied his policy of cooperation with the Communists to the teachings of Pope John XXIII.[38] To look for justification in papal statements and to be originally or predominantly influenced by them are very different matters, however. The broad inclusiveness of papal statements and the ability of men of vastly different political persuasions to justify their positions in terms of the statements indicate that the apparent strength of papal authority is often more a matter of justification than of predominant influence.

Despite the ambiguity and limited effectiveness of Vatican messages, in some situations papal decrees can have an innovative ef-

34. Jerónimo José Podestá (Obispo de Avellaneda), *Sobre la encíclica "El desarrollo de los pueblos": Conferencia pronunciada en el Teatro Roma de Avellaneda, el día 6 de mayo de 1967* (Avellaneda: Artes Gráficas B. U. Chiesino, S. A., 1967), p. 4.
35. Geraldo de Proença Sigaud, S.V.D., Antonio de Castro Mayer, Plinio Corrêa de Oliveira, and Luis Mendonça de Freitas, *Reforma agrária, questão de consciência*, 4th ed. (São Paulo: Editôra Vera Cruz, 1962), pp. 194–95.
36. Pedro Badanelli, *Perón, la Iglesia y un cura*, 4th ed. (Buenos Aires: Editorial Tartessos, 1960), p. 141.
37. Douglas J. Roche, "Nicaragua: Sunny Land of Rot," *The Sign* 41, no. 12 (July, 1962): 31.
38. *Camilo: Presencia y destino* (Bogotá: Editores Publicidad, Servicios Especiales de Prensa, 1967), pp. 156–59.

215

fect. They are by no means the source of all insight and innovation as some clerical rhetoric claims, but they do affect the attitudes and actions of a large body of clergymen and laymen whose institutional loyalty is directed toward Rome. All papal pronouncements gain wide publicity. Progressive churchmen relate encyclicals to their national situations, as when Father Martínez Galdeano interprets *Populorum Progressio* as "a dramatic and urgent criticism of how the capitalist system has been carrying things out in the third world."[39] Through the flurry of activity that accompanies papal messages and such interpretations of them, churchmen gain a newsworthy tool with which to restate or reformulate their ideological orientation. Papal powers of appointment give the Vatican even more leverage, as a pope can put conservative or avant-garde candidates into positions of national Church leadership. The influence of John XXIII was progressive not simply in terms of his pronouncements but also in terms of crucial appointments which have worked to influence Latin American affairs even after his death.

Vatican II worked to strengthen this orientation within Latin American Catholicism, although Catholic diversity and Church politics limited innovation through the council just as they limit the possibilities of papal initiative. The split evident in the Latin American Church between the ultraconservatives, the progressives, and the Catholic left is clearly apparent in Europe as well, where the liberal bishops of northern Europe contrast the conservative faction that controls *L'Osservatore Romano*. Opposition between European factions became especially clear at Vatican II,[40] but this hardly means that the 600 Latin American bishops who came to Rome for the council developed their differences from observing European factionalism or from placing different interpretations on Pope John's calls for reform. To the extent that European Catholi-

39. Fernando Martínez Galdeano, S.J., "La encíclica social de Paulo VI," *Sic* 30, no. 295 (mayo, 1967) : 219.

40. For an insider's summary of the factional conflicts at Vatican II, see Rynne, *Letters from Vatican City,* esp. pp. 223–41. A summary of Latin American positions taken at the council may be found in Hellmut Gnadt Vitalis, *The Significance of Changes in Latin American Catholicism Since Chimbote, 1953* (Cuernavaca, Mor.: CIDOC, 1969), chap. 9, "Latin America and the Vatican Council II."

cism and Vatican directives actually did influence the Latin American prelates, those influences were themselves set in motion by the very trends toward economic and ideological change in the secular world that have shaped the evolution of the Church in Europe as well as Latin America.

In retrospect, Vatican II seems to have been one stage in the decentralization of Church power. In anticipation of Vatican II, Pope John XXIII unprecedentedly called for a discussion of proposals made by the bishops themselves; after Vatican II, some liberal reforms have won partial implementation even though they failed to gain the council's endorsement. In the view of Cardinal Suenens, the Primate of Belgium and leader of liberal bishops at Vatican II, one such reform has been the retirement age limit for bishops that he himself proposed. When he said at the Council that the age limit should be instituted, a stiff silence met his remarks and they were not discussed again, but, several years after the Council, Pope Paul, ostensibly on his own initiative, suggested a voluntary retirement age for bishops.[41] Such an evolution of policy, put in motion by the public and journalistic as well as the formal ecclesiastical debates of Vatican II, may ultimately lead to the general acceptance of a married diaconate in dioceses where bishops allow it, and to the expansion of the power of individual bishops at the expense of papal authority in other ways.

Although the Vatican Council thus stimulated the movement for Catholic reform, it did not take the decisive actions that would have more fully satisfied the progressives and alienated the traditionalists. The council led some bishops to proclaim the need for Catholics to become responsible citizens and to participate actively in the "restructuring of the world," and bishops often describe the council as the direct impetus for such messages.[42] But, on the other hand, traditionalists now see themselves as being in a battle that Vatican II made more difficult, and they quote selected statements of Pope Paul VI to show that the council cannot really change

41. Comments of Leo Jozef Cardinal Suenens at the third plenary session, Eighth World Congress, International Political Science Association, Munich, Germany, Sept. 3, 1970.

42. See Manuel Talamás Camandari (Primer Obispo de Ciudad Juárez), *IV carta pastoral sobre la renovación de la vida cristiana* Feb. 2, 1966, p. 3.

the traditional orientations of the Church.[43] As in numerous conflict situations, a purposeful ambiguity has allowed churchmen of opposing persuasions to join in supporting pleas for "renovation," which they interpret in different ways. As Bishop Alberto Devoto summed up the open-endedness of the council, "Vatican II is not a Council which has dictated laws, but one which has indicated orientations and attitudes."[44] By indicating an orientation without laws, the council at least stirred an increasing awareness of change; it aired issues that will be difficult to neglect until far broader reforms are realized. One of its major effects has been to educate Church leaders in contemporary progressivism as well as in the diversity of viewpoints that exist among them.

The intellectual influence of European Catholicism extends well beyond the effects of Vatican II. Belgian Catholic thought, for instance, has added an action orientation and an intellectual depth to discussions of change in Latin America. In a study of connections between democracy and development that has been circulated in Latin America, Dr. Rezsohazy of the Catholic University of Louvain characteristically denounces the "stumbling block of sterile academicism." Rejecting the "simplistic assumption" that communism and capitalism provide the only models of development, Rezsohazy tells Latin Americans to search for new paths of development and to search for them actively outside the confines of purely academic debate.[45] This same message has been carried in the activist training that Father François Houtart and his colleagues at the University of Louvain have provided for Latin American priests.

With its European background, the study of sociology in Catholic universities now encourages a new generation of Catholics to see social relationships in analytical rather than doctrinal terms. Because it does this effectively, it also arouses criticisms from the older Church hierarchy such as that which forced the resignation

43. Antonio de Castro Mayer (Bispo de Campos), *Considerações a propósito da aplicação dos documentos promulgados pelo Concílio Ecumênico Vaticano II: Carta pastoral* (São Paulo: Editôra Vera Cruz, 1966), pp. 10–11.
44. Alberto Devoto (Obispo de Goya), untitled pastoral letter, Goya, Navidad de 1965.
45. Rudolf Rezsohazy, *Democracia y desarrollo,* Colección Desarrollo Integral, no. 7 (n.p.: Secretariado Social Mexicano, n.d.), p. 12.

of Dr. J. E. Miguens as the director of the Sociology Department at the Catholic University of Argentina in 1966.[46] Latin Americans do not regularly question the inherent credibility of Catholic dogma, but they do question its relevance to the problems that they face. The issue is, in the phrase of Ricardo Arias Calderón, "not whether the Christian message can be believed, but whether it ought to be believed."[47] To meet this criterion of ethical relevance, Catholics have been adapting traditional elements of their message to make it more effective in dealing with contemporary problems.

Besides confronting the test of ethical relevance, the Latin American Church has been forced to face new ideological challenges from Europe and North America. During the colonial period and much of the nineteenth century, state support gave the Catholic Church an exclusive monopoly in the moral guardianship of Latin Americans. That monopoly bred complacency and allowed the pattern of nominal Catholicism to arise among the great majority of citizens. The Church had to reorient its position in order to retain loyalty and support, however, when secular ideologies began to contest its moral authority. Liberalism and positivism provided the challenge in the nineteenth century, even though many liberals respected the Church while wanting to lessen its secular power. During the twentieth century communism has more overtly advocated the antireligious viewpoint. Now Latin American churchmen react not only to societal change and shifts in Catholic thought outside Latin America, therefore, but also to more general ideological currents. Although the attitudes sometimes relate in a specific sense to the foreign policies of Russia, Britain, or the United States, they are more intimately bound up with the issues of state ownership, social welfare legislation, and the feasibility of violent revolution as a lever of change that the domestic experience of these nations suggests.

The tolerance that characterizes contemporary Catholic thought

46. For an analysis of the crisis over the teaching of sociology in Argentina, see Rafael Braun, "Crisis en la Universidad Católica Argentina," *Criterio* 39, no. 1515–16 (19 enero, 1967).

47. "The Intellectual Challenge to Religion in Latin America," in John J. Considine, M.M., ed., *The Religious Dimension in the New Latin America* (Notre Dame, Ind.: Fides Publishers, 1966), p. 67.

has arisen in part as a reaction to intellectual pluralism and the intolerance of the past. Arnold Toynbee interprets the decline in commitment to Christianity during the past three centuries as a reaction against the excesses of the religious wars of the sixteenth and seventeenth centuries, suggesting that men have rejected spiritual fervor in order to "immunize" themselves against the fanaticism that allowed the atrocities of those wars. With the rejection of Christian fanaticism, men have been tempted to support with displaced fervor the tenets of nationalism, communism, or individualism, which Toynbee calls the "post-Christian ideologies."[48] The antagonistic and frequently self-destructive tendencies of Hitler's perversion of nationalism, the Communist sacrifice of life under Stalin and Mao Tse-tung, or the ruthless self-centeredness of individualistic robber barons have more recently indicated the dangers of fervor among these newer ideologies also. In this context, many Catholics in Latin America are coming to see the progressive yet tolerant tendencies of *freista* thought as having real merit. The zeal of the new thought is not directed against Protestants, who are increasingly seen from an ecumenical standpoint. Instead, zeal is directed against the common human afflictions of poverty, disease, and social inertia. Channeling activity against these plagues encourages men to work through joint effort, and so builds tolerance among them.

In the debate over secular ideologies Latin Americans have found champions among the progressive leaders of European Catholicism. Just as the secularism of nineteenth-century French thought profoundly affected Latin America, so the thought of twentieth-century Frenchmen has had wide repercussions among Latin American Catholics. The example of Father Pierre Teilhard de Chardin provides the dual example of a life spent in scientific endeavor and of a firm dedication to human progress on earth. As Father Teilhard declared, "Our faith imposes on us the right and the duty to throw ourselves into the things of the earth."[49]

48. Arnold J. Toynbee, *Change and Habit: The Challenge of Our Time* (New York: Oxford University Press, 1966), pp. 169–70.
49. Pierre Teilhard de Chardin, *The Divine Milieu: An Essay on the Interior Life*, trans. D. M. MacKinnon and others (New York: Harper & Row, 1965), p. 69.

Despite vicious attacks on Jacques Maritain by Catholic conservatives in Latin America,[50] his concepts of Christian humanism have also been widely accepted in the area. In Brazil, Jackson de Figueiredo actively disseminated the doctrine of Maritain. Jackson had rejected Catholicism in his student days, and as a law student in Bahia even stoned a group of priests who landed there after being expelled from Portugal in 1910.[51] With his conversion to Catholicism in 1918, however, he became one of its most ardent defenders against socialism and materialism. Besides energetically spreading Maritain's doctrines, Jackson played a part in the conversion to Catholicism of Alceu Amoroso Lima, the philosopher who was to become the greatest intellectual champion of Catholic humanism in Brazil. In turn, Amoroso Lima is credited with having shaped the thinking of such Brazilian leaders as Carlos Lacerda. Lacerda, as the man whose opposition most influenced the suicide of Getúlio Vargas in 1954, the resignation of Jânio Quadros in 1961, and the ouster of João Goulart in 1964, has been a powerful political figure. While the degree to which Christian convictions actually impinge upon Lacerda's political actions has often been questioned, his alleged support for Catholicism and the principles of Amoroso Lima points up at least the outward pervasiveness of Maritain's thought.

Maritain also influenced Giovanni Montini long before he became Pope Paul VI. In 1928 Montini translated Maritain's *Three Reformers* into Italian, and as a leader of liberal Italian Catholics during Mussolini's regime Montini relied upon Maritain's precepts in the ideological debate with fascism. When Maritain served as French ambassador to the Holy See after World War II, he made frequent contacts with Montini through the Vatican Secretariat of State. Maritain's prestige has been so great that Pope Paul has called himself a disciple of Maritain.[52] The French humanist also shaped the chances for Catholic progressivism in Latin America

50. See "Jacques Maritain," chap. 3 in Jorge Iván Hübner Gallo, *Los católicos en la política* (Santiago de Chile: Zig-Zag, 1959), pp. 35–46.
51. [João] Cruz Costa, *Panorama of the History of Philosophy in Brazil*, trans. Fred G. Sturm (Washington, D. C.: Pan American Union, 1962), p. 95.
52. *Time*, April 21, 1967, p. 69.

by his influence upon Eduardo Frei. Frei first listened to Maritain while traveling in Europe as a student during the 1930's, and the political approach that Frei had drawn from Catholic humanism by the end of that decade has remained the core of his position ever since. Although the Catholic left now finds the thinking of Maritain to be dated, Maritain and his message remain an impressive basis for the progressive movement.

CHURCH POWER AND THE FEAR OF CHANGE

Fear works as one of the prime motivating forces in human affairs and, although its effects are now muted in the material abundance of the developed societies, it continues to underlie change in the Catholic Church. Catholics fear secularism, Protestantism, and communism; as they become more acutely aware of the forces of the secular world, they fear the population explosion as well. Each of these forces appears to threaten the Church in both an institutional and an ideological sense. Since the response of Catholic progressivism derives from the particular ways in which clergy and activist laymen perceive these threats to their position, Catholic interpretations bear as much relevance to the process of adaptation as do the threats themselves.

From a concern to increase or at least to maintain the authority of the Church, Catholic leaders champion the new lines of social doctrine. Such priest-sociologists as Fathers Houtart and Pin recognize that, in terms of religious motivation, most Latin Americans see religion as protecting them from the potent forces of nature rather than seeing it as a guide to their moral action. This desire for protection may coincide with desires to avoid hell in the afterlife, to conform to the superficial pattern of religious values in one's village or nation, or to enjoy a sense of participation and belonging in a religious community.[53] Functionally, the Catholic religion has thus operated more in terms of the psychological benefit that individuals derive from it than it has as a device to control behavior in the

53. François Houtart and Émile Pin, *The Church and the Latin American Revolution,* trans. Gilbert Barth (New York: Sheed and Ward, 1965), chap. 15.

222

larger context of society. If this is true and if men continue to gain more control over the forces of nature and to derive their sense of participation from membership in newly arisen interest groups or national communities, then the force of religious loyalty in Latin America may be expected to decline. Observing one or more of the tendencies leading toward this decline, Latin American Church leaders have felt an urge to make Church doctrines and attitudes more directly relevant to the lives of ordinary citizens.

Such adaptation requires coming to terms with the force of secularism, as churchmen appreciate that the old values of Christian meekness and resignation have lost their meaning for many Latin Americans. In the words of a Colombian report on the children of peasant families who moved to Bogotá, "The 'Christian resignation' which had justified their parents' way of life means nothing to them."[54] At the same time, some of the most influential social reformers in Latin America, such as President José Batlle y Ordoñez of Uruguay in the early twentieth century, have combined emphasis on secularism with their advocacy of social welfare legislation. Christmas in Uruguay is officially called Family Day, and *El Día,* the great newspaper founded by Batlle, still maintains its atheistic character by spelling God with a small "g" and mentioning Pope Pius XII only as Señor Pacelli.[55] The new Catholic concern for material progress responds pragmatically to the evaporation of older Catholic values and to the advocacy of reform by secular leaders.

Opponents of religion have long applauded the trend toward secularism, but in doing so they have exaggerated its speed and misjudged the role of fear in the process of religious transformation. In the early 1920's, Bertrand Russell wrote that "religion, since it has its source in terror, has dignified certain kinds of fear, and made people think them not disgraceful. In this it has done mankind a great disservice: *all* fear is bad, and ought to be overcome not by fairy tales, but by courage and rational reflection."[56] Terror, however, is a more permanent and a more beneficial part of the human

54. "Report on Colombia," *Inquietudes* 2, no. 12 (Dec., 1966), as reprinted in *CIF Reports* 6, no. 2 (Jan. 16, 1967): 12.
55. John J. Considine, *New Horizons in Latin America* (New York: Dodd, Mead & Company, 1958), p. 106.
56. *What I Believe* (New York: E. P. Dutton & Company, 1925), p. 13.

condition than Russell allows. In Latin America and elsewhere man's feelings of powerlessness against the forces of nature have now receded, but fear is hardly absent from areas where abject poverty, inefficient and repressive governments, and warfare or civil strife prevail. Far from being bad or disgraceful, fear can be socially useful if it encourages men to overcome the potential destructiveness of the caprice of nature or their own tendencies toward repressiveness or self-destruction. Even if men lose credence in the "fairy tales" of religion, the imperfection of their environment encourages some reliance upon faith, either secular or religious, in addition to their reliance upon pure rationality. Although the influence of religion and quasi-religious sentiment has not passed away, the fear that the old forms of religion are passing away has centrally motivated the modification of those forms.

In addition to counteracting the growth of secularism, Catholic spokesmen feel a need to adjust to other ideological, religious, and political currents in Latin America. Catholic intellectuals reiterate concern for equality and human well-being partly as a defensive reaction. Since the colonial period, the great majority of the leading intellectuals and philosophical movements in Latin America has failed to identify themselves first and foremost as Catholic. Just as concern for the failure to achieve intellectual preeminence has encouraged Catholics in the United States to accept many of the norms and values of non-Catholic intellectuals,[57] so Latin American Catholics adopt some of the values of secular social thinkers not only by osmosis but also in order to gain more standing among the recognized leaders of the community. Protestantism and communism have also threatened the Church through the promises of material benefit that their ethics convey, and the shifts in Catholic activity reflect these challenges. Communist conspiracies have not produced the trend of Catholic progressivism, although some observers of Communist tactics have assumed such subversion. As Thomas Sanders cogently argues, the view that Catholic leftists have become dupes of international Communism neglects the essential conservatism of

57. Edward Wakin and Joseph F. Scheuer, *The De-Romanization of the American Catholic Church* (New York: Macmillan Company, 1966), pp. 252–63.

the official Communist parties in Latin America.[58] Progressivism has not arisen through subservience to communism; on the contrary, a fear of both Communist and Protestant competition has potently motivated the evolution of Catholic thought.

Feelings of individual frustration and the assumption that reforms must be massive in order to succeed have further encouraged the rise of the Catholic left. In the late 1950's members of the National Student Union in Brazil concluded that reform could not really be effective in Brazilian universities until broader reforms came to Brazilian society, and in conjunction with the university branch of Catholic Action the students began to debate the issue of Catholic responsibility in leftist movements.[59] Opposing the view that the Church should stay out of politics, some Catholic periodicals in Latin America have come to press that involvement. *CIF Reports* lets an atheist voice the sentiment that it would be unpolitic for Catholics to proclaim so forthrightly; it approvingly reprints C. Wright Mills's critique that "if you do not get the church into politics, you cannot confront evil and you cannot work for good. You will be a subordinate amusement and a political satrap of whatever is going. You will be the great Christian joke."[60]

The action orientation seems necessary to those who take heed of the religious situation in the Soviet Union, as the victory of Bolshevism remains—for those who learn from the experience of countries and periods other than their own—a most forceful example of the devastation of religion. Peasants in pre-Bolshevik Russia were especially bothered by arbitrary and unresponsive uses of wealth and power by Orthodox bishops.[61] Russian clergymen lost their concern for the immediate lives of their parishioners, as the Orthodox Church wrapped itself in ritual and allegiance to autocratic secular leaders. As a result, it lost the underlying allegiance of the Russian people long before 1917, and the Bolsheviks' sense of quasi-religious

58. Thomas G. Sanders, "Catholicism and Development: The Catholic Left in Brazil," in Kalman H. Silvert, ed., *Churches and States: The Religious Institution and Modernization* (New York: American Universities Field Staff, 1967), p. 98.
59. *Ibid.*, p. 90.
60. "C. Wright Mills's Pagan Sermon," *CIF Reports* 1, no. 8 (Jan., 1963): 364.
61. Paul B. Anderson, *People, Church and State in Modern Russia* (New York: Macmillan Company, 1944), p. 37.

idealism and secular mission filled a void left by the sterile formalism of religion. As S. M. Kravchinskii commented long before the rise of the Bolsheviks:

> This does not mean that the Russian peasants are by nature inclined to religious indifference. They have their full share of the human faculty for intense enthusiasm, which, in dealing with masses, is most readily converted into religious zeal. . . .
>
> All we wish to point out is that with the orthodox Russian peasantry, which up to the present day has formed three-quarters of our rural population, religious feeling is almost entirely dormant. . . .
>
> It has lain there, hidden in the breasts of the toiling millions, as an enormous potential force, which, however, may be awakened some day, and appear as a new and important agent of our national history. We, for our part, venture to express the opinion that here, in the presence of this latent force, which has never yet been tested, lies perhaps the greatest enigma of Russia's future.[62]

The same force lies dormant in Latin America today, and churchmen wish to capitalize upon it before it becomes the tool of antireligious movements.

The Church enters this struggle from a position of weakness and decline. In 1563 Chile had one priest for every 600 inhabitants,[63] and in 1969 it had one priest for every 3,443 inhabitants. In 1956 half of the Catholics in the world lived in Europe and were served by 66 per cent of the world's priests, while the third of the world's Catholics who lived in Latin America were served by only 8 per cent of the world's priests.[64] Critics of Catholicism like Paul Blanshard point out that the missionary status of Latin America and the predominance of foreign priests in many areas shows the total failure of Catholicism really to capture popular loyalties.[65] Furthermore,

62. S. M. Stepniak [Sergei Mikhailovich Kravchinskii], *The Russian Peasantry: Their Agrarian Condition, Social Life and Religion* (London: George Routledge & Sons, 1905), pp. 379–80.

63. Renato Poblete, S.J., "La situación religiosa en Chile," *Teología y Vida* 3, no. 4 (octubre–diciembre, 1962) : 231.

64. Arturo Gaete, S.J., "Un Cas d'Adaptation: Les 'Pentecostales' au Chili," in Aron and others, *L'Église, l'Occident, le Monde*, p. 149.

65. Paul Blanshard, *American Freedom and Catholic Power*, 2d ed. (Boston: Beacon Press, 1958), pp. 315–16.

while the Catholic faith could be passed on by the older members of the extended family in the traditional rural societies of Latin America, the pattern of increasing urbanization and social mobility now interferes with familial transmission of religious values. Still another impetus to change comes from the very lack of change in the past, from the fact that churchmen have reason to fear for the continuance of the institution that they serve because of the maintenance of such rules as that on priestly celibacy. Pope Paul VI has decried the lack of priests in Latin America,[66] but he has not altered the celibacy rule which, in the sexually conscious Latin American environment, might significantly increase priestly vocations.

Churchmen recognize the position of Catholic weakness. The Church is especially weak in Uruguay, traditionally one of Latin America's most progressive countries, where Father Segundo estimates that only about 60 per cent of the Uruguayan people is now even baptized by the Church.[67] Catholic influence is threatened even in Ecuador, a traditional bastion of its strength. In the aftermath of Fidel Castro's victory in Cuba, the bishop of Ambato admitted that Catholicism in Ecuador, like that in Cuba, could serve as no bar to a Communist takeover. Ecuador was once so devoutly Catholic that, in 1873, Congress approved President Gabriel García Moreno's consecration of the republic to the "Sacred Heart of Jesus." By 1961, however, Bishop Echeverría Ruiz declared that the Catholicity of Ecuador had changed decisively in the last twenty years, and that now the "truly Catholic people are such an insignificant minority that in a moment of crisis they could do nothing."[68]

Despite Church weakness and the barriers to direct Church leadership, clergymen could still realize major influence through their example, their pronouncements, and their effect on secular leaders. The personalities of some of the *abiertos* have notably increased their leadership and therefore aided the cause of progressivism. As Landsberger notes in the case of Chile, for example, "the

66. *La acción pastoral en América Latina trazada por el Papa Paulo VI,* pp. 9–10.
67. Juan Luis Segundo, S.J., "The Future of 'Cristianismo' in Latin America," *CIF Reports* 2, no. 2 (May, 1963) : 69.
68. Bernardino Echeverría R., O.F.M. (Obispo de Ambato), *Carta pastoral a propósito de los ejemplos de Cuba,* June 24, 1961 (Ambato: Editorial "Pío XII," 1961), p. 3.

progressive bishops have been helped by their being generally impressive as persons: Widely traveled, knowledgeable, evidently moved by humanitarian concerns, and generally radiating a feeling of love and acceptance, even toward adversaries."[69] In order for this experience to be more widespread, however, many more churchmen would have to increase their personal prestige. The prestige of the native clergy has traditionally been low, especially in countries like Guatemala which have produced virulent anticlericalism. Although in some countries members of wealthy families have continued to assume high Church positions, Mary P. Holleran concludes for Guatemala that the people have looked down on the native clergy because its members have risen from very poor backgrounds. On the basis of field research in 1946, she observed that even when a devout family of upper-class Catholics decided that a family member might be ordained, they would say, "but, of course, not in Guatemala."[70] The extreme difficulty which the Church continues to have in arousing native vocations in all of the Latin American countries emphasizes the low appeal of the priesthood, and the opposition of contemporary anticlericals to any direct political role for the clergy reinforces the barrier which low prestige creates for effective Church leadership. The inheritors of the anticlerical tradition are especially likely to reject the Church where an alliance continues between secular and ecclesiastical conservatives.

The type and content of education that is available in Latin America similarly work to limit clerical vocations and recruitment. With lower levels of literacy and secondary education than in Europe or the United States, comparatively few boys possess the education required to become a priest. Educational deficiencies are as much qualitative as they are quantitative because, despite lower levels of general education than in some other Catholic countries, boys wishing to enter the Latin American priesthood are welcomed and strongly encouraged in Catholic schools and seminaries. Students who are concerned to reshape the societies in which they live can

69. Henry A. Landsberger, "Time, Persons, Doctrine: The Modernization of the Church in Chile," in Henry A. Landsberger, ed., *The Church and Social Change in Latin America* (Notre Dame, Ind.: University of Notre Dame Press, 1970), p. 81.

70. *Church and State in Guatemala* (New York: Columbia University Press, 1949), p. 244.

find little to attract them in strictly religious training or in an un-constructive ethic of sheer anticommunism. As Father Serafín Azáceta suggests in explaining the acceptance of communism by some French Catholics, part of the blame rests on simplistic educa-tion that allows individuals to grow up believing that the world is divided into what he calls the "good guys" and the "bad guys."[71] As Catholics thus call for more personal discernment in order to fight Communist propaganda, they inculcate attitudes of discernment which may easily be turned on Catholic doctrines as well.

The surprising lack of priestly vocations also relates to a question of sexual prestige on which Catholic ethics and Latin American re-alities have never become reconciled. With many boys introduced to houses of prostitution at the age of fourteen and many families crowded into one-room sleeping accommodations where children early learn the "earthy side of life," Father James A. Clark is right in pointing to a widespread acceptance of sexuality that precludes boys from choosing the chaste life of a priest.[72] Latin American re-spect for masculine prowess and sexual accomplishment sharply con-trasts the religious ethic of asceticism and sexual abstinence. Because of this, men may inwardly fear appearing effeminate or childish if they undertake actions such as a vocation or regular Church attend-ance which would associate them too directly with the ethic of abstinence. The old practice of priestly concubinage allowed priests to conform to the norm of prowess and gave them natural sexual outlets, but it also created tension between their actions and their professions of belief. Although churchmen have overcome the repu-tation for promiscuity which they enjoyed in Mexico and elsewhere, they have not done so in such a way as to increase their influence to the widest extent. As priestly concubinage has decreased, priestly actions conform to religious ethics but diverge even more sharply from the ethic of sexual prestige.

From an understanding of the likely impact of the population explosion on their societies and on the Church itself, other clergy-men have come to champion the new Church policies. Father Renato

71. Serafín Azáceta, O.F.M., "El 'ala izquierda' del catolicismo francés," *Verdad y Vida* 17, no. 66 (abril–junio, 1959) : 355.
72. *The Church and the Crisis in the Dominican Republic*, p. 29.

Poblete finds that the quantitative growth of Latin American populations "implies a tremendous change—a total and rapid change which has affected all human social structures and all human activities."[73] While population growth endangers the amount of direct contact which Catholics can have with their priests, the amount of that contact is already more tenuous than it would at first appear. Father Poblete notes that in national censuses the number of citizens who identify themselves as Catholic varies from 65 per cent in Uruguay to 98 per cent in Colombia and Peru. Attendance at mass is only 1 or 2 per cent of the adult population in the working-class districts of many burgeoning Latin American cities, however, and it rises to only 30 per cent of the adult population even in middle- and upper-class districts. As these figures and the shrinking proportion of priests to total populations endanger Church influence, Father Poblete and other Catholic leaders have chosen to interpret them as a challenge. They are "in a way a blessing from God," because they have spurred reassessment of Church activities and occasioned the new tendencies of Catholic social policies. Specifically and programmatically, Father Poblete suggests that the demographic situation in Latin America means that the Church will have to cooperate with other groups to achieve its objectives by promoting cooperatives, trade unions, and rural institutes.[74] While papal encyclicals and ecumenical councils have promoted these policies, an ally of the encyclicals and councils has been the population explosion which Church policies have unintentionally encouraged.

It would be inaccurate as well as uncharitable to see the basic motivation of Church leaders resulting from fear for the institutional position of the Church or from a need to bring Church pronouncements and policies into line with economic possibilities. One of the most consistent results of my interviews with members of the Catholic clergy in Latin America has been the conviction that they have

73. Renato Poblete, "The Great Resurgence in Today's Latin America," in John J. Considine, M.M., *The Church in the New Latin America* (Notre Dame, Ind.: Fides Publishers, 1964), p. 22. For a general discussion of social changes which the population explosion is producing, see Frederick C. Turner, "The Implications of Demographic Change for Nationalism and Internationalism," *Journal of Politics* 27, no. 1 (Feb., 1965).

74. Poblete, "The Great Resurgence in Today's Latin America," pp. 25–30.

come personally to believe in the doctrines of progressivism, rather than merely to espouse them in a Machiavellian manner in order to gain influence for the Church. The ethic of Christian humility and service into which clergymen have been socialized has molded the directions of the progressive movement. Dom Hélder Câmara is not merely reacting to secular informality, for example, when he urges bishops to suppress the use of such titles as "excellency" and "eminence," to stop using coats of arms, to live in modest housing, and to replace their black limousines with less expensive automobiles.[75] These suggestions try to tie the leadership of the Church more closely to the common people, and they seem particularly appropriate in a century when formal titles of address or coats of arms appear stylized and old-fashioned. But, in a modern sense, Dom Hélder's viewpoint also expresses his own feelings of Christian humility. A central precept of traditional Christianity here coincides in its influence with the social forces that now underlie Catholic progressivism.

75. St. Clair, "The Battling Bishop of Brazil," pp. 44–45.

VI ~

Some Implications
of the New Catholicism

What is the future of Catholic progressivism? Ivan Illich writes that "it is blasphemous to use the gospel to prop up any social or political system,"[1] but this is exactly what the gospel has traditionally done in Latin America and probably what in a general sense it will continue to do. What has changed is that those who expound the gospel most sincerely have come to agree less and less on the sort of system that churchmen ought to support. For their own self-preservation and that of the institution they serve, churchmen will continue to work under all but the most repressive regimes. They will continue to advocate a broad spectrum of governmental and social systems, so that the real issue is not merely whether some churchmen try to prop up the status quo or to impose North American or Marxist solutions. Instead, the future of progressivism will depend on the means and effectiveness with which Catholic activists work to carry through their new concern for equality, economic development, and ethical humanism in the differing environments of the Latin American republics.

1. Ivan Illich, "The Seamy Side of Charity," *America* 116, no. 3 (Jan. 21, 1967): 90.

Study of Latin American Catholicism points unmistakably to the fact that the alleged monolith of the Catholic Church contains an extraordinarily diverse and contradictory array of viewpoints on social and political questions. Churchmen frequently say that outsiders should not judge the nature of Latin American Catholicism by the religious practices and institutions of Europe or the United States, but in fact this warning on generalizations applies as much within Latin American Catholicism itself. Although the Church faces numerous common problems in the area as a whole, the ways advocated for it to meet these problems differ radically among countries and among progressive, conservative, and avant-garde segments of the Church within each country.

Within this context of diversity, the trend has become what Thomas Sanders rightly calls "cautiously progressive." Sanders correctly points out that an institution whose primary function is to attend to the religious needs of its members cannot be expected to provide the chief leadership for secular social change.[2] More and more actively, however, the Church has come to back efforts for agrarian reform, for a more egalitarian society, and for broader political participation. Widespread Church approval for specific reformist policies legitimizes them and provides a sense of continuity and reassurance for Latin Americans who desire what they suppose to be the ultimate results of change but fear the disrupting and uncertain process of change itself. Churchmen, as respected ideologues and as directors of an extensive organizational structure, can significantly influence the speed and the direction of social innovation. On some issues, in some localities, and under some clergymen, the old reluctance to sanction change will continue. Alternatively, while innovations are not likely to come with the speed or in each of the directions advocated by Dom Hélder, Camilo Torres, or Ivan Illich, their ideas already challenge the lines of *freista* thought. As avant-garde and *freista* ideas become even more pervasive, they should continue to add democratic, egalitarian, and humanistic tendencies to the contemporary process of change.

Even now, parts of the Latin American Church have become far

2. Thomas G. Sanders to Richard H. Nolte, July 17, 1967 (TGS-2 in series of field reports distributed by the Institute of Current World Affairs), p. 10.

more progressive than is generally recognized. In Brazil, Father Vaz sums up one thrust of contemporary thought in his desire to give men "a profoundly humanistic interpretation of their origins," an inspiration to counteract the "dehumanizing" tendencies in modern society.[3] In Peru, as Fredrick Pike concluded in 1966 after extensive field research, clergymen have come to be "as much in the vanguard of change and modernization" as their better-publicized Chilean counterparts. The complexities of social change in Peru have simply made the efforts of Peruvian churchmen more difficult and harder to understand.[4] One of the most encouraging signs of the new force within the Church is that progressives stress the need for active, broadly based participation. In the analogy of Bishop Talamás Camandari, just as new electric power being generated in northern Mexico is useless unless it is connected to industrial machines, so the spirit of Vatican II is useless unless it reorients the actions of individual Catholics.[5]

Another sign of the growing strength of the progressive movement has been the traditionalist reaction against it. Although the *freista* ethic grew out of traditionalism, many conservatives vigorously denounce the *freistas*. As other conservatives have gradually been won over, part of the conservative viewpoint has maintained considerable sway and appeal in its compatibility with progressivism. Conservatives point out that to love the poor one does not have to hate the rich,[6] and this reminder counteracts the twisted ethic of altruism that has often turned idealists into revolutionaries. In contemporary Latin America, where many of the rich remain self-satisfied, hatred builds up against them among lower groups that reject the poverty in which they themselves live. The problem for the *freistas* has become not simply to rechannel the hatreds of lower groups, but also to change the thinking of middle and upper groups

3. Henrique C. de Lima Vaz, S.J., "Cristianismo e consciência histórica," *Síntese* 3, no. 9 (janeiro–março, 1961): 63.
4. See Fredrick B. Pike, "The Catholic Church and Modernization in Peru and Chile," *Journal of International Affairs* 20, no. 2 (1966): esp. 277.
5. Manuel Talamás Camandari (Primer Obispo de Ciudad Juárez), *IV carta pastoral sobre la renovación de la vida cristiana*, Feb. 2, 1966, p. 4.
6. Antonio de Castro Mayer (Bispo Diocesano de Campos), *Carta pastoral prevenindo os diocesanos contra os ardis da seita comunista*, May 13, 1961, 2d ed. (São Paulo: Editôra Vera Cruz, 1961), p. 18.

and to alter the relationships that have led to the discontent. It is here that Catholic progressives, rather than the traditionalists, have more realistic answers.

Like the compromise with conservative nonviolence, the Catholic debate over agrarian reform and labor unions is less advanced than it would at first appear to be. Churchmen here debate how the economic pie is to be divided rather than how it is to be made larger. Only a small number of clergymen join Father Mario Zañartu in understanding that, in the distribution of productive resources, "one's neighbor is best loved by giving to the most capable persons rather than to those who need them most or to those who please one more."[7] This orientation works, not to justify elitism, but to increase the resources of society as a whole. However, most clergymen think in terms of the individual welfare of the property owner, the peasant, or the factory worker rather than in terms of productivity. Churchmen with very different points of view praise "economic development" and "social progress" and, if asked directly, most would agree that Latin American productivity needs to be raised. By thinking in terms of the individual welfare of property owners who want to keep their land, or peasants who want to divide up the land, or factory workers who want higher wages and social service benefits, however, the churchmen regularly overlook the importance of higher farm and factory production and the dangers that uneconomic farming and manufacturing practices pose for the realization of productivity increases. It is only natural that churchmen should react as humanists rather than as businessmen, but it is unfortunate if their humanism causes them to focus on short-term goals rather than on the productivity increases that would allow the broadest realization of humanist goals in the future.

Even while going only somewhat beyond the regressive tendencies of traditionalism, the progressive movement has begun to overcome the older criticisms of the Church. Critics have often charged that Catholicism is antiscientific and that its influence has retarded the growth of technology, science, and free inquiry in Latin America.

7. Mario Zañartu, S.J., "Religious Values in Latin America: An Appraisal," in John J. Considine, M.M., ed., *The Religious Dimension in the New Latin America* (Notre Dame, Ind.: Fides Publishers, 1966), p. 42.

Paul Blanshard, in one of his typical denunciations of Catholicism, finds that the Church keeps "the masses of the people in Catholic countries in a perpetually depressed cultural condition. They have an unbalanced diet of too much sentiment and too little science, and the result of their cultural malnutrition is that they are kept permanently immature because they have never learned the art of mental growth in freedom."[8] In order to counteract such criticisms and to help Latin American countries to adapt to technological innovations, however, Catholic schools and universities have begun to place far more emphasis on science and technology.

The Church has also adapted to the force of contemporary nationalism. In Southeast Asia, where the spread of Christianity never became as pervasive as in Latin America, nationalist leaders have repeatedly tried to create a sense of nationalism and common culture by promoting a return to Buddhism or Islam for the entire population.[9] Latin Americans cannot shake off their European inheritance, however, in the way that Asians try to shake off "cultural imperialism" from Europe or North America. Where nationalism is linked to religion in Latin America, it is linked to Catholicism. The region contains as many forms of nationalism as it does of Catholicism, and men with very different attitudes toward social change justify their attitudes in terms of both religious and nationalist rhetoric. Neither nationalism nor Catholicism is an inherently progressive force, but they are forces which people now regularly tie together for either progressive or conservative ends. The degree to which progressive Catholics can convince other Latin Americans to accept their interpretations of nationalism and Catholicism will significantly shape the social effects of these forces.

The relationship of the Church to secular nationalists and authoritarians has become more problematical than it was in the aftermath

8. Paul Blanshard, *Communism, Democracy, and Catholic Power* (Boston: Beacon Press, 1951), p. 234.

9. See Winburn T. Thomas and Rajah B. Manikam, *The Church in Southeast Asia* (New York: Friendship Press, 1956), esp. pp. 8–9. On the interplay of nationalism and Catholicism in the different Latin American republics, see Frederick C. Turner, "Catholicism and Nationalism in Latin America," a paper presented at the Eighth World Congress of the International Political Science Association, Munich, Germany, Sept., 1970.

of the victory over Juan Perón in 1955. Although events in Venezuela and Colombia temporarily confirmed the feasibility of Church opposition to dictatorship, the Paraguayan experience demonstrated the dangers of such opposition. Argentine clergymen long remained diplomatically "nonpolitical" in their approach to the regime of General Onganía. Churchmen have even relaxed their early denunciations of Cuban *fidelistas* and the Brazilian military, and the contrasting patterns of both Brazilian and Cuban authoritarianism can count on a core of staunch defenders within the Church.

Given the context of Latin American politics, this policy of ambiguity toward authoritarianism is probably all that can be expected from the Church. Catholic progressivism has proved strong in Chile, but Chile remains distinctive in its traditions of military nonintervention, respect for electoral decisions, and general openness to innovation. Venezuela manifests similar Christian Democratic strength, but in most other Latin American states neither the Christian Democrats nor progressive churchmen are powerful enough to wield decisive political power. The mantle of the Church can protect Christian Democratic parties under regimes like that of General Stroessner in Paraguay, where Church sponsorship is more open because of the suppression of parties not backed by forces as influential as the Church. Catholic activists can also stand ready to fight against authoritarians who energetically repress civil or religious rights, who fail to bring economic advances, and who generate enough popular antagonism to give their opponents a chance of success. But, where these conditions are not met, doctrinaire resistance to authoritarianism appears to counteract so many Catholic interests as to make churchmen reject it.

Genuine political neutrality can be a great asset for the Church, for individual priests, and sometimes for the community as a whole. In Paraguay, for example, Frederic Hicks's field research has shown that rural priests win prestige and power by maintaining real indifference between the interests of the Liberal and Colorado parties. The parties themselves have no proclerical traditions, since each has grown out of the tradition of nineteenth-century liberalism after Dr. Francia crushed the power of the Church. Paraguayan priests naturally gain power in this context when, as impartial arbiters working in the interests of their local community, they prevent conflicts of interest from going for settlement beyond the village where partisan criteria would determine the outcome.[10] The advantages of priestly neutrality become evident when one contrasts this situation with that of the Colombian Conservative party, which has traditionally tied priests into its own partisan politics and thereby prevented them from working more effectively to stem such problems as *la violencia*. Even toward the successful Christian Democratic party of Eduardo Frei, the Church prudently tried to remain in the background, advocating support for humanist principles and opposition to violence while not burdening lay reformers with the old millstone of clerical direction.

Like political neutrality, the tolerance of Catholic diversity in Latin America creates both strengths and weaknesses. Georg Simmel found the rise of Christianity to be one of the great turning points for religion because Christianity did not tolerate particularistic religions as they had previously tolerated one another, or, as Simmel said, because "the God of the Christians was the first to extend His sphere of influence from those who believed in Him to those who did not."[11] Simmel's insight illustrates a cause for the messianism of Catholicism in colonial Latin America, but the most significant tendency in more recent Catholicism derives from a different and in a sense contradictory tendency. While Christians claim universal jurisdiction for their God, they in fact support very different conceptions of who He is and what He wishes in the economic and social sphere. Catholics in Latin America are not overly forbearing toward spiritualism or Protestantism, but they do countenance an extraordinarily wide diversity of religious beliefs so long as the beliefs are alleged to be Catholic. Although Simmel is right in showing that the Christian faith is externally intolerant, its Catholic version in Latin America has proved exceptionally lenient in terms of its own subcultures. This allows Latin American Catholicism to persist at different levels

10. See Frederic Hicks, "Politics, Power, and the Role of the Village Priest in Paraguay," *Journal of Inter-American Studies* 9, no. 2 (April, 1967).
11. Georg Simmel, *Sociology of Religion,* trans. Curt Rosenthal (New York: Philosophical Library, 1959), p. 69.

of society, but it weakens the force that Catholicism can exert in the direction of any particular social change. Future economic developments will affect the chances to spread such tolerance outside the Church, since it becomes increasingly feasible in a society of comparative abundance.

Even with the Catholic policy of tolerance, the question arises as to whether the philosophies and programs of Dom Hélder and Hübner Gallo, or of Guatemalan and Dutch Catholicism,[12] can really remain under the same ecclesiastical authority and structures. They can probably do so only if that authority is so ambiguous as to allow their extreme divergencies, and if their own internal dynamics do not push them even further apart. If the process of reform continues, as it almost surely must, one of its primary effects may be the growth of a new Church whose solidarity is assured not by common assent to religious doctrines and social ambiguities, but by the generalization of a progressive or conservative viewpoint and the disaffection of the factions that cannot adhere to it. Such an evolution would occasion substantial departures in the membership, doctrines, and power of the Church.

For the time being, the esoteric nature of much Catholic debate allows the overall impact of the Church to be more unified and pervasive. Pareto rightly observed that theologies which are at all complicated belong only to restricted classes of people, and that in doing so they depart from popular interpretations.[13] Theological debates in Latin America reach comparatively few citizens, although their long-run impact is much greater than Pareto's comment might lead one to believe. While only the well-educated segment of the Latin American population can follow the intellectual complexities of the new Catholic thought, members of this educated group like Eduardo Frei sometimes reach positions of great influence. The very restrictiveness of the Latin American educational system increases the potential influence of those who receive higher education. Further-

12. For survey research and informed commentary on the much-discussed topic of contemporary religious belief in Holland, see G. H. L. Zeegers, G. Dekker, and J. W. M. Peters, *God in Nederland* (Amsterdam: van Ditmar, 1967).

13. Vilfredo Pareto, *The Mind and Society: A Treatise on General Sociology*, trans. Andrew Bongiorno and Arthur Livingston, 4 vols. (New York: Dover Publications, 1963), 1: 215.

more, the changing nature of the theological debates is allowing types of popularization which fit the social needs of Latin Americans. The thinking of Father Vaz, Pedro Badanelli, or Camilo Torres remains unknown to most *latinos,* but citizens all over the area recognize that churchmen now demonstrate active concern and disagreement over the best ways to reach the illusive goal of social justice. Just as intellectuals like Bartolomé de Las Casas, Manuel Gamio, or José Enrique Rodó have shaped lines of popular culture in the past, so contemporary Catholics may set in motion patterns of group interaction and reaction which go well beyond their original impetus.

The future of progressive Catholicism is assured as the influence of reformist priests passes from man to man. Dr. Podestá, the bishop of Avellaneda, Argentina, tells the story of Father Ángel Herrera, a Spanish priest who proclaimed that the allegedly Christian, Western civilization in which most Catholics live is genuinely neither Christian nor humanistic. Father Herrera was a militant lay reformer before the Spanish Civil War and became a priest-sociologist only after the Republican defeat; he deeply impressed Bishop Podestá with the reformist ethic when the bishop was a young student of canon law in Spain.[14] The same force of example has operated in Eduardo Frei's contact with Jacques Maritain and in the general diffusion of the new Catholic ethics. Just as European clerics and laymen impressed leaders of the present reform movement in Latin America, so the example of contemporary churchmen and Christian Democrats is now shaping the attitudes of Catholic students. The example for students is by no means uniform, but the influence of the progressives is pervasive and visible enough to insure the growth of a new generation that will also work for reform in the name of the Church.

Granting the possibilities of intellectual innovation and the force of example, factionalism still means that the overall Catholic impact on the process of social change will not be as large as the leaders of the various ideological wings within the Church would like. As Ivan

14. Jerónimo José Podestá (Obispo de Avellaneda), *Sobre la encíclica "El desarrollo de los pueblos": Conferencia pronunciada en el Teatro Roma de Avellaneda, el día 6 de mayo de 1967* (Avellaneda: Artes Gráficas B. U. Chiesino, S.A., 1967), p. 14.

240

Vallier points out, a group must be fairly unified and able to operate cohesively at the national level in order to be effective in Latin American politics.[15] Internal dissention dissipates energy and weakens the effects of shifts in Catholic ideology. Although the new predominance of official Catholic pronouncements in favor of innovation works to legitimize the process of change, Catholic statements vary tremendously in the degree to which they advocate programs for land reform or the proletarianization of political power. Catholics in Mexico, Chile, and Venezuela have developed comparatively broad consensus on specific social innovations, but Catholics in the majority of Latin American countries have not achieved comparable agreement. In most republics Catholics do not seem likely to develop striking new levels of consensus, and their impact in shaping their national societies will consequently be limited.

The failure of the Church to collaborate more effectively in the process of peaceful change rests at least as much upon secular factionalism and secular leaders as it does on Church personnel. The close collaboration between Russian Orthodox clergymen and the Soviet state after Hitler's attack on Russia in 1941 indicates that, if secularists and religionists believe that the danger of their common enemy is great enough,[16] even persecution and fundamentally opposed positions cannot prevent joint actions. Collaboration among groups both inside and outside the Church would increase in Latin America, if political leaders convinced the wealthy that failure to spur economic growth and to make political systems more responsive are at least as dangerous to their position as the invasion of a foreign army. Following President Frei's example, imaginative leaders could try to build unity by attacking such common problems as poverty and the threat of mass revolution in the same way demagogues have built unity by attacking foreigners. The fact that more leaders have not done this should not be blamed so much on an unwillingness of the Church to collaborate, but rather on the more general failure to develop effective leadership in the secular sphere.

15. "Religious Elites: Differentiations and Developments in Roman Catholicism," in Seymour Martin Lipset and Aldo Solari, eds., *Elites in Latin America* (New York: Oxford University Press, 1967), pp. 197–98.
16. See John Shelton Curtiss, *The Russian Church and the Soviet State, 1917–1950* (Boston: Little, Brown and Company, 1953), pp. 290–303.

While Catholic factionalism manifests disunity at the present time, the issues that it brings out into the open may lead to a lessening of conflicts in the long run. Ivan Illich's outspoken criticism of missionary priests has occasioned a heated debate, but it reflects the views of other churchmen who differ sharply from him in their vision of the good society. Such nationalists as the late Archbishop Rossell Arellano of Guatemala have likewise opposed large influxes of foreign priests, although the scarcity of Latin American vocations has caused other bishops to welcome foreign priests, religious, and lay volunteers. The ratio of priests to laymen in the Latin American populations will almost surely decline further as the population explosion continues, and resentment of foreign clergymen could become more pervasive if increasing numbers of them should be recruited. It is unlikely that the Church outside Latin America can assemble and send a much higher proportion of priests than it has done in the past, however, and, if some of Illich's criticisms are heeded, the priests who are sent should be better adapted to fill constructive social roles. Although some churchmen have bitterly attacked Illich's ideas, those ideas in time should come to appear far less radical than they are now said to be.

Despite the remarkable advance of Protestantism in Brazil, the Protestants also face severe difficulties in Latin America. Such groups as the American Bible Society try to spread Christian teachings in Latin America, as in 1961 the society distributed 541,696 copies of the Bible and 8,688,336 copies of various selections from it. On Thursday of Holy Week in 1962 some 10,000 copies of an Easter selection from the Bible were given free at toll stations to Venezuelans driving along the superhighway from Caracas to La Guaira.[17] The effects of such distributions in terms of changing Latin American political orientations are neither great nor uniform, however, not only because there are so many illiterates, but also because those who do read the material rarely pay enough serious attention to it to let it reshape their attitudes and beliefs.

In the context of limited ecclesiastical influence, one way to gain

17. W. Stanley Rycroft and Myrtle M. Clemmer, *A Factual Study of Latin America* (New York: Commission on Ecumenical Mission and Relations, United Presbyterian Church in the U. S. A., 1963), pp. 230, 236.

immediate attention is to advocate violent revolution. Just as, in the early stages of the French Revolution of 1789, the French clergy wanted reform rather than the massive revolution that followed, so modern Catholic progressivism can be interpreted as a prelude to violence. If the United States should refrain from intervention and if such forces as population pressure, highly skewed income distribution, inadequate levels of economic development, and inflated expectations should continue, then Latin American churchmen could find that their calls for reform will lead to reconstructions of the social system that go well beyond their current plans. This possibility remains highly problematical at the present time, however. Religious observers in Latin America have long predicted the coming of mass revolution, but their predictions have so far proved mistaken and still seem premature. After nearly twelve years of missionary activity in Latin America, as astute an observer of Latin American affairs as Richard Shaull wrote in 1955 that the situation in Brazil "is every day more critical" and that "the revolution threatens to break at any moment."[18] After the situation looked much the same for almost a decade, the Brazilian army took direct control in 1964 to make mass revolution impossible in the short run. Men who have sincerely feared the imminence of revolution have used it as a device to arouse Christian concern and to wean foreign aid funds from the United States Congress, but in reality their fears have proved groundless more because of the counter-pressures and inertia of Latin American politics than because of the Christian activities or foreign aid which their calls occasioned.

Although Catholic Christianity has approved of violence in many contexts, it is doubtful that violence will come to be more widely supported as the necessary prerequisite to contemporary change. The pope's crowning of Charlemagne, the blessings on the Crusades, and overt backing for such violence-based regimes as those of Maximilian or Rafael Trujillo—all these Church actions sanctioned violence in particular contexts. The question is not whether the Church will sanction violence, therefore, but whether it will sanction violence for the particular purpose of furthering certain kinds of social

18. M. Richard Shaull, *Encounter with Revolution* (New York: Association Press, 1955), p. viii.

change. In the cases of Charlemagne, the Crusades, Maximilian, or Trujillo, the men whose violence the Church approved appeared to be furthering the institutional interests of the Church itself. In the case of Latin American social change, however, the direct benefit to the Church remains much more in doubt. For this reason and because violence does such immediate damage to the people for whom it is allegedly perpetrated, few Catholic leaders can be expected to support it.

The security-conscious report of Governor Nelson Rockefeller to the Nixon administration may thus exaggerate the revolutionary tendencies of the contemporary Church in Latin America. Rockefeller declares that the Church is now "a force dedicated to change—revolutionary change if necessary," and that, like Latin American students, churchmen now show "a profound idealism" that, in some cases, makes the Church "vulnerable to subversive penetration."[19] While the Church's increased dedication to reform represents an apparent break with its traditional support for the status quo, a less obvious but more deeply significant tendency is the profound split among Catholic factions over social programs. Some churchmen do not favor social change, while many others simply refuse to meddle in social and political issues. Among those who favor reform deep gulfs separate the programs and techniques advocated by different factions. In this context, it is not so much subversion as disunity that will prevent Catholic advocates of change from realizing their separate goals.

In contrast to both Nelson Rockefeller and the revolutionary wing of the Catholic left, most Latin American Catholics agree with Eduardo Frei's evaluation of contemporary guerrilla movements. The guerrillas do not seem likely to win popular backing despite the wide publicity that their raids receive. To Frei and to the great majority of Catholic activists, the raids and the guerrilla movements behind them "are desperate manifestations of 'out' groups or agents of an absurd propaganda. They have no destiny: only frustration and failure."[20] In this context of presumed frustration, Catholic moder-

---

19. Nelson A. Rockefeller, "Quality of Life in the Americas," mimeographed (n.p.: n.p., 1969), p. 17.

20. Quoted in "El presidente Frei habla con: The Economist," *The Economist* (edición para América Latina), Nov. 17, 1967, p. 11.

ates criticize the left on the grounds that it pushes for reform so adamantly as to become ineffective. Priests who preach revolution in a wealthy parish or under a staunchly conservative bishop are regularly sent out of the country for study or training, so that their immediate impact on the community is lost. Moderates argue that, if these reformers were more diplomatic in the presentation of their convictions, they would become far more effective. Since the moderates are sincere in their desire for change and do not simply advise caution to preserve the old order,[21] the chief feature distinguishing them from the radicals remains a patience in method rather than an opposition in goals.

Paradoxically, however, and in stark contrast to the tendencies of the New Testament, the pervasiveness of Catholicism in Latin America also works to increase conflict among some social groups. Psychologists generally agree that, as in religious wars, religion becomes a socially disruptive force when it encourages individual aggressiveness to be turned outward against foreign groups.[22] Religion can also set one group against another in the context of a single society, and it can do so even when the members of that society share nominal allegiance to the same religious convictions. In the past, Latin American Catholicism occasioned conflict through the suppression of indigenous religions during the Spanish conquest and through the struggle between Church and State in the nineteenth and early twentieth centuries. At present, revolutionary reformers and archconservatives put forward diametrically opposed programs in the name of Catholic teachings and then conspire to employ the amount of violence required to unseat an alien regime and realize their programs. By condoning the aggressiveness that is directed against opposing groups, self-justification in terms of Catholic doctrine undergirds conflict and prevents compromise between secular conservatives and revolutionaries.

Among the moderates, the ethic of Christian humanism has shaped a contrasting attitude toward conflict and revolution. By making social reform more acceptable to them, it leads them to

21. My belief in the sincerity of the moderates derives from interviews with priests from Venezuela, Mexico, Colombia, Chile, Guatemala, Bolivia, and Brazil between 1964 and 1970.
22. See Mortimer Ostow and Ben-Ami Scharfstein, *The Need To Believe: The Psychology of Religion* (New York: International Universities Press, 1954), p. 142.

interpret the danger of violence as a reason that opposition to reform must be overcome. Conscientious liberals overstate the danger of "explosion" or "revolution" in order to make a convincing case for what they believe on humanitarian grounds to be right. C. Wright Mills has gained great popularity among Latin American intellectuals, only in part because his general thesis of a "power elite" seems to fit the concentration of power in the region within narrow elite groups. His popularity also derives from the underlying and sometimes carefully concealed idealism and humanitarianism of the intellectuals, and this same idealism leads them to stress the dangers of mass revolution. Members of the democratic left and their North American allies have based Latin American reforms and United States foreign aid on the supposition of dire consequences arising from mass revolution and Communist subversion. As Church leaders have swung increasingly behind social reform, they too have come to see violent revolution not so much as a threat to the privileged position of secular aristocrats or the Church itself but as a threat to the realization of constructive social action.

Catholicism's weathering of anticlericalism in the French Revolution of 1789 and the Mexican Revolution of 1910 suggests that the Church will later come to terms with revolutionary regimes if massive revolution does come to Latin America. Between a government and the Catholic Church just as between nation-states, mutual interest is the surest bond for cooperation. Mutuality of interests between Church and State can overcome stringent opposition to compromise among factions in both organizations. In 1801 Napoleon and Pope Pius VII concluded a concordat to regularize relations between the revolutionary French regime and the Holy See. They acted because it was in their interests to do so, even though they received exceptionally heavy opposition from cardinals who wanted no accommodation with the French Revolution, from the monarchist clergy who opposed Napoleon, from French freethinkers, and from supporters of the Constitutional Church in France including Talleyrand and Bishop Grégoire.[23] The reconciliation between Church and State in Mexico which began under Lázaro Cárdenas

23. See E. E. Y. Hales, *Revolution and Papacy, 1769–1846* (Garden City, N. Y.: Doubleday & Company, 1960), pp. 139–54.

shows that compromise is equally possible in the midst of Latin American anticlericalism. Even after the most massive revolutions, secular leaders simply demand that the Church adhere to the principles of the revolution. These demands may be harsh, but they do not in themselves preclude cooperation between Church and State. Mutual adjustment between communism and Catholicism in Eastern Europe indicates that Communist victories do not prevent eventual tolerance, and a process of Church accommodation with Fidel Castro's regime in Cuba has already begun. In the case of future Church-State conflicts, as in those of the past, both religious thought and the relationship of ecclesiastical to secular authority will probably change; the Church will adapt in order to survive.

During the present period, the Catholic debate over the uses of force and violence demonstrates that the Church is reacting to the same trends that have molded the secular ideologies of the twentieth century. In 1944 Pryns Hopkins suggested that totalitarian ideologies of Soviet communism or Nazi and Italian fascism had become emotional substitutes for traditional religion, and that two primary features differentiated totalitarianism from religion. First, totalitarians found their goals in the present world rather than in heaven. Secondly, totalitarianism allowed the use of force as well as persuasion to achieve its goals.[24] Although Hopkins failed to suggest that religion itself might come more and more to adopt these distinguishing features, this is in a sense what has happened in the case of Latin American Catholicism.

The apparent concern for human welfare which now figures so prominently in Catholic pronouncements underlines the importance that religious leaders attribute to worldly problems, while the example of Camilo Torres and Ação Popular indicates an increasing Catholic willingness to use force to obtain worldly objectives. The advocates of violence remain a distinct minority among Latin American Catholics, and the *freistas* adamantly oppose them. But the nature of the new approval of violence differs categorically from that traditionally encouraged by religion, as its objective is social change rather than the conversion of pagans or the conquest

24. *From Gods to Dictators: Psychology of Religions and Their Totalitarian Substitutes* (Girard, Kansas: Haldeman-Julius Publications, 1944), p. 7.

of infidels. It should certainly not be seen in the prejudicial terms which the expansionist policies of Hitler and Stalin have associated with the word "totalitarian," and it should not be confused with the common claims of a people at war that their gods approve of the warfare. Instead, through concern to overcome what is defined as economic exploitation by a conservative elite, the themes of the Catholic reformers bear a striking resemblance to the early Bolshevik desire to forcibly end capitalist exploitation or the Nazi desire to end the menace of the Jewish financiers. Besides showing how far the avant-garde of Latin American Catholicism has come from the traditional position of defending an elite of which the Church itself was a major part, the new secular concerns and the debate on force indicate the adaptability of Catholicism.

The most dynamic factor behind the ideological shift from individualism to socialism has been the broadening possibility of material advancement. Adam Smith and his followers interpreted individual self-interest as the best motivation for economic advancement, because they lived in an early stage of the Industrial Revolution when a comparatively small number of individuals could reap substantial benefits from the processes of economic change. When capitalism encouraged huge disparities in living conditions and when substantial material advancement became feasible for a much broader range of workers, socialism came to the fore. Those individuals who felt particularly secure under capitalism and potentially threatened under the new ethic of mass sharing have clung to the older capitalist ethic, but socialist attitudes have spread out of avowedly socialist states to traditional democracies like Britain and the United States and even to the developing countries. The dilemma of Latin America is that the ethic of mass sharing has come to the area before the material capability to realize the ethic has been fully achieved. As Catholic spokesmen join secular leaders in preaching the ethic, however, they press harder and harder for economic growth and a wider distribution of wealth. If these goals are not achieved through the pacific means that most churchmen now advocate, then the impact of their message will encourage more violent attempts at change. Violence—at least in the short run—will prevent the group cohesion and economic initiative that are required to attain a society in which mass sharing is possible.

The threats of pentecostal Protestantism and Fidel Castro's revolution can be easily exaggerated as forces behind Catholic adaptation. In evaluating the reasons for change in the Latin American Church, Ivan Vallier assigns particular importance to pentecostal movements that, he says, have forced the Church to pay increasing attention to the religious as opposed to the political aspects of its position and doctrine.[25] Religious competition may not be as significant an influence as are the fundamental shifts in the economic possibilities and secular expectations of Latin American societies, however, especially because of the limited areas and groups among which pentecostals have so far found success.[26]

Similarly, instead of being a major catalyst of change, the Cuban revolution has deepened the attitudes toward reform that the various segments of the Church already had. Conservatives use the case to show how devious international communism really is, and from it they draw the easy lesson that Catholics cannot afford to collaborate with any movement that might be Communist-inspired. Numerous churchmen, reacting to Castro, give more verbal support to social reform, but it remains for many of them a nebulous generalization rather than a commitment to programmatic action. Catholic nationalists object to Fidel's aid to movements that try to overthrow their governments, while anti-Communist reformers use the Cuban case to show that Communist revolutions may fail to deliver the political and economic reforms that they promise. A major impact of Communist Cuba on Latin American Catholicism, therefore, has been not so much to create new attitudes as to activate and confirm the attitudes that were already present.

In a world that has become increasingly secular, Catholic attitudes have simply come to deal more directly with the secular problems of development. Christian concern to relieve poverty operates as a major impetus behind clerical calls for reform. The growing

25. Ivan Vallier, *Catholicism, Social Control, and Modernization in Latin America* (Englewood Cliffs, N. J.: Prentice-Hall, 1970), esp. pp. 150–52.
26. See Frederick C. Turner, "Protestantism and Politics in Chile and Brazil," *Comparative Studies in Society and History* 12, no. 2 (April, 1970).

possibilities of reform underlie such calls, but the attitudes of Catholics also depend upon care for their neighbors' welfare. The attitudes of both clerics and laymen are shaped by political realities, and in turn they set in motion popular expectations that affect those realities.

Secular orientations pose an underlying threat to the position of the Church, as the Christian Democrats' hostility to authoritarianism has led some Catholics to question the structure of authority in their own ecclesiastical hierarchy. Thomas Molnar, openly making an accusation that some Latin Americans have made in private conversations, finds that the avant-garde priests of Latin America are "trying to dismantle the Church from within."[27] Such an undermining coincides with the effects of evolving patterns of interpersonal relationships. Max Weber observed that skepticism and indifference to religion have uniformly arisen when traders and financiers gained prominence,[28] and Latin Americans are becoming more preoccupied with the values of trade, finance, and development.

The new Catholic thought works in another sense to undermine the traditional power of the Church. In a special study designed to explain the role of religion and the Church to Peace Corpsmen serving in the Andean countries, Richard H. Stephens suggests that rural priests wield considerable temporal and spiritual authority because of their conflict-reducing role. Since life is hard and aggressive tendencies are strong among rural villagers, adherence to traditional modes of behavior is maintained in order to prevent the release of aggressiveness and the breakdown of community life. Deference paid to the priest reduces conflict between the various segments of the community and helps to preserve the precarious pattern of community accommodation.[29] What happens to this role of the Church when priests like Camilo Torres advocate violent revolution and stir up conflict within communities, however? As the position of the Church comes to be less supportive of the status quo, the Church jeopardizes its own traditional position.

27. "Christian Socialism's Day," *National Review* 19, no. 13 (April 4, 1967) : 349.
28. *The Sociology of Religion,* trans. Ephraim Fischoff (London: Methuen & Co., 1965), p. 92.
29. Richard H. Stephens and others, *Religion,* unit 1 in *Cross-Cultural Understanding* (Washington, D. C.: International Study Center, n.d.), p. 6.

The restrictions on the influence of the Church lead to the question of whether Catholic influence or even Catholicism itself will pass away in Latin America. For psychological as well as social reasons, however, such a disappearance remains highly unlikely. Despite the Reformation and despite the doubts of antireligious skeptics, Catholicism as an ideology and as an institution has proved itself through history to be most resilient. The tempo of social change in the nineteenth and twentieth centuries has increased enough to make the process of adaptation more difficult, but so far it has worked to lessen rather than extinguish the power of the Church. Even a large number of Latin American nominal Catholics derive a sense of security from their religious beliefs. Far from laying traditional beliefs and belief systems open to doubt as some critics have suggested, changes in the liturgy and regalia of the Church make the trappings of religion more compatible with an individual's nonreligious experience. In the future as in the past, Latin American Catholicism is more likely to adjust than to disappear.

Despite sweeping changes in the Church and in Catholic thought, both continue to be major influences on the process of change itself. Some secularists disagree with this interpretation, and they will probably continue to do so. Pierre Burgelin, for example, after defining the "profane" as a threshold where "reverential fear ceases and curiosity begins," finds that the evolution from the sacred to the profane which began at the height of the Middle Ages will ultimately "establish all our activities within the embrace of a single completely human world, without reference to the immanence of the supernatural."[30] Even if the theological rubric of Catholicism should fall away as he implies, however, human relationships of the future will be shaped by the Catholic doctrines developing in the present period. The humanism which motivated clerical care for the Latin American Indians or clerical support for the early principles of the French Revolution also appears in the social

---

30. "On the Transition from the Sacred to the Profane," *Diogenes* 33 (Spring, 1961): 119–20. For a more devout interpretation of the secularization process, see Giuseppe de Rosa, "Secularización y secularismo," *Criterio* 43, no. 1596 (28 mayo, 1970).

doctrines of contemporary Catholicism. If this humanism is maintained—whether or not it remains tied to formal theology—Catholic ethics will continue to shape forcefully the direction and nature of change in Latin America.

As in other organizations, questions of organizational adaptation in the Catholic Church depend in considerable part on the staffing of leadership positions. If outspoken reformers are raised to positions of influence, then the Church can adapt much more rapidly to its milieu. In Latin America, progressive churchmen have taken over numerous positions in the hierarchy, and the press of events and Catholic opinion seem likely to increase their number. Even if conservatives continue to direct some Church organizations outside Latin America, they may someday have to ratify the shifts in Catholic positions which occur there among the rank and file. If so, Latin America will become a genuine innovator both in ecclesiastical affairs and political development.

While the evolution of Catholic progressivism naturally concerns Latin Americans most directly, it also has major implications for social science research and for United States foreign policy. In order to clarify and expand our understanding of Catholic thought, specific interrelationships need to be tested in a series of Latin American countries. More empirical, short-range studies of Catholic attitudes need to be made. How do patterns of attitude correlate with income, class status, age, sex, membership in lay organizations, membership in particular religious orders, and degrees of religious authority? Does advocacy of authoritarian tenets in Catholicism coincide with support for secular autocrats? How do degrees of Catholic progressiveness differ among countries, both in terms of the numbers of individuals actively motivated by such attitudes and in terms of their influence within their political systems? To what extent are specific Catholic groups willing to collaborate with other groups in order to promote change, and among what groups and for what reasons does collaboration seem possible? Although a series of empirical studies of these questions would not provide definitive answers to the issues of Latin American Catholicism, they would at least yield a body of firm data through which a more valid level of generalization could be reached.

The United States would do well to recognize the importance of the Catholic progressives much more than it has. With their preoccupations in Southeast Asia, Europe, and the Middle East, the administrations of Lyndon Johnson and Richard Nixon have shown comparatively little concern for Latin America. Frictions between Christian Democrats and the United States government have impeded rapport between them, as when Christian Democrats sharply condemned United States involvement in the Dominican crisis of 1965. Fuller appreciation of the Christian Democratic approach would not only modify such policies as the Dominican "invasion," it would also encourage the United States to back more adequately the non-Communist groups that are the most dedicated to reform and the most likely to effect it. The United States should grant recognition to all Latin American governments but provide the heaviest aid to those countries that are best able to use it. Patterns of political and social development leading to eventual political stability with steady growth in per capita income are decidedly in the national interest of the United States as well as the Latin American republics. Through agrarian, educational, and fiscal reforms, the Chilean and Venezuelan Christian Democrats have shown themselves to be dedicated implementors of the necessary type of development programs. Furthermore, they work indirectly for the aims of other North American groups as well as for the interests of their own people through their insistence on representative government, their strong encouragement of political participation and "intermediate groups," and their programs of compensated nationalization rather than outright expropriation of foreign holdings.

In this situation, the United States government should back such groups as the *freistas* even more heavily than it has done in the past. Effective reformers are all too rare in Latin America and, if aid is not provided when a country can make the best use of it, the real opportunity to further North American and Latin American interests may be lost. Prospects for more massive foreign assistance are reduced by United States commitments at home and in other parts of the world, by Washington's caution in regard to the more extreme faction in the Christian Democratic parties, and by the Latin Americans' natural chariness of too close a dependence on financing by a foreign power. Channeling most aid through international agencies, as President Nixon advocates, would help to prevent the assistance from compromising the regimes to which it went. If funds were channeled through the World Bank or the United Nations, the political opponents of the Latin American progressives could not so easily attack them for accepting "tainted" dollars. North American statesmen should not put too many strings on foreign aid when it is being used to support worthwhile reform programs, and they should recognize, as did President John F. Kennedy during the short Brazilian regime of Jânio Quadros, that the democratic left can steal the fire of the radicals most effectively by making some concessions to them. North Americans need to recognize the full force of foreign nationalism, admitting and even stressing that the impetus for innovation comes from the Latin American nations involved. If this policy orientation is correct, then the United States government should quietly but less reservedly welcome the growth of Catholic progressivism and stand willing to provide much more substantial aid for the progressives in a case like that of Chile where they win power and try to put through effective, albeit costly, reforms. Such a policy would work toward a more genuine inter-American community by placing the United States far more squarely and decisively behind the forces for genuine reform.

Bibliography

It is difficult to locate many of the important sources of information on Latin American Catholicism. Although the libraries of the major North American universities and seminaries contain English language publications on the Catholic Church, they regularly lack copies of the Catholic books, journals, and pastoral messages published in Latin America. Some libraries, like that at the University of Connecticut, have developed special acquisitions programs for these Latin American materials, but the range of sources available at most libraries remains uneven and severely limited. Among the best institutions in Latin America where these specialized documentary materials may be consulted are those at the Centro Intercultural de Documentación (CIDOC) in Cuernavaca, Mexico, and such Jesuit research institutes as the Centro Bellarmino in Santiago, Chile, and the Centro Gumilla in Caracas, Venezuela.

Scholars have so far done comparatively little systematic research in the pastoral messages, factional broadsides, and periodical literature of Latin American Catholicism. Many Latin American bishops issue individual and collective pastoral letters on social problems as well as on more strictly religious topics; the letters range in size from single mimeographed sheets to long booklets. Episcopal offices in the capital of each Latin American country regularly contain files of the major pastorals issued in that country. I have made a personal collection of social and political pastorals, which now contains important messages issued by more than ninety bishops over the past two decades, but more complete sets of pastorals for most of the Latin

Bibliography

American countries can be more easily consulted at CIDOC. That center also offers researchers an excellent collection of periodical literature and position statements by different factions in the Church, although the number of books available at CIDOC remains comparatively small.

In addition to more thoroughly researching these traditional types of sources, scholars in the future will undoubtedly make better use of statistical data and survey research. The statistics that appear in the *Annuario Pontificio* and in the more than forty volumes published since 1958 by the Federación Internacional de Institutos Católicos de Investigaciones Socio-religiosas y Sociales (FERES) represent only part of the religious data already collected in each Latin American country. Cooperation with social scientists interested in survey research seems far more feasible to Church leaders than it does to the members of such other elites as the Latin American military; both questionnaire surveys and informal interviews carried out among clerical groups should considerably increase our understanding of Latin American Catholicism during the decade ahead. As improvements occur in both the range of data collected and the techniques of their collection, social scientists can use the data to develop new hypotheses and to test the hypotheses on Catholicism that they have already devised.

The following, highly selective bibliography makes no attempt to list the range of studies consulted and footnoted in the present volume. It does not present general works on religious sociology, for instance, nor does it refer again to most of the sources cited on such subjects as Chilean Christian Democracy or the ideas of Camilo Torres and other spokesmen. Instead, it suggests some of the books of most general interest for students of Latin American Catholicism; these volumes variously contain interpretations of Catholicism and development, historical analyses, statistical information, and the results of attitude surveys. In the last section of the bibliography, there is an enumeration of some of the most important journals and documentation services that regularly publish discussions of the Church in Latin America.

BOOKS

Alfaro, Carlos. *Guía apostólica latinoamericana.* Barcelona: Herder, 1965.
Alonso, Isidoro, *La Iglesia en América Latina.* Fribourg: FERES, 1964.
Annuario Pontificio per l'Anno 1970. Città del Vaticano: Tipografia Poliglotta Vaticana, 1970.
Badanelli, Pedro. *Perón, la Iglesia y un cura.* 4th ed. Buenos Aires: Editorial Tartessos, 1960.
Bialek, Robert W. *Catholic Politics. A History Based on Ecuador.* New York: Vantage Press, 1963.

256

Boza Masvidal, Eduardo. *Revolución cristiana en Latinoamérica.* Santiago de Chile: Editorial del Pacífico, 1963.

Caldera, Rafael. *El bloque latinoamericano.* Santiago de Chile: Editorial del Pacífico, 1961.

Câmara, Hélder. *The Church and Colonialism: The Betrayal of the Third World.* Denville, N. J.: Dimension Books, 1969.

Clark, James A. *The Church and the Crisis in the Dominican Republic.* Westminster, Md.: Newman Press, 1967.

Coleman, William J. *Latin-American Catholicism: A Self-Evaluation.* Maryknoll, N. Y.: Maryknoll Publications, 1958.

Considine, John J., ed. *The Church in the New Latin America.* Notre Dame, Ind.: Fides Publishers, 1964.

——, ed. *The Religious Dimension in the New Latin America.* Notre Dame, Ind.: Fides Publishers, 1966.

——, ed. *Social Revolution in the New Latin America: A Catholic Appraisal.* Notre Dame, Ind.: Fides Publishers, 1965.

Courlander, Harold, and Rémy Bastien. *Religion and Politics in Haiti.* Washington, D. C.: Institute for Cross-Cultural Research, 1966.

D'Antonio, William V., and Fredrick B. Pike, eds. *Religion, Revolution, and Reform: New Forces for Change in Latin America.* New York: Frederick A. Praeger, 1964.

Dewart, Leslie. *Christianity and Revolution: The Lesson of Cuba.* New York: Herder and Herder, 1963.

Directorio católico latino-americano, 1968. Bogotá: Secretariado General del CELAM, 1968.

Einaudi, Luigi, Richard Maullin, Alfred Stepan, and Michael Fleet. *Latin American Institutional Development: The Changing Catholic Church.* Santa Monica, Calif.: Rand Corporation, 1969.

Fichter, Joseph H. *Cambio social en Chile: Un estudio de actitudes.* Santiago de Chile: Editorial Universidad Católica, 1962.

Foy, Felician A., ed. *1970 Catholic Almanac.* Garden City, N. Y.: Doubleday & Co., 1970.

Frei Montalva, Eduardo. *Sentido y forma de una política.* Santiago de Chile: Editorial del Pacífico, 1951.

——. *La verdad tiene su hora.* Santiago de Chile: Editorial del Pacífico, 1955.

Gibbons, William Joseph, and others. *Basic Ecclesiastical Statistics for Latin America.* Maryknoll, N. Y.: Maryknoll Publications, 1958.

Guzmán, Germán. *Camilo Torres,* trans. John D. Ring. New York: Sheed and Ward, 1969.

Haddox, Benjamín Edward. *Sociedad y religión en Colombia* (*estudio de las instituciones religiosas colombianas*), trans. Jorge Zalamea. Bogotá: Ediciones Tercer Mundo, 1965.

Bibliography

Holleran, Mary P. *Church and State in Guatemala.* New York: Columbia University Press, 1949.

Houtart, François, and Émile Pin. *The Church and the Latin American Revolution,* trans. Gilbert Barth. New York: Sheed and Ward, 1965.

Hübner Gallo, Jorge Iván. *Los católicos en la política.* Santiago de Chile: Zig-Zag, 1959.

Kadt, Emanuel de. *Catholic Radicals in Brazil.* London: Oxford University Press, 1970.

Kennedy, John J. *Catholicism, Nationalism and Democracy in Argentina.* Notre Dame, Ind.: University of Notre Dame Press, 1958.

Labelle, Yvan, and Adriana Estrada. *Latin America in Maps, Charts, Tables. No. 2: Socio-Religious Data (Catholicism).* México: CIDOC, 1964.

Landsberger, Henry A., ed. *The Church and Social Change in Latin America.* Notre Dame, Ind.: University of Notre Dame Press, 1970.

Larraín E., Manuel. *Escritos sociales.* Santiago de Chile: Editorial del Pacífico, 1963.

Marsal S., Pablo. *Perón y la Iglesia.* Buenos Aires: Ediciones Rex, 1955.

Mecham, J. Lloyd. *Church and State in Latin America. A History of Politico-Ecclesiastical Relations.* Rev. ed. Chapel Hill, N. C.: University of North Carolina Press, 1966.

Mendes, Cândido. *Memento dos vivos: A esquerda católica no Brasil.* Rio de Janeiro: Tempo Brasileiro, 1966.

Pike, Fredrick B., ed. *The Conflict Between Church and State in Latin America.* New York: Alfred A. Knopf, 1964.

Pin, Émile. *Elementos para una sociología del catolicismo latinoamericano.* Bogotá: FERES, 1963.

Poblete Barth, Renato. *Crisis sacerdotal.* Santiago de Chile: Editorial del Pacífico, 1965.

Ponce García, Jaime, and Óscar Uzin Fernández. *El clero en Bolivia, 1968.* Cuernavaca, Mor.: CIDOC, 1970.

Proença Sigaud, Geraldo de, Antonio de Castro Mayer, Plinio Corrêa de Oliveira, and Luis Mendonça de Freitas, *Reforma agrária, questão de consciência.* 4th ed. São Paulo: Editôra Vera Cruz, 1962.

Sanders, Thomas G. *Catholic Innovation in a Changing Latin America.* Cuernavaca, Mor.: CIDOC, 1969.

Segundo, Juan Luis. *Función de la Iglesia en la realidad rioplatense.* Montevideo: Barreiro y Ramos, S.A., 1962.

Sexto mensaje del Presidente de la República de Chile, don Eduardo Frei Montalva, al inaugurar el período de Sesiones Ordinarias del Congreso Nacional. Santiago de Chile: Dirección de Informaciones y Radiodifusión de la Presidencia de la República, 1970.

Smith, Donald Eugene. *Religion and Political Development.* Boston: Little, Brown and Company, 1970.

Tiseyra, Óscar. *Cuba marxista vista por un católico.* Buenos Aires: Jorge Álvarez, 1964.

Torres, Camilo. *Revolutionary Writings.* New York: Herder and Herder, 1969.

Vallier, Ivan. *Catholicism, Social Control, and Modernization in Latin America.* Englewood Cliffs, N. J.: Prentice-Hall, 1970.

Vekemans, Roger, and others, *América Latina y desarrollo social.* 2 vols. Barcelona: Centro para el Desarrollo Económico y Social de América Latina, 1966.

Vitalis, Hellmut Gnadt. *The Significance of Changes in Latin American Catholicism Since Chimbote, 1953.* Cuernavaca, Mor.: CIDOC, 1969.

Wayland-Smith, Giles. *The Christian Democratic Party in Chile.* Cuernavaca, Mor.: CIDOC, 1969.

Williams, Edward J., *Latin American Christian Democratic Parties.* Knoxville, Tenn.: University of Tennessee Press, 1967.

JOURNALS AND DOCUMENTATION SERVICES

Catolicismo (Campos, Brazil)
CIAS (Buenos Aires, Argentina)
CIDOC Informa (Cuernavaca, Mexico)
CIF Reports (Cuernavaca, Mexico, 1962–1967)
Criterio (Buenos Aires, Argentina)
Fiducia (Santiago, Chile)
Friends of Latin America (Louvain, Belgium)
Informaciones Católicas Internacionales (Mexico City)
Latin America Calls! (Davenport, Iowa)
Mensaje (Santiago, Chile)
Nadoc (Lima, Peru)
Notiziario della Pontificia Commissione per l'America Latina (Vatican City)
Pastoral Popular (Santiago, Chile)
Reportaje DESAL (Santiago, Chile)
Revista Eclesiástica Brasileira (Petrópolis, Brazil)
Sic (Caracas, Venezuela)
Social Compass (Louvain, Belgium)
Teología y Vida (Santiago, Chile)
Verbo (Buenos Aires, Argentina)
Víspera (Montevideo, Uruguay)
Vozes (Petrópolis, Brazil)

Index